FIFE,
PERTHSHIRE
AND ANGUS

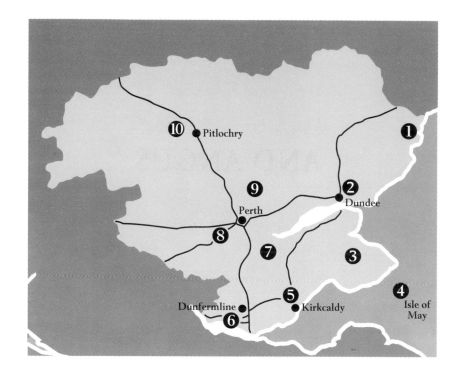

EXCURSIONS

EXPLORING SCOTLAND'S HERITAGE

RCAHMS

FIFE, PERTHSHIRE AND ANGUS

SECOND EDITION

• •

Bruce Walker and Graham Ritchie

Series Editor: Anna Ritchie

EDINBURGH: HMSO

Cover photography: Historic Scotland (Culross and Edzell)

End papers by Elisa Trimby

British Library Cataloguing in Publication Data

A catalogue record for this book is available from the British Library

Applications for reproduction should be made to HMSO. Many of the photographs are from the collections of the Royal Commission on the Ancient and Historical Monuments of Scotland; copies may be obtained from the Secretary:

Royal Commission on the Ancient and Historical Monuments of Scotland

John Sinclair House, 16 Bernard Terrace, Edinburgh EH8 9NX

0131-662 1456

The Royal Commission, which was established in 1908, is responsible for compiling a national record of archaeological sites and historic buildings of all types and periods. The Royal Commission makes this record available both through its publications (details of which can be obtained from the above address) and through the maintenance of a central archive of information, known as the National Monuments Record of Scotland. This contains the national collection of pictorial and documentary material relating to Scotland's ancient monuments and historic buildings and is open Monday to Friday for public reference at the above address.

HMSO Bookshops
71 Lothian Road, Edinburgh EH3 9AZ
0131-228 4181 Fax 0131-229 2734
49 High Holborn, London WC1V 6HB
(counter service only)
0171-873 0011 Fax 0171-831 1326
68-69 Bull Street, Birmingham B4 6AD
0121-236 9696 Fax 0121-236 9699
33 Wine Street, Bristol BS1 2BQ
0117 9264306 Fax 0117 9294515
9-21 Princess Street, Manchester M60 8AS
0161-834 7201 Fax 0161-833 0634
16 Arthur Street, Belfast BT1 4GD
01232 238451 Fax 01232 235401
The HMSO Oriel Bookshop
The Friary, Cardiff CF1 4AA
01222 395548 Fax 01222 384347
Published by HMSO and available from:

HMSO Publications Centre
(Mail, fax and telephone orders only)
PO Box 276, London SW8 5DT
Telephone orders 0171-873 9090
General enquiries 0171-873 0011
(queuing system in operation for both numbers)
Fax orders 0171-873 8200

HMSO's Accredited Agents
(see Yellow Pages)
and through good booksellers

ALSO PUBLISHED

THE HIGHLANDS

GLASGOW, CLYDESIDE AND STIRLING

ABERDEEN AND NORTH-EAST SCOTLAND

ARGYLL AND THE WESTERN ISLES

OTHER TITLES IN PREPARATION

DUMFRIES AND GALLOWAY

EDINBURGH, LOTHIANS AND BORDERS

ORKNEY

SHETLAND

ISBN 0 11 495286 8

CONTENTS

FOREWORD

Twentieth-century Scotland has a heritage of human endeavour stretching back some nine thousand years, and a wide range of man-made monuments survives as proof of that endeavour. The rugged character of much of the Scottish landscape has helped to preserve many antiquities which elsewhere have vanished beneath modern development or intensive deep ploughing, though with some 10,200 km of coastline there has also been an immeasurable loss of archaeological sites as a result of marine erosion. Above all, perhaps, the preservation of such a wide range of monuments should be credited to Scotland's abundant reserves of good building stone, allowing not only the creation of extraordinarily enduring prehistoric houses and tombs but also the development of such remarkable Scottish specialities as the medieval tower-house and the iron-age broch. This volume is one of a series of nine handbooks which have been designed to provide up-to-date and authoritative introductions to the rich archaeological heritage of the various regions of Scotland, highlighting the most interesting and best preserved of the surviving monuments and setting them in their original social context. The time-scale is the widest possible, from relics of World War II or the legacy of 19th century industrial booms back through history and prehistory to the earliest pioneer days of human settlement, but the emphasis varies from region to region, matching the particular directions in which each has developed. Some monuments are still functioning (lighthouses for instance), others are still occupied as homes, and many have been taken into the care of the State or the National Trust for Scotland, but each has been chosen as specially deserving a visit.

Thanks to the recent growth of popular interest in these topics, there is an increasing demand for knowledge to be presented in a readily digestible form and at a moderate price. In sponsoring this series, therefore, the Royal Commission on the Ancient and Historical Monuments of Scotland broadens the range of its publications with the aim of making authentic information about the man-made heritage available to as wide an audience as possible. This is the second edition of the series, in which more monuments, museums and visitor centres have been added in order to reflect the way in which the management and presentation of Scotland's past have expanded over the last decade. The excursions section proved very popular and has been both enlarged and illustrated in colour.

The authors were both brought up in Tayside and have been involved in the architecture and archaeology of eastern Scotland throughout their working careers. Bruce Walker lectured in the School of Architecture, University of Dundee, from 1963, and from 1990 has been seconded to Historic Scotland, acting first as a district architect and currently as an architect in the Technical Conservation, Research and Education division. He has a special interest in vernacular buildings, both rural and industrial, and in the materials used in their construction. Graham Ritchie has been an

Investigator with the Royal Commission on the Ancient and Historical Monuments of Scotland since 1965; his excavations in Fife and Tayside include the stone circle at Balbirnie, and he is closely concerned with the recording of Pictish stone-carving in the area; he is Head of the Archaeology Division of the Royal Commission.

Monuments have been grouped according to their character and date and, although only the finest, most interesting or best preserved have been described in detail, attention has also been drawn to other sites worth visiting in the vicinity. Each section has its own explanatory introduction, beginning with the most recent monuments and gradually retreating in time back to the earliest traces of prehistoric man.

Each major monument is numbered and identified by its district so that it may easily be located on the end-map, but it is recommended that the visitor should also use the relevant 1:50,000 maps published by the Ordnance Survey as its Landranger Series, particularly for the more remote sites. Sheet nos 42, 43, 44, 45, 51, 52, 53, 54, 57, 58, 59, 65 and 66 cover the area of this volume. The National Grid Reference for each site is provided (eg NO 670598) as well as local directions at the head of each entry.

An asterisk indicates that the site is subject to restricted hours of opening; unless attributed to Historic Scotland or the National Trust for Scotland (NTS), the visitor should assume the monument to be in private ownership and **should seek permission locally to view it**. It is of course vital that visitors to any monument should observe the country code and take special care to fasten gates. Where a church is locked, it is often possible to obtain the key from the local manse, post office or general store.

We have made an attempt to estimate how accessible each monument may be for disabled visitors, indicated at the head of each entry by a wheelchair logo and a number: 1=easy access for all visitors, including those in wheelchairs; 2=reasonable access for pedestrians but restricted access for wheelchairs; 3=restricted access for all disabled but a good view from the road or parking area; 4=access for the able-bodied only.

Many of the sites mentioned in this handbook are held in trust for the nation by the Secretary of State for Scotland and cared for on his behalf by Historic Scotland. Further information about these monuments, including details of guidebooks to individual properties, can be obtained from Historic Scotland, Longmore House, Salisbury Place, EH9 1SH. Information about properties in the care of the National Trust for Scotland can be obtained from the National Trust for Scotland, 5 Charlotte Square, Edinburgh EH2 4DU. The abbreviation NMS refers to the National Museums of Scotland, Edinburgh, whose collections include important material from Fife, Perthshire and Angus.

ANNA RITCHIE
Series Editor

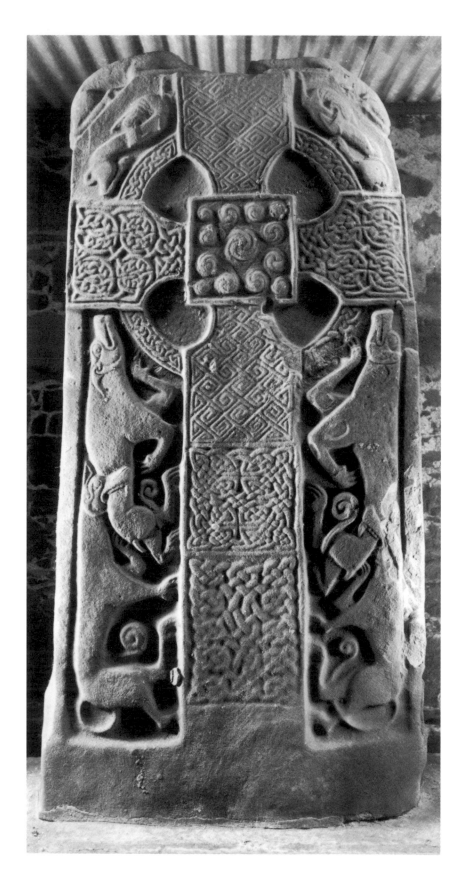

St Madoes cross-slab
(in Perth Museum and Art Gallery)

ACKNOWLEDGEMENTS

Many friends and colleagues have helped during the preparation of the second edition of this volume. The records of the Royal Commission on the Ancient and Historical Monuments of Scotland and the National Monuments Record of Scotland have been an invaluable source of information, and we are grateful to the Record staff for assistance, particularly to Mrs Lesley Ferguson, Mr Kevin McLaren, Ms Veronica Steele and Mrs Ruth Wimberley. The achievements of the Photographic Department of the Royal Commission, under Mr G B Quick and Mr J D Keggie, are gratefully acknowledged; we are grateful in particular to Mr J M Mackie, Mr S Wallace, Mr A G Lamb, Ms A P Stirling and Mr R M Adam. The drawings of Pictish monuments by Mr J Borland and Mr J N Stevenson provide an invaluable record of their decoration. We are grateful to Mr J White of the Photographic Library of Historic Scotland and Dr I G Brown of the National Library of Scotland for all their help. Mr I F C Fleming kindly checked the National Grid References and excursion routes.

We are grateful to Dr D J Breeze and Mr G S Maxwell for advice on Roman Tayside, and for Dr Breeze's permission to use the drawing of a Gask Ridge watch-tower. Miss J E M Comrie, Mr S P Halliday and Mr J B Stevenson provided information about Perthshire monuments, and Mr N Atkinson, Ms A Reid and Mr W G Watson advised on Tayside museums. In addition, we should like to thank Mr G J Barclay, Professor G W S Barrow, Mrs J Campbell, Mr C H Channon, Mr A J Cooke, Mrs J Docherty, Mr J G Douglas, Mr T Drysdale, Mr I Fisher, Dr R Fawcett, Mrs M Henderson, Mr J R Hume, Mr R Leitch, Mr C McGregor, Mr R J Mercer, Dr M K Oglethorpe, Mr W Payne, Mrs E V W Proudfoot, Mr R Stuart, Mr D M Spence, Mr G Stern, Miss L M Thoms and Miss D Tindall. We are also grateful to the staffs of Angus Folk Museum, Fife Folk Museum, Signal Tower Museum Arbroath, Scottish Fisheries Museum and the Library of Duncan of Jordanstone College of Art. Mr J G Dunbar made many helpful comments on the original text, and the series editor, Dr Anna Ritchie, has been supportive throughout the preparation of the volume.

Herring drifters in St Monans harbour around 1900

St Monans Church

INTRODUCTION

Iron-age fort on
Barry Hill, Perth
and Kinross

Rich natural resources and a central location have together ensured that
Fife and Tayside possess some of the most outstanding monuments in
Scotland. They range from earliest prehistoric times to the present century,
and the area is particularly noted for its Dark Age sculpture, for its
medieval tower-houses and burghs and for its elegant bridges and numerous
harbours. The area covers Fife, Angus, Dundee, and Perthshire and Kinross.

Fife and Tayside are bounded by the Grampian Mountains to the north and
west, the North Sea to the east, and the Firth of Forth and Carse of Stirling
to the south. The main lines of land communication run south-west to

north-east, parallel to the major physical features. These features comprise: the Grampian Mountains to the north-west of the Highland Boundary Fault; the great valley known as Strathmore when north, and Strathearn when south, of the River Tay; the Sidlaw Hills forming a lesser barrier between Strathmore and the Angus Coastal Plain to the east, and the Carse of Gowrie to the south; the Ochil Hills forming a similar barrier between Strathearn and the Loch Leven basin and, after turning along the south shore of the Firth of Tay, the Howe of Fife; the Lomond Hills starting to the north-east of Loch Leven and extending into a spinal ridge through the eastern end of Fife separate the Howe of Fife from the south Fife Coalfields.

The basic rock formations creating these features are: Dalradian metamorphic rocks in the Grampian Mountains; Devonian Old Red Sandstones in Strathearn, Strathmore and the Howe of Fife; igneous rocks in the Ochil Hills, Sidlaw Hills and parts of the Lomonds; and Carboniferous rocks along the south coast of Fife. Strangely, the drainage pattern bears little direct relationship to the structure of the underlying rocks, with the River Tay at times running across the grain of the land and the Firth of Tay occupying what should be an anticline between the Sidlaw Hills and the Ochil Hills. Many other important streams are discordant and it is generally agreed that the drainage system has been imposed from above, from a surface which has now disappeared. This variation in rocks, physical form, and discordant drainage creates a rich and varied landscape with considerable divergence of rock textures and colours. This in turn has affected the colour and texture of the buildings erected in each district. The gneiss and granite of the Highland area produces a range of sparkling greys. The Old Red Sandstone belt has walls ranging from deep warm reds to cooler pinkish-greys. The igneous rocks produce deep blue-black and purple whinstone; and the carboniferous rocks range in colour from pale creams to deep honey coloured and brown limestones. In all of these areas there are intrusive rocks often in the form of glacial boulders which when split can add a range of colours to any wall.

Roofing materials follow similar patterns. The availability of various types of flagstone and slate in Angus and Perthshire and the complete lack of these materials in Fife led to different approaches to the roofing of utilitarian vernacular buildings. All four counties had clay available for the manufacture of building materials in the 18th and 19th centuries but only in Fife and parts of Kinross were pantiles produced in quantity for the roofing of outbuildings and steadings. The other areas utilised their natural resources for inexpensive roof coverings and restricted the manufacture of clay building-products to bricks and drainage tiles.

The varying landscape is also reflected in the types of agriculture practised: hill farming in the glens of the Grampian Mountains and on the highest areas of the Sidlaw Hills; stock farming with a little arable land along the Highland Boundary Fault and on the other ranges of hills; and arable and feeding farms in Strathearn, Strathmore, the Angus Coastal Plain, Carse of Gowrie, East Neuk and Howe of Fife and along the south-facing slopes of south Fife.

Many of the areas now providing the richest of the agricultural land, namely Strathearn, Strathmore, Carse of Gowrie and Howe of Fife, were, until the 18th or more commonly the 19th century, areas of shallow lochs and bog. Consequently, early settlement usually occurred on areas of gently sloping ground where the land drained naturally. Place-names in the area tend to confirm this fact. The study of place-names is far too complex to discuss in this volume, but a word about common prefixes and suffixes may help the visitor to understand elements of the more common nomenclature. Starting with the most recent period, English place-names in the area tend to be composite and easy to understand, being generally descriptive of situation. Examples include: Bogside, Hillend, Blackwater and Greystone. In addition to these is a whole category linked to medieval farm and settlement types. These associate an English descriptive phrase with an earlier place-name. These include: Milton (Mill town) of-, Haton (Hall town) of-, Cotton (Cot or Cottar town) of-, Kirkton (Church town) of-, Mains (principal farm) of-, Upperton (Upper or north town) of-, Netherton (Lower or south town) of-, Easterton (East town) of-, and Westerton (West town) of-. The towns refer to the old Scottish 'ferm-toun' (farm town), a multiple tenancy farm which might contain a mill and a farmers' hall, or which might be entirely composed of cot houses, or be the principal farm or be geographically situated in one of the ways described.

View of St Andrews Pier by T Allom

The name-type most representative of the Gaelic-speaking period is that containing *baile*, a 'farm-stead or township', usually taking the form of the prefix 'bal'. These names are normally found close to the larger rivers and their tributaries and the density of their distribution is particularly impressive on the upper reaches of the Tay and the Tummel and in the valleys of the North and South Esk. There is also a considerable concentration between Dundee and the Sidlaw Hills. These are all slightly less productive areas than those with earlier names, suggesting that Gaelic-speakers occupied land not already settled prior to their arrival. This implies a peaceful intrusion rather than a violent one. It is worth noting that the names of several of the important settlements in the region appear to belong to this period. These include Angus, Brechin, Dundee, Montrose and Perth.

Earlier Pictish place-names often begin with the element *Pit*, meaning 'a share, a piece' of land, although in many cases the second part of the name is Gaelic, implying that it belonged to a bilingual period in the 9th or 10th century. Another significant place-name element in this area is *Aber*, applying to the mouth of a watercourse or the confluence of two streams. Pre-Celtic names are linked to the major watercourses such as the Tay. This derives from *Ta*—'to melt, to dissolve, to flow'. It can be seen in other British river names such as Thames, Tame, Team, Thame, Tearn, and Tamer.

Place-names are one illustration of the chronological and cultural depth of settlement in Fife and Tayside; traces of burial and ritual sites from prehistoric times show that the area was intensely occupied from the third millennium BC, from times when archaeology alone can provide evidence. Indeed excavation has revealed traces of some of the earliest settlement in Scotland at Morton on Tentsmuir, where the tools have been found of nomadic hunters who made their campsites there some eight thousand years ago. A dug-out canoe or logboat of Scots Pine belonging to this period was discovered at Friarton, near Perth. Campsites or middens have also been found at Dundee and Broughty Ferry, for example, but settlement is likely to have been sparse. The earliest agricultural folk have not left such clear evidence of settlement as in other areas, but the distribution of stone axes and the discovery from air photographs of possible ritual sites mean that early settlement was not as sparse as appears from the few sites visible on the ground. Only a few burial sites have been found; Clach na Tiompan (no. 107) acted as a burial place for a small agricultural community over several centuries. The great ritual complexes of the third millennium BC, often centred on henge monuments as at Balfarg (no. 95), have been seen as indicating a more complex social order capable of large-scale public works. The range and distribution of settlement, burial and ritual monuments of broadly second millennium BC date show that settlement was widely spread throughout the region. Each year in the course of ploughing farmers uncover cist burials (burials in slab-built graves), and archaeologists salvage as rapidly as possible the information that such burials yield about bronze-age traditions. These cists often contain distinctive pottery vessels known as Beakers and Food Vessels. Both cist burials and cremations buried in Cinerary Urns are found mostly on lower ground, but contemporary domestic hut circles and field-systems (eg Craighead, NW of Alyth, NO 195549) extend the distribution of settlement into upland areas. Some round cairns and barrows may be of neolithic date, as may some standing stones; cupmarked boulders were being created from this time, for a fine example was found in the neolithic long barrow at Dalladies in Kincardine.

The first millennium BC saw the formation of powerful tribal units with the social and military organisation necessary for the construction of hillforts. By this time Celtic was the dominant language but it is clear that an older tongue was still remembered. The underground storehouses, or souterrains, of broadly first century AD date were probably associated with rich farms, and they are one of the most remarkable groups of monuments in our area.

The Roman advance into Scotland began in about AD 79 when the governor of the province of *Britannia*, Gnaeus Julius Agricola, marched through the Southern Uplands to the Forth-Clyde isthmus, and perhaps, penetrated as far as the estuary of the *Tavus,* or River Tay. The Roman historian Tacitus, who was Agricola's son-in-law, included an account of these northern campaigns in his biography of the governor; according to Tacitus, the army met with no resistance, and some of the troops spent the winter in the area, for there appeared to be no reason to fear attack. Agricola marched into Strathearn and Strathmore in about AD 82-83; in the wake of the various phases of the advance a line of forts was constructed from Camelon to Ardoch (no. 81), and then via Strageath to Bertha at the confluence of the Tay and Almond; the north-west flank was eventually protected by a screen of forts blocking the mouths of most of the river-valleys that pierce the south-east bulwark of the Grampian massif, but it is still uncertain precisely when these, and the installations along the main route, were first constructed. The site of the fortress of Inchtuthil may have been first occupied about AD 82-83, the first season of campaigning north of the Forth, but the real task of consolidation could not commence until the close of the next campaign, during which Agricola advanced further into Grampian, where he met the combined forces of the northern tribes, under their leader Calgacus and defeated them at the famous battle of *Mons Graupius,* the location of which has tantalised Scottish antiquaries for centuries.

The strategy of Roman occupation of eastern Scotland from the time of *Mons Graupius* to about AD 87 or 88 may be seen in the disposition of the forts between Ardoch and Stracathro (the most northerly fort in the Empire), with the outlying chain of forts to the north-west at the mouths of several Highland glens. Between Ardoch and Bertha the forts were complemented by a chain of timber watch-towers, the best preserved of which are to be found on the Gask Ridge (no. 83). By AD 87 or 88 Roman forces had been withdrawn from northern Scotland and the forts dismantled; by the beginning of the 2nd century the northern frontier of the province began to take a more cohesive form on the Tyne-Solway line.

In the AD 140s southern Scotland was again invaded and taken under Roman sway, and the great frontier barrier known as the Antonine Wall was built between the Forth and Clyde; in Tayside the forts of Ardoch, Strageath and Bertha were rebuilt as forward posts and were occupied, with one brief interval, till the mid 160s. In the final period of campaigning in AD 208-11 after an invasion of the province by the northern tribes, the Emperor Septimius Severus led a massive army into Scotland, using bases that could be serviced by sea from South Shields: on the Forth, Cramond was rebuilt, and on the Tay a new legionary base was constructed at Carpow, although there are now practically no surface traces of what must have been a substantial military installation. The field monuments are among the most impressive in the Roman Empire; the Roman advances also had a political effect on the native population and helped to create the powerful confederacy we know today as the Picts.

Pictish symbol stone from Dunnichen, Angus
(now in McManus Galleries, Dundee)

The Picts are mentioned in Roman literary sources from AD 297 onwards as enemies of Roman Britain, whose aggression contributed to Roman withdrawal from the province, and it is clear from these sources that the political entity that was to become the kingdom of the Picts by the 6th century began as a federation of iron-age tribes. Pictish art owes much to this Celtic ancestry as well as to Northumbrian styles absorbed through ecclesistical contact from the 7th century onwards. Perthshire, Angus and Fife formed the southern part of the kingdom of the Picts, and many fine examples of Pictish stone-carving survive, both in the open air and in museums. Christianity was firmly established in the course of the 7th century and became a potent influence upon the style and repertoire of Pictish sculptors; not only were cross-slabs adopted, but a range of other Christian motifs appears on the stones, most notably scenes from biblical stories of David. The major work of converting the Picts to Christianity was carried out from Iona by Columba and his missionary successors in the late 6th and 7th centuries, but the southern fringes of Pictland along the shores of the Firth of Forth had probably received some experience of Christianity through the efforts in the 5th century of Nynia, or St Ninian, and his followers from Whithorn in Galloway.

Pictland proper lay to the north of the Forth, though some scholars have argued for a Pictish presence south of the Forth. History records the appointment of Trumwine as bishop of the Picts in AD 678, based at Abercorn near South Queensferry, but Dark Age monasteries were frequently sited on territorial boundaries and it would only be prudent, if the Forth were the southern Pictish boundary, to house an Anglian cleric from Northumbria on the 'safe' side of the estuary. His responsibilities included Anglian communities in Lothian as well as the Picts to the north. Fife and Tayside were thus particularly susceptible to ecclesiastical and political influence from northern England. In the mid 650s the Pictish king is known to have had a Northumbrian father, and subsequently, for some thirty years after about 658, southern Pictland lay under Northumbrian domination. The battle of Nechtansmere, near Dunnichen, in 685 was a great victory for the Picts and put an end to the Northumbrian presence though not to Northumbrian influence. Bishop Trumwine withdrew with his monks from Abercorn. Yet by about 710 the Pictish king, Nechtan, was eager to bring the Pictish Church into line with that in Northumbria and to invite Northumbrian architects into Pictland to help build a stone church.

Documentary sources also record battles between the Picts and both the Scots of Dalriada (Argyll) and the Britons of Strathclyde, and a gradual ascendancy of Scottish influence in Pictland during the late 8th and early 9th centuries led finally to a political union of Scots and Picts under the kingship of Kenneth mac Alpin from about AD 843. Thereafter Pictland had become Scotland and, although fine stone sculpture continued to be created, the distinctive Pictish symbols were gradually dropped from the artists' repertoire, presumably having become politically unacceptable.

The ceremonial and symbolic centre of the kingdom of Alba, created by the union of the Picts and Scots, was at Scone in the heart of the area covered by this volume. Here the high kings were inaugurated and here lay the hub of political authority. The ecclesiastical importance of the region at this formative time is underlined by the establishment of religious houses at Brechin (no. 69) and Abernethy (no. 70) and later at Dunkeld (no. 64) and St Andrews (no. 67).

As royal power was consolidated, however, and the territories of the kingdom of Scotland increased with the annexation of the land as far south as the Tweed in 1018 and the acquisition of Strathclyde also in the early 11th century, the centre of royal authority moved south, ultimately to Edinburgh. The 12th-century monarchs continued to favour the area, for Alexander I founded a royal abbey at Scone in 1120; with the organisation of bishoprics by David I, the territorial holdings of the bishops appear to hark back to earlier times, and the seats themselves were all at existing religious centres, for example Brechin, Dunkeld and St Andrews. Royal authority may be seen in the creation of burghs, such as Perth and Montrose, and through the activities of sheriffs, important regional officers of crown administration. In the 12th century royal patronage was responsible for the foundation of the Abbeys of Arbroath (no. 66) by William I in 1178 and Lindores in 1191.

Leuchars Church by D Roberts, 1831

In Scottish terms this region has always been a relatively prosperous area. During the medieval period there was a considerable concentration of royal burghs, particularly along the south facing coast of Fife. Many of these burghs ceased to develop during the post-medieval period, causing a fossilisation of their structures which resulted in the survival of considerable numbers of late-medieval and post-medieval buildings, albeit in a much altered condition. These buildings formed the early focus of activity for the NTS Little Houses Scheme in towns such as Culross, Dysart, Pittenweem and St Monans. At the other end of the scale, the surviving road and feu pattern shows that the medieval plans of the burghs of Dundee, Perth and St Andrews were as ambitious as any in Scotland. Dundee, in particular, grew in importance throughout the medieval period and, by the early 17th century, was considered to be the richest and most secure burgh in the country. The town was twice sacked in the mid 17th century, first by an army led by the Duke of Montrose, when the destruction was limited due to the approach of a relief force, then in 1651 by an army led by General Monk.

The damage was considerable and a large proportion of the townsfolk were put to the sword. This ended Dundee's first period of prosperity and effectively halted the town's growth for at least fifty years. Even after this fifty-year period, expansion was slow until the early years of the 19th century when the town again began to develop, this time under the combined impetus of the Industrial and Agrarian Revolutions.

The rural area accommodated the dwellings of about ninety-five per cent of the medieval population, yet the surviving medieval rural buildings are representative of less than five per cent of the rural population. These are the former dwellings of rich landlords, taking the form of fortified dwellings such as tower-houses. Little is known of the dwellings of the remainder of the rural population other than that these were mainly constructed of turf, stone and turf, wattle and daub or timber-frame. Few descriptions survive for other than the dwellings of the very rich and of the very poor. The middle classes, including farmers, rural tradesmen, and other similar groups, are virtually ignored in contemporary documents.

Blair Castle

In Fife and Tayside, the principles of Classical architecture and planning were introduced in the 1540s with the erection of Falkland Palace (no. 42), but it was not until the late 17th century that these principles were generally accepted by the majority of the region's landowners. During the 18th and 19th centuries the mansion houses, parks, estate buildings and lodges were either extended or rebuilt. 18th-century mansions were generally built to Palladian principles and, although there were a number of changes in architectural style in the 19th century, estate organisation generally followed the rules set down by Palladio in his *Four Books of Architecture*. This was based on the system existing in the vicinity of Venice in Italy in the 16th century when Palladio operated there. This estate organisation involved the landowner exercising control through a 'factor' who dealt directly with the tenant farmers, pendiclers and sub-tenants, on the individual holdings.

The 'great rebuilding' of farms started in the mid 18th century in the richer agricultural areas where there was easy access to a good market. In general, however, this rebuilding took place in the 19th century, in tandem with the establishment of an adequate road, rail and sea transport system, and the development of manufacturing industries both in the burghs and in estate-controlled manufacturing villages.

In more recent years the manufacturing base has changed from textiles and heavy industry to electronics and oil related industries. But, although there has always been an industrial base in the region, the primary occupation and source of wealth, continues to be in agriculture.

EXCURSIONS

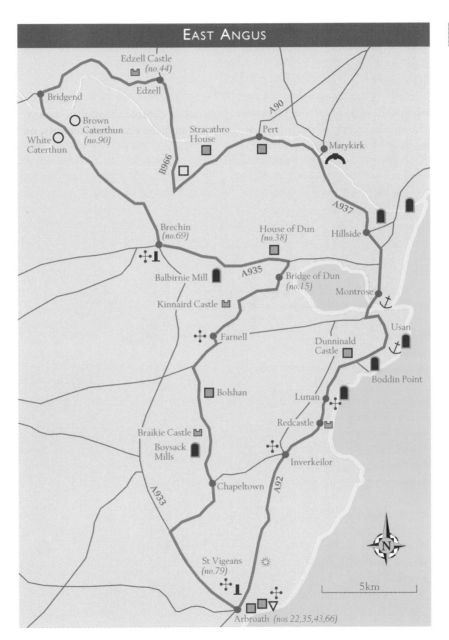

EAST ANGUS

Edzell Castle *(no.44)*
Edzell
Bridgend
Brown Caterthun *(no.90)*
White Caterthun
Stracathro House
Pert
A90
Marykirk
B966
A937
Brechin *(no.69)*
House of Dun *(no.38)*
Hillside
Balbirnie Mill
A935
Bridge of Dun *(no.15)*
Montrose
Kinnaird Castle
Usan
Farnell
Dunninald Castle
Boddin Point
Bolshan
Lunan
Redcastle
Braikie Castle
Boysack Mills
Inverkeilor
A933
Chapeltown
A92
St Vigeans *(no.79)*
5km
N
Arbroath *(nos 22,35,43,66)*

KEY

Bridge	
Castle	
Church	
Fort	
Harbour	
Henge	
House, rural building	
Industrial Monument	
Mercat Cross	
Military Monument	
Miscellaneous later monument	
Miscellaneous prehistoric	
Motte	
Pictish Stone	
Roman Monument	
Round Cairn	
Standing Stone	
Stone Circle	
Town, village	

From Arbroath take the A 92 road towards Montrose, noting the location of the bronze-age cairn on the summit of Dickmontlaw (NO 654435) to the east of the road. At Inverkeilor make a right turn to the Lunan road. To the north of this road junction stands Inverkeilor Parish Church (NO 664496) containing some fine panelled balcony fronts. About 0.5 km north of Redcastle crossroads, pass Redcastle (NO 687510) on the east side of the road. Redcastle was built by King William the Lion in the 12th century as a royal hunting seat and the surviving section of barmkin wall may date from that period.

After crossing a narrow bridge over the Lunan Water and passing Lunan Parish Church (NO 687515) and the entrance to Lunan House, the road to the right leads to a car park, past the ruins of a dovecote and an icehouse (privately owned). The icehouse is built into the bank of the side of a small pond and has an interesting tower feature forming the entrance porch. The main chamber is subterranean, but the mound of earth covering the barrel vault can be seen clearly. This is a commercial icehouse built to serve the salmon fishing station at Lunan Bay.

Continuing northwards from Lunan to the Dunninald crossroads (NO 696538), turn east towards Usan. The road skirts the south boundary of the Dunninald Castle park, passing some simple early 19th-century lodges and estate-workers cottages. The first road to the right leads south-east to Boddin Point (NO 713533) with its 18th-century limekilns (now ruinous and collapsing into the sea) and harbour and 19th-century salmon fishing station, icehouse, fishhouse and bothy. The limekilns are about 0.25 km from the car park down a reasonably steep incline. Care must be taken, particularly if there are children in the party, as the cliff edges are dangerous and the tops of the limekilns have no balustrades either to the edge or to the kiln-bowls.

Return to the Usan road and then turn right, then almost immediately right again to the farmyard of Seaton of Usan and to Fishtown of Usan with its Coastguard Station, ruined village, harbour, and icehouse/saltpan (no. 8).

Return to Seaton of Usan and continue northwards; from the hilltop at Barns of Craig can be seen the full extent of the Montrose Basin and the Royal Burgh of Montrose, with its beautiful mid 19th-century parish church steeple (NO 714577). Continue to Montrose itself. The large medieval market square is worthy of note, although most of the buildings surrounding the square were rebuilt in the 19th century or later.

From Montrose follow the A 92 road towards Aberdeen passing: a former brewery (NO 715590), on the junction of the A 92 and A 935 Brechin Road, now used as a distillery; Montrose Airfield (NO 719595) with its World War I aircraft hangars; and the North Toll house (NO 716596) at the junction of the A 92 and A 937 Aberdeen roads. Approximately 2 km north of this junction on the A 92, turn right for Kinnaber. Kinnaber House (NO 725617) is a late 17th-century mansion showing a transitional phase between the earlier tower-house style and the later classical mansionhouse style. To the south of the house and close to the road is a field containing what appears to be the remnants of a pre-improvement fermtoun. Continue past the house and Kinnaber dovecote to Fisherhills salmon fishing station with its icehouse.

Return to the A 92 and turn northwards towards Aberdeen, in 0.25 km turn west to Hillside, passing a distillery on the north side of the road. At Hillside turn north towards Aberdeen on the A 937 road. Approximately 5 km north of Hillside the A 937 road makes a sharp right turn under a railway bridge to cross Marykirk Bridge (NO 686650) with its integral toll-house. The bridge and toll-house were designed by John Smeaton in 1813.

Continue along the west side of the railway embankment towards Pert and North Water Bridge past the fine late 17th-century house known as Gallery (NO 673656). North Water Bridge (NO 652661) was completed in 1539 and until recently carried the A 94 Perth-Aberdeen road.

Edzell Castle

On reaching the A 90 turn south-west towards Brechin and Perth. After passing Stracathro Hospital, occupying the grounds of Stracathro House, a neo-classical mansion by the Aberdeen architect, Archibald Simpson, take the B 966 to Edzell. This road passes to the west of the site of Stracathro Roman temporary camp (NO 613656).

Enter Edzell under the triumphal arch erected to celebrate Queen Victoria's visit and continue to the far end of the main street. Turn left opposite the Panmure Arms Hotel following the signposts for Edzell Castle (no. 44). The elaborate Edzell Castle dovecote (NO 588690) stands to the north of Mains of Edzell farmhouse.

Continue westwards to Bridgend then south-east towards Brechin, through a saddle between the Brown and White Caterthuns (no. 90). Continue into Brechin (no. 69).

From Brechin follow the A 935 for Montrose. Approximately 3 km from Brechin the road passes to the north of Balbirnie Mill (NO 631585), a former corn (oats) mill which is open to the public as a restaurant-coffee house linked to the former milling floor. Approximately 4 km beyond this, on the north side of the road, is the House of Dun (no. 38).

Turn back towards Brechin for 0.1 km then turn south to Bridge of Dun (no. 15), and take the Farnell road about 1 km to the south of the bridge. This road passes Haughs of Kinnaird (NO 644574), the home farm for the Southesk Estates, once famous as a model farm used to illustrate ideal farm

St Vigeans Museum, detail of stone no.1 with hunter with crossbow and animals

buildings in *Encyclopaedia Britannica*. The building has now been remodelled to suit modern farming practice. The road then follows the park wall round the east and south sides of Kinnaird Castle. In Farnell village turn south past Farnell Parish Church (NO 627554), a neo-Gothic building by James Gillespie Graham, to the A 934 Montrose-Forfar road. Turn south-west towards Forfar for approximately 1.8 km then turn south past Bolshan (NO 619520), a farm with the stump of a former threshing wind-mill, now used as a water tower. Continue south for about 0.9 km, turn towards Kinnell for 0.1 km then south towards Boysack Mills, past Braikie Castle (NO 628508), a 16th-century tower-house now becoming ruinous. Boysack Mills (NO 626491) is a good example of a small corn (oats) mill which retains its mill dam and water wheel. Continue southwards towards Arbroath through Chapelton. 1 km beyond Chapelton turn south-west to Colliston then south-east towards Arbroath on the A 933. Pass HMS Condor, the Royal Marine Commando base, then detour north-east to St Vigeans Museum (no. 79) and church.

Hospitalfield House

On reaching the outskirts of Arbroath on the A 933, turn right at the Western Cemetery gates to follow the by-pass road to Dundee. The ceme-tery (NO 624417) contains the Patrick Allan Fraser Mausoleum, a Gothic folly of extraordinary vigour. On leaving the cemetery continue towards Dundee for about 1.5 km to Hospitalfield House (no. 35).

Other monuments within the town of Arbroath include Arbroath Abbey (no. 66), the Abbot's House (no. 43) and the Bell Rock Signal Tower (no. 22) containing the Signal Tower Museum.

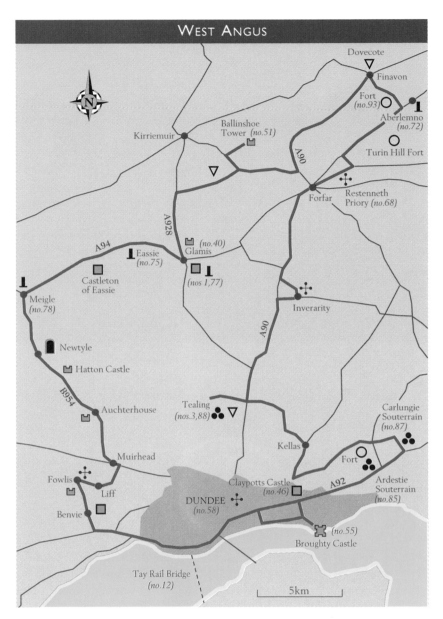

From Dundee take the A 92 towards Arbroath then the A 930 for Broughty Ferry to visit Broughty Harbour and Broughty Castle (no. 55). Return along the shore road to Westfield Road (B 978), turn north and cross the traffic lights into Claypotts Road for Claypotts Castle (no. 46). Take the A 92 towards Arbroath for 5 km to Ardestie souterrain (no. 85), and after a further 2 km turn north to Carlungie following the signpost for Carlungie souterrain (no. 87). Continue north to the T-junction, turn west to Templehall crossing the B 962 and following the B 961 back towards Dundee for about 0.8 km then turn south to Laws of Monifieth farm, where permission to visit the fort should be sought. On the hilltop, to the south of the farm, is an extensive timber-laced fort (NO 491349), which was later overlain by one of the few brochs in Tayside. Take the B 961 back towards Dundee to Baldovie, turning north on the B 978.

Tealing Souterrain

On reaching Kellas turn west towards Tealing, crossing the A 929 to Tealing dovecote (no. 3) and souterrain (no. 88). Follow the A 929 and A 932 to Forfar. The road passes within 1.5 km of the wide-bodied church at Inverarity (NO 452443), which can be approached from Gateside or by the B 9217 Douglastown-Arbroath road.

In Forfar visit the Meffan Institute Museum to see the Pictish stones from Kirriemuir and an excellent introduction to the archaeology and history of the area. Then turn right at the traffic lights through the centre of the town, following the B 9113 Montrose road to Restenneth Priory (no. 68). Continue towards Montrose for 0.75 km then turn north to meet the B 9134 Forfar-Brechin road. Turn north-east towards Brechin and follow the road to Aberlemno Pictish stones (no. 72). This road passes Turin Hill (NO 514535) on which are the remains of a complex fort and three later small stone-walled fortifications; there are also several cup-and-ring marked outcrops.

Turn back on the B 9134 towards Forfar; after 1 km take the Finavon road to the north-west past Finavon fort (no. 93). On reaching the A 90 turn north-east towards Aberdeen for approximately 1 km to Finavon dovecote (NO 490570), possibly the largest double-chambered lectern type dovecote in Scotland. Follow the A 90 back towards Forfar and take the A 926 road to Kirriemuir. After passing Padanaram School take the second road on the right to Ballinshoe. Pass Ballinshoe steading to Ballinshoe Tower (no. 51). Return to Padanaram School and take the road to the west to North Mains of Ballindarg (NO 406513), a fine 18th-century farm steading dated 1761. Continue west to Roundyhill School then south on the A 928 to Glamis Castle (no. 40), the Angus Folk Museum (no. 1), the Glamis Pictish stones (no. 77), parish church and churchyard. The wild garden, the 'cathedral' around St Fergus' Well, is a beautiful sight in Glamis Den.

From Glamis take the A 94 road towards Perth, leaving the road at Eassie to visit the Pictish stone (no. 75). About 1.5 km west of Eassie is the moated site of Castleton of Eassie (NO 333466), former site of Nairne House Home Farm now Castleton Hotel. On reaching Meigle follow the B 954 road towards Dundee stopping at the Meigle Museum to see the collection of Pictish stones (no. 78). Follow the B 954 to Newtyle where the terminus of the Dundee and Newtyle Railway can be seen by turning left at the crossroads towards Glamis then second right to the terminus building (NO 300414). Continue on the B 954 towards Dundee passing the extended tower-house known as Hatton Castle (NO 301410) on the east side of the Glack of Newtyle. The road runs parallel to the line of the Dundee and Newtyle Railway to Auchterhouse. Turn right at Auchterhouse crossroads to the Mansion House Hotel, formerly Auchterhouse (NO 331372), an extended tower-house built round a courtyard and in close proximity to a second ruined tower-house.

The B 954 meets the A 923 in Muirhead. Immediately after the junction turn south and follow the signposts to Liff and then Fowlis. Fowlis Easter Church (NO 322334) is a fine example of a collegiate church with the remains of a rood screen and wall paintings. Take the road south through Benvie passing Fowlis Castle (NO 321333), a 16th-century tower-house on the east side of the road; Benvie Mill (NO 328315), a simple corn (oats) mill; and a cast of the Benvie cross-slab in the graveyard (the original is in the McManus Galleries, Dundee).

On reaching the A 85 turn east to Dundee. At the Invergowrie roundabout follow the A 85 for Dundee Airport to the Invergowrie service road. Invergowrie toll-house (NO 349303) stands on the south side of the former Dundee-Perth turnpike road. Continue to Dundee following the A 85 past Dundee Airfield to the Tay Rail Bridge (no. 12). Other monuments in Dundee include St Andrews Church (no. 58), the Polar research ship *Discovery* and the early 19th-century frigate *Unicorn*.

Aberlemno, front face of cross-slab at the roadside

Aberlemno, symbol stone
(Left)

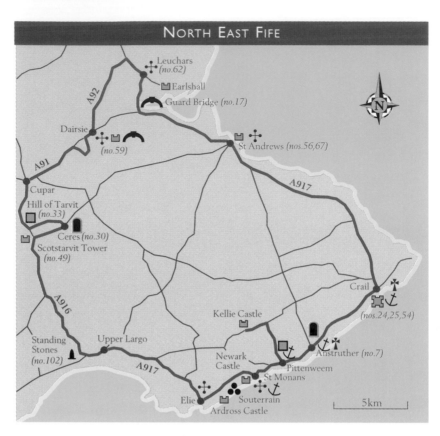

NORTH EAST FIFE

From St Andrews follow the A 91 Cupar road, passing a number of cast-iron mile markers (no. 21) and a toll-house (NO 463188)—extended by the addition of a second apsidal ended wing—on the north side of the road. Turn north for Guardbridge Hotel and park for views of and access to Guard Bridge (no. 17). Follow the A 919 to Leuchars Church (no. 62). Earlshall (NO 464210), a 16th-century tower-house restored by Sir Robert Lorimer, is situated approximately 1 km east of Leuchars Church and has a fine topiary garden.

From Leuchars continue north-west on the A 919 towards Dundee. Turn southwestwards at St Michael crossroads, stopping to examine the comprehensive list of places on the cast-iron distance plate. Follow the A 92 for Dairsie and Cupar. This road has a number of fine early 19th-century cast-iron mile markers (no. 21), the most obvious being situated on the St Michael side of the roundabout at the junction of the A 92 with the A 91. Follow the A 91 to Dairsie then turn south for Pitscottie. Approximately 1.5 km from the junction in Dairsie, turn westwards avoiding crossing Dairsie Bridge and park at Dairsie churchyard for Dairsie Church (no. 59), castle and bridge. Continue north-west from the churchyard to rejoin the A 91 road, turning towards Cupar. There is a good cast-iron mile marker on the east side of this junction.

On entering Cupar stop short of the junction of the A91 and B940 where there is a fine example of an early 19th-century toll-house (NO 378146). Follow the A 92 road through Cupar then the A 916 to

**Leuchars Church,
detail of arcading**

Scotstarvit Tower (no. 49) and Hill of Tarvit (no. 33). Leave Hill of Tarvit by the south drive and turn east to Ceres and Ceres Weigh-house (no. 30).

From Ceres follow the B 939 westwards to its junction with the A 916 at Craigrothie; turn south for approximately 4 km then south-east along a minor road for Lundin Links standing stones (no. 102). Follow the A 915 eastwards through Lundin Links to Upper Largo, then the A 917 for Elie Church (NO 491001) in the centre of Elie. Continue on the A 917, passing: the ruins of Ardross Castle (NO 508007); Ardross souterrain (NO 503009); Newark Castle (NO 518012), to St Monans harbour (NO 526015) and church (NO 522014).

On returning to the A 917 continue east to Pittenweem; follow the signs for the harbour to visit The Gyles (NO 550024) and other NTS Little House projects and Kellie Lodging. Kellie Castle (NO 520052) is situated to the north of St Monans.

Return to the A 917 and continue to Anstruther for the Scottish Fisheries Museum (no. 7), passing the market cross at the beginning of the west harbour. Continue through Anstruther to Cellardyke and back to the A 917 for Crail market cross (no. 25), Market Square, and harbour (no. 24).

From Crail follow the A 917 to St Andrews, which contains a remarkable group of monuments including: the Castle (no. 56); the Cathedral (no. 67) with its precinct walls, St Rule's Tower and St Mary of the Rock; the Harbour; Blackfriars Aisle in South Street; the West Port; and St Salvator's Chapel in North Street.

**St Andrews
Cathedral**

**St Andrews
Cathedral and
Castle from
the air**

ISLE OF MAY

Fog Siren

The Low Light

Lighthouse base

Lighthouse

Priory

Fog Siren

Landing Place

500m

A visit to the Isle of May makes a fascinating excursion from the points of view of natural history, industrial archaeology, and early medieval remains. The ferry leaves from Anstruther, just opposite the Scottish Fisheries Museum (no. 7), weather permitting, on most days in the summer (for ferry times phone 01333 310103). The island is a National Nature Reserve managed by Scottish Natural Heritage and the warden will advise visitors about paths and access, particularly during the breeding season. The crossing takes about an hour and depending on the trip and the tide conditions the visitor can enjoy between one and three hours on the island. Warm and waterproof clothing and footwear is essential; take refreshments.

Set on a commanding position is the lighthouse built by Robert Stevenson in 1816, with the base of the earlier tower at its side (no. 23). Foghorns at each end of the island were operated by compressed air and the system of pipes that were needed is an unusual feature of the archaeology of navigational aids.

The ruined Priory was founded by David I in about 1145, as a daughter house of Reading, but the recorded Christian history of the island is much older for in 875 St Ethernan and his followers were reputedly murdered by the Vikings and his shrine was to become the object of pilgrimage in medieval times. Excavations have revealed the depth of evidence that remains to be uncovered, including the cloister area and long cist burials.

**Isle of May,
Lighthouse**

**Base of earlier
lighthouse**

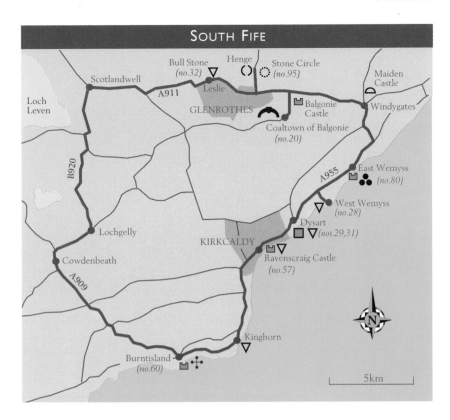

SOUTH FIFE

From Kirkcaldy High Street follow the A 921 Dundee road to the traffic lights overlooking Ravenscraig Castle (no. 57). There is an excellent beehive type dovecote in the park to the east of the Castle (NT 293924). Continue on the A 955 for approximately 1 km then turn east into Dysart to visit: Dysart Tolbooth (no. 29); Pan ha' Little Houses project, and Bay Horse Inn (no. 31); harbour and museum. Return to the A 955 and proceed to the north-east, turning south to West Wemyss to visit the tolbooth (no. 28). Continue through West Wemyss to East Wemyss, parking at the cemetery to visit Macduff's Castle (NO 344971) and Wemyss Caves (no. 80).

Kirkcaldy, Sailor's Walk (Left)

Well Cave, Wemyss and Macduff's Castle

Continue on the A 955 to the outskirts of Buckhaven then turn north on the B 930 for Windygates joining the A 915 south of the town. Follow the A 915 to the centre of Windygates then the A 916 towards Kennoway. On leaving Windygates, down a steep hill, the motte known as Maiden Castle (NO 349015) stands to the east of the road. Backtrack to the centre of Windygates then follow the A 911 to Markinch. At the west end of Milton of Balgonie follow a minor road to Coaltown of Balgonie and Balgonie Castle (NO 312006), a large tower and courtyard castle, and Coaltown of Balgonie Bridge (no. 20).

Follow the B 9130 to Markinch and beyond, turning north on the A 92, towards Dundee. The henge monument of Balfarg and the restored stone circle of Balbirnie (no. 95) are sited on either side of the A 92 about 1.1 km north of Glenrothes. From Balfarg take the B 969 to Leslie and the Bull Stone (no. 32). Continue on the A 911 to Scotlandwell, turn south on the B 920 to Lochgelly then join the A 910 for Cowdenbeath. Turn south on the A 909 for Burntisland. In Burntisland visit: Rossend Castle (NT 228857), a recently restored tower-house, and Burntisland Parish Church (no. 60). Return to Kirkcaldy on the A 921 road by Kinghorn noting the 19th-century tolbooth and jail (NT 270871). In Kirkcaldy note the Sailor's Walk buildings (NT 284920) at the north cnd of the High Street; these are good examples of early 17th-century townhouses.

**Ravenscraig
Castle**

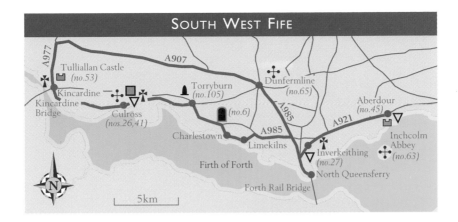

SOUTH WEST FIFE

From Dunfermline Abbey and Palace (no. 65) follow the A823 towards North Queensferry using the B980 and B981 to the former ferry piers (NT 130802 and 128802) between the Forth Road Bridge and Forth Rail Bridge. Return by the B981 to Inverkeithing to visit the tolbooth (no. 27) and market cross. Continue north on the B981 till its junction with the A921, following this road east to Aberdour. Visit Aberdour Castle (no. 45), dovecote and gardens.

From North Queensferry, take the boat (timetable allowing) to Inchcolm Abbey (no. 63), enjoying views of the Forth Road and Rail Bridges. On return follow the A985 road for Kincardine Bridge. Take the loop south through Limekilns to Charlestown harbour and limekilns (no. 6). Continue west, rejoining the A985 road to Torryburn standing stone (no. 105) and Culross.

**Dunfermline
Abbey, interior**

Aberdour Castle
(Top)

Inchcolm Abbey

Culross has a number of important monuments including the Abbey (NS 989862), Palace (no. 41), Market Cross (no. 26), Tolbooth (NS 985859) and NTS Little Houses project. Full details may be obtained from the NTS information office in the Tolbooth.

Follow the B 9037 west to Kincardine on Forth to view: Kincardine Bridge (NS 925871) opened in 1936; Kincardine Market Cross (NS 931875) and, off the A 977 north of the town, Tulliallan Castle (no. 53). Continue north on the A 977 through Kilbagie returning to Dunfermline by the A 907.

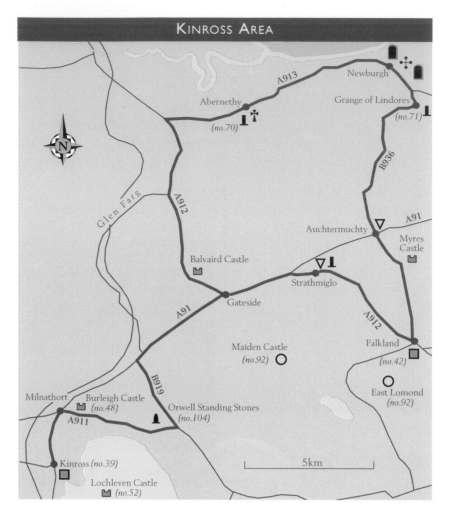

KINROSS AREA

From Kinross follow the A 922 to Milnathort, turning east on the A 91 for 0.25 km, then south-east on the A 911 to Burleigh Castle (no. 48). Continue eastwards on the A 911 to Orwell standing stones (no. 104) on the north side of the road, then to Wester Balgedie. Turn north-west on the B 919 to its junction with the A 91. Follow the A 91 north-east to Gateside, turn north-west on the A 912 road for Glen Farg. Balvaird Castle (NO 169115), a 15th-century L-plan tower-house with later extensions, stands on a hill-top on the east side of the road approximately 2.5 km from Gateside. Continue northwards on the A 912 to Baiglie Inn, turn east on the A 913 for Abernethy with its market cross (NO 190163) and round tower (no. 70).

From Abernethy continue to Newburgh on the A 913. Newburgh was an important shipping centre for Tay salmon in the late 18th century, after Richardson of Pitfour established a trade with Billingsgate, London for fresh Tay salmon packed in ice. This trade started in 1765 and soon Newburgh was exporting fresh fish from fishing stations as far apart as Rockhall, St Cyrus, Loch Tay and Stirling; the icehouse survives at the southern edge of a modern housing development to the south of the main street. It is a large rectangular structure built against the north retaining wall of a road running parallel to the main street (NO 235181).

Abernethy Round Tower

To the east of Newburgh are the ruins of Lindores Abbey (NO 243184) and Parkhill Mill (NO 245185), a former three-storey corn (oats) mill and kiln used, by the farmer at Parkhill farm, for the bruising of cattle feed. The dam which supplies the water to the overshot wheel is situated on the opposite side of the road from the mill building.

The ruins of Denmylne Castle (NO 249175), on the east side of the A913 road about 1 km from Newburgh, represent a simple rectangular tower with a later extension to the back creating an unorthodox L-plan form. Just south of Denmylne Castle, turn south on the B936 then east through Grange of Lindores to Abdie Pictish stone (no. 71).

Follow the B936 road south to Auchtermuchty, to see the tolbooth (NO 238117) situated in the centre of the town; this 18th-century structure incorporates a tower as the centre piece of the composition, the council chamber on the first floor, and a gaol on the ground floor (now the local library and citizen's advice centre).

Kinross House and Loch Leven

Falkland Palace
(Bottom)

From Auchtermuchty follow the B936 south to Falkland, passing to the east of Myres Castle (NO 241109), approximately 0.5 km south of the town. This tower-house with later extensions is the birthplace of Dr Reginald Fairlie, architect for the restoration of Leuchars Church (no. 62) and other important ecclesiastical buildings in the region. In Falkland, visit the Palace (no. 42) and some fine examples of 17th- and 18th-century town houses. The Lomond Hills to the south of Falkland contain several prehistoric monuments including the forts of East Lomond and Maiden Castle (no. 92).

From Falkland follow the A912 northwest to Strathmiglo, passing the tolbooth (NO 214102) in the centre of the High Street. This is a building of similar age and style to the tolbooth at Auchtermuchty. A fine Pictish symbol stone may be seen beside the churchyard gate at NO 216102, in Kirk Wynd, south of the High Street. Return to Kinross by the A91, B996 and A922. Kinross House (no. 39) is entered from the High Street, and Lochleven Castle (no. 52) can be reached by boat from the pier to the east of the burgh.

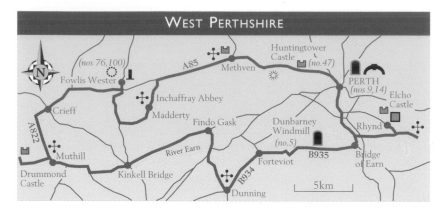

WEST PERTHSHIRE

From Perth follow the A85 to Huntingtower Castle (no. 47), then continue westwards to Methven passing a large prehistoric burial mound (NO 069249) on the south side of the road about 1.2 km from the Huntingtower Castle road-end. Methven Castle (NO 041260) is a large symmetrical rectangular building with turretted corners. In Methven village visit the parish churchyard (NO 025260) which contains an unusual neo-Classical mausoleum of extraordinary quality, sited close to the south wall of the church. This is one of the last works by Robert Playfair prior to his premature death in 1794.

Continue westwards on the A85 road towards Crieff then turn south for Madderty and Inchaffray Abbey (NN 953225). From Madderty continue southwards to a crossroads. Turn west towards Crieff for approximately 2.5 km, then north to Fowlis Wester to see the cross-slabs (no. 76) and the cairn, standing stone and stone circle (no. 100) to the north of the village.

Return to the A85 and turn west to Crieff, passing a toll-house at the junction of the A85 with the Madderty road (NN 868216). On reaching the Square, turn south on the A822 road to visit the fine parterre-type formal gardens at Drummond Castle (NN 844179). Continue south to Muthill Old Church (NN 867170) with its tall tower and late Anglo-Saxon type windows.

From Muthill follow the Kinkell Bridge road to the east crossing the course of a Roman road (NN 887165) about 2 km from the village. Cross Kinkell Bridge turning north on the B8062 for 0.1 km, then north-east for Findo Gask following the Gask Ridge with its Roman watch-towers (no. 83).

Fowlis Wester

From Findo Gask take the road south to join the B9141 road to Dunning. Dunning Church tower (NO 019144) is a powerful structure, again displaying late Anglo-Saxon type windows. From Dunning, follow the B934 to Forteviot, then the B935 towards Bridge of Earn, visiting Dunbarney Windmill (no. 5).

In Bridge of Earn turn north towards Perth on the A912 road. Cross the bridge over the River Earn and turn east for Rhynd. At Mains of Kinmonth continue eastwards for Easter Rhynd churchyard (NO 182185) which contains some interesting salmon fishermen's tombstones. These are illustrated with low relief plans and three-dimensional representations of the salmon cobles and fishermen at work.

Backtrack to Mains of Kinmonth, continuing north-westwards towards Rhynd. Turn north for Elcho Castle (NO 164210), passing Elcho farmhouse and steading (NO 163208) now much altered from its 1830s model farm condition. To the north of the steading is a beehive type dovecote and beyond that Elcho Castle, an extended L-plan tower-house of substantial proportions.

Return to Perth by the A 912 passing Perth Prison on the east side of the road. Cross the South Inch to Marshall Place to visit Perth Water Works (no. 9). Perth Bridge (no. 14) is situated at the north end of Tay Street. The impressive old Council Chambers building is at the corner of Tay Street and High Street.

Elcho Castle

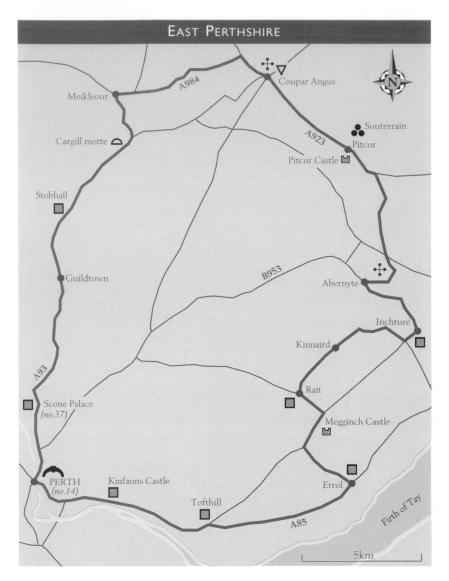

EAST PERTHSHIRE

From Perth cross Perth Bridge (no. 14) taking the A93 to Scone Palace (no. 37) with its agricultural implements collection, market cross, gateway and chapel. Continue north on the A93 past Balboughty farm steading (NO 124275), the impressive home farm of the Scone Palace Estates erected in 1853 to an Italianate design. After passing through Guildtown visit Stobhall (NO 132343), an interesting house containing a fine painted ceiling in the chapel, probably painted between 1625 and 1648.

On leaving Stobhall continue northwards past Cargill motte (NO 157374), over Bridge of Isla to Meikleour Beech Hedge (NO 161387), a remarkable hedge being approximately 20 m in height. The village of Meikleour (NO 157395) is a good example of a mid 19th-century estate village.

From Meikleour follow the A984 and A923 to Coupar Angus. Leave Coupar Angus on the A923 road over the level crossing and past the 18th-century tolbooth and the ruins of Coupar Angus Abbey (NO 223397).

Perth Bridge

Pitcur souterrain (NO 252373) and Pitcur Castle (NO 251369) are on either side of the road about 3.25 km from Coupar Angus Abbey.

Continue on the A923 and a minor road to Abernyte churchyard (NO 266311), where there are some fine 18th-century tradesmen's tombstones, particularly the flesher's stone on the south side of the church. Join the B953 road at Abernyte and proceed south-eastwards towards Inchture visiting the late 18th-century estate village of Baledgarno (NO 276302), comprising a long street of single-storey estate workers' cottages. Those to the north of the Rossie Priory Gates were two-room cottages, those to the south, single room. The early 19th-century village school stands in the field to the south and the Factor's House and Baledgarno steading occupy the hillside to the east.

Inchture (NO 280287) is a good example of a 19th-century estate village built in two stages in the 1830s and 1860s. The 1830s houses are all pattern-book types grouped in single-storey ranges of three or four dwellings. The 1860s houses are mainly of one and a half storeys with upper floor dormer windows. At the west end of the village, detached from the other 19th-century buildings, is a long single-storey range with a large doorway at the west end of the south facade. This was the terminus of the Inchture horse tramway linking the village to the Inchture railway station approximately 2 km to the south.

Join the A85 road on the north side of Inchture following the road to the south-west towards Perth. Turn north-westwards to Rait village (NO 226268). The west end of this village is one of the best surviving examples of a pre-agrarian improvement 'ferm-toun' with single-storey thatched cottages bending on plan and running with the level of the ground to reflect the nature of the natural features of the locality. Return to the A85 towards Perth, past the gates to Megginch Castle, then turn to the south-east for Inchcoonans. Inchcoonans Brick and Tile Works (NO 238233) is one of the last surviving 19th-century brickworks in Scotland. The former clay pit on the east side of the road has now been back filled and returned to agricultural use. Errol village (NO 252228) is the

**Kinfauns Home
Farm Dairy**

centre of one of the largest concentrations of *pisé* walled houses (a form of consolidated tempered earth) in Scotland. Slightly battered walls in the High Street and Cowgate indicate the use of this material behind modern harl.

Rejoin the A85 for Perth passing Tofthill farmhouse (NO 177210), an early 20th-century neo-vernacular farmhouse based on an extended tower-house design. The A85 passes to the south of Kinfauns Castle (NO 150226), an 1830s house by Sir Robert Smirke, designer of the British Museum in London, in a castellated style. On either side of Kinfauns Castle is a tower folly rising from the crags penetrating the wooded slopes of the hills. These were erected as 'ruins' to accentuate the similarity between this stretch of the River Tay and the River Rhine at its confluence with the Moselle. Between the house and road is situated the walled gardens and home farm. The home farm has a splendid dairy and scullery designed by Sir Robert Lorimer in 1927.

Continuing towards Perth, the A85 passes under Friarton Bridge to Barnton Toll (NO 128220) with its Classical facade, tariff board and the remains of the toll bar.

Blair Castle

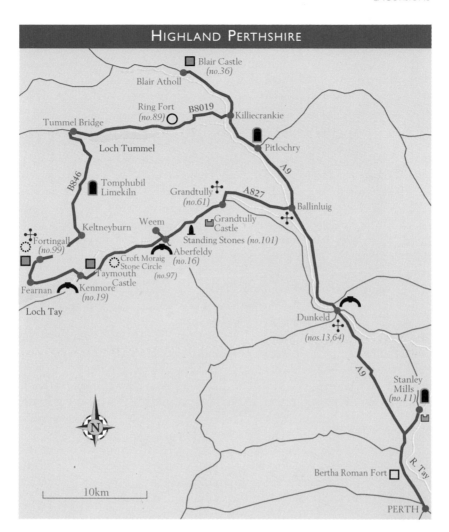

HIGHLAND PERTHSHIRE

Blair Castle (no.36)
Blair Atholl
Ring Fort (no.89)
B8019
Killiecrankie
Tummel Bridge
Loch Tummel
Pitlochry
A9
B846
Tomphubil Limekiln
Grandtully (no.61)
A827
Ballinluig
Keltneyburn
Weem
Grandtully Castle
Fortingall (no.99)
Standing Stones (no.101)
Croft Moraig Stone Circle (no.97)
Aberfeldy (no.16)
Taymouth Castle
Fearnan
Kenmore (no.19)
Loch Tay
Dunkeld (nos.13,64)
A9
Stanley Mills (no.11)
R. Tay
Bertha Roman Fort
10km
PERTH

N

From Perth follow the A9 road for Inverness; after crossing the River Almond the road passes to the west of the site of Bertha Roman fort (NO 097268). Take the B9099 for Stanley Mills (no. 11) and planned village. To the east of the mills is a pleasant walk to the end of a promontory formed by a bend in the River Tay. At the end of this promontory is the ruin of a former tower-house (NO 122329).

Return to the A9 continuing northwards and take the detour to Dunkeld crossing Dunkeld Bridge (no. 13) to the town centre. Visit the NTS Information Centre and Little Houses project in the High Street; Dunkeld Cathedral (no. 64); and Dunkeld House icehouse (NO 029427). The icehouse is a domestic type with a pit below the entrance level to contain the ice. It is situated in the side of a wooded hill to the west of the north carpark.

Either follow the tourist route north on the line of the 18th-century military road or the A9 to Ballinluig. Turn west on

Dunkeld Cathedral

the A 827 towards Aberfeldy visiting Logierait churchyard with its early cross-slab and mortsafes (see no. 74). Continue following the A827 through Grandtully to St Mary's Church (no. 61) about 3.5 km beyond the village. Returning to the A827 there is a dramatic view of Grandtully Castle (NN 891513), a Z-plan tower-house with Victorian extensions. The A827 road passes near Lundin standing stones (no. 101).

Pass through Aberfeldy to the crossroads at the west end of the town. Turn north on the B846 for Weem and Kinloch Rannoch. Stop at the Victoria Park walking south-west along the south bank of the River Tay for views of Aberfeldy Bridge (no. 16). Backtrack to Aberfeldy turning west on the A827 road to Kenmore, visiting Croft Moraig stone circle (no. 97). From Croft Moraig the road climbs to a considerable height above the valley floor. From this vantage there is a good view of Taymouth Castle (NN 784465), one of the largest 19th-century houses in the region.

After entering Kenmore turn north-east through the Taymouth Castle Gates for the Chinese Bridge (no. 19) and close-up views of Taymouth Castle. Backtrack to Kenmore. An ambitious reconstruction of a crannog is underway at Croft-na-Caber at the NE end of Loch Tay (NN 769448), which will offer a unique impression of a widespread type of settlement of later prehistoric and early historic date. Again, back to Kenmore. Follow the A827 for Fearnan and Killin. As the road passes the east end of Loch Tay it crosses Kenmore Bridge (NN 771455), an early 19th-century structure.

At Fearnan turn north for Fortingall. The thatched cottages fronting the north side of the road are known as Balnald Cottages (NN 739470) and are the work of James Marjoribanks MacLaren. These incorporate features of vernacular buildings found in the Kinross area in the second half of the 19th century. Fortingall Parish Church was remodelled by the same architect and Fortingall Hotel, the work of his successors, Dunne and Watson. All were significant buildings in the development of later Scottish architecture by architects as diverse as Dr Reginald Fairlie, Sir Robert Lorimer and Charles Rennie Mackintosh. There are stone circles (no. 99) at the east end of the village.

Continue north-eastwards to Keltyneyburn to the T-junction with the B846 and turn north towards Kinloch Rannoch following the line of General Wade's Military Road. Approximately 5.5 km from this junction is the farm of Tomphubil which has an old limekiln (NN 787545). At Tummel Bridge T-junction turn east for Killiecrankie on the B 8019. Stop at Queen's View, Loch Tummel to visit the ring-fort (no. 89).

Continue on the B8019 to Bridge of Garry then north through the Pass of Killiecrankie to the NTS Visitor Centre (NN 917626) and The Soldier's Leap over the River Garry. From Killiecrankie follow the A9 north-westwards to Blair Atholl and Blair Castle (no. 36).

Return to Perth by the A9 and the Tourist Route through Pitlochry, visiting the Hydro Electric dam and fishladder (NN 937577).

AGRICULTURE, FISHING AND INDUSTRY

St Andrews around 1900

AGRICULTURE

Fife and Tayside contain some of the richest agricultural land in Scotland. This land is at present the subject of a second agricultural revolution just as radical and far reaching as the first and involving sweeping changes. Field and farm size is increasing as the workforce decreases. Changes in agricultural technology and machinery are causing a demand for larger, more flexible, buildings and the old order is being replaced by the new.

Prior to this recent change there were few high quality agricultural buildings erected this century. The ogee-roofed dairy and adjoining scullery at Kinfauns Castle Home Farm (NO 149224), designed by Sir Robert Lorimer and erected in 1928, is outstanding in this class. This building is in private ownership but is readily visible from the A 90 Dundee/Perth road a little to the east of Friarton Bridge.

The second half of the 19th century saw a general expansion of the farm buildings dating from the first half of the century. The most common extension was the provision of root stores and the roofing of cattle wintering courts. A number of fine neo-vernacular and Scots Baronial farmhouses were erected at this time, usually as replacements for earlier houses. Tofthill (NO 177210), also on the A 90, was erected in 1910 to designs by F L W Deas of Edinburgh. This is a neo-vernacular house based on the detail and proportions of an extended tower-house. This house replaced a two-storey, peind-roofed, Georgian farmhouse by Sir Robert Smirke. The farmhouse at Pittormie (NO 417185) in north Fife also started life as a Georgian house. This building was remodelled in 1867 by John Milne of St Andrews to be a fine example of a Scots Baronial style farmhouse. This was achieved by the addition of new wings, crowstepped gables, dormer windows, castellated parapets and turrets. A large landscaped garden was established to help the romantic illusion by framing views of the house and accentuating its vertical elements. In the rich agricultural areas these romantic houses were mainly replacements for earlier improved houses built in the late 18th or early 19th century, whereas in the Highland districts they often formed the first major improvement. This resulted in greater numbers of romantic houses in the Highlands making the standard houses appear less severe than their Lowland counterparts.

Lochore field pattern with ridge and furrow

One Highland site of particular interest is the Glenlyon Estate in the parish of Fortingall. The buildings on this estate were built in a number of neo-vernacular styles representing various stages in the development of agricultural buildings in Lowland districts. The Glenlyon farmhouse, steading, laundry, kennels and, although not agricultural, the Fortingall Hotel are all based on forms associated with Scottish tower-houses. The groups of agricultural and estate workers' houses known as Balnald Cottages in the village of Fortingall (NO 739470) are based on pre-agricultural improvement Lowland vernacular buildings from lowland Perthshire. All these agricultural buildings were erected to the designs of James Marjoribanks MacLaren between the years 1886 and 1890. The last class of buildings in this group is represented by Balnald farmhouse and steading (NO 736470). This farmhouse is a version of the type of asymmetrical neo-vernacular farmhouse first designed by William Mackenzie, burgh architect of Perth, circa 1830. Mackenzie designed the farmhouse and steading at Elcho (NO 163208) and this design was illustrated in J C Loudon's *Cottage Farm and Villa Architecture* in 1833 and 1842. A similar design by Mackenzie appeared in Loudon's *Encyclopaedia of Agriculture*. They served therefore as models for many later buildings in all parts of Britain and abroad. This design was particularly popular in the rich agricultural districts of Tayside and Fife, varying in its architectural complexity with the size of farm served. Unfortunately both the farmhouse and steading at Elcho have been remodelled in recent years and have lost much of their value as historic monuments. This is the situation with many other important mid 19th-century farm steadings in the region and illustrates a principle worth bearing in mind—that specialised buildings, erected in areas where there is only one occupation, are at risk when requirements change. A number of other Tayside farm buildings appeared in important publications. Not all were specifically identified, appearing as 'farm in Strathmore' or 'farm in the Carse of Gowrie'. Identified farms include: Haughs of Kinnaird steading (NO 644574) built in 1861 and appearing in *Encyclopaedia Britannica* in 1878; Inverquharity steading (NO 403577) and Drumkilbo steading (NO 302447) appeared in *The Book of Farm Buildings*, 1861, and in various editions of Stephen's *Book of the Farm*. Only Drumkilbo has remained largely unaltered externally.

Buildings representing the first phase of agricultural improvement still survive as farmhouses or as former steadings on some mansion house sites where later development was located further away from the house, leaving the first phase buildings intact. This is the case at Pitmuies House (NO 567497), built in 1770, and North Mains of Ballindarg (NO 406513), 1761. Fragments do survive on many traditional steadings but unfortunately these are disappearing at an alarming rate especially on the richest agricultural land. Possibly the most complete collection of agricultural buildings from the late 18th century are the farms, pendicles and estate workers' houses on the Glamis Estate in Central Strathmore. These buildings, mainly constructed between 1771 and 1776, are still working farms and therefore unsuitable for the casual visitor but the layout of the pendicles known as Plans of Thornton (NO 4046) can be observed from the Forfar/Glamis section of the A 94 road. Pendicles are agricultural holdings where the tenant is expected to have a supplementary occupation such as weaver, wright, mason, cobbler or, on the Glamis Estate, a quarryman of stone slate. At Plans of Thornton, the relationship between the pendicle buildings and the fields served by them is particularly obvious. Some idea of the internal arrangement of these dwellings and steadings can be obtained at the Angus Folk Museum (no. 1) at Glamis.

Finavon Castle dovecote, nesting boxes

The typical house erected during the first phase of the agricultural revolution is symmetrical in appearance as are the farm buildings. Houses are normally situated to the south-west of the steading or, in very early examples, to the east. The earliest houses are usually found on the largest farms as these were first to 'improve'. They are large, two-storey houses with three bay fronts, occasionally having single-storey, peind-roofed wings against the gables of the main house. The main characteristic of these houses is their wide and generous proportions, with gabled roofs and windows which are small in proportion to the wall area. These buildings are normally only one room deep and access is through a door in the principal facade. The accommodation consists of a kitchen to one side of the entrance and a family bedroom to the other. The parlour is over the kitchen and another bedroom over the family bedroom. There is sometimes a small room over the entrance and the base of the stair. The attic could be occupied by younger members of the family or by servants. The wings were entered independently, one containing the milk parlour, the other the henhouse, privy and fuel store. The henhouse usually backed the kitchen fireplace for warmth in winter as hens stop laying when they are cold. Gradually this form of building moved down the social scale and, as the pace of improvement increased, smaller farms were provided with one-and-a-half or single-storey houses. In these buildings the kitchen and parlour were at opposite sides of the entrance with the bedrooms above. These early small houses had no dormers but were occasionally lit from windows in the gable. The farm buildings associated with all of these farmhouses were normally organised around the U-shaped court, open to the south unless the holding was very small when an L-shape or single range was sufficient. The midden or cattle wintering court was always placed centrally.

Throughout the region farmhouse roofs are normally slated but may have been thatched when originally constructed. The situation with steadings and outbuildings reflects the availability of cheap roofing materials. Stone or grey-slate is readily available along the entire length of the Sidlaw Hills and this material is used for roofing in Strathmore, the Sidlaws and the coastal plain of Angus. In Fife and Kinross there was no natural, cheap roofing material and there steadings and outbuildings are normally pantiled. William Adam, architect and entrepreneur, designer of Aberfeldy Bridge (no. 16) and father of the internationally renowned Robert Adam, claimed to have introduced the manufacture of pantiles to Fife in 1723. The idea and prototypes possibly came from the Low Countries but the story that they came as ballast cargoes cannot be substantiated as there are no bills of lading and no stamped tiles—a common practice in the Low Countries tileworks.

Although the majority of these buildings are constructed with masonry walls, many of the first phase buildings have walls of brick, clay and bool, or tempered clay. The largest concentrations of these buildings are to be found round Errol (NO 2522) in the Carse of Gowrie and from Brechin (NO 5960) and Montrose (NO 7157) north-eastwards to the boundary with Aberdeenshire.

Some of the first improved buildings were constructed of less permanent materials and have since almost disappeared. The village of Pitmiddle (NO 243296) in the Braes of Carse is typical of this group and appears as a jumble of low rubble walls, linear mounds where turf walls have stood and corner stones. The Angus and Perthshire glens contain considerable numbers of deserted settlements from both before and after the agricultural revolution. Field patterns formerly associated with these settlements are still to be seen particularly when the sun is low or when there is a light dusting of snow. In many instances the former field patterns have been destroyed by later agricultural activity and in the rich lowland areas the former ridge and furrow was deliberately levelled by double digging by spade.

The only pre-improvement farm buildings to survive in considerable numbers are dovecotes or pigeon-houses. From medieval times onwards landowners set up deer parks, rabbit warrens and dovecotes to ensure a supply of fresh meat over the winter months. By the 17th and 18th centuries these were being constructed in stone, beehive types being popular in Fife and lectern types in Angus, Kinross and Perthshire. The preference for beehive forms in Fife may reflect the shortage of cheap natural roofing materials.

Dovecotes were occasionally housed in disused structures, an example being the south-east tower of Dairsie Castle (NO 413160), now restored to its former domestic function, and the church tower at Inchcolm Abbey (no. 63). Melville House Doocot (NO 302126) was also converted from a disused building. It occupies the tower of a former windmill, similar to Dunbarney (no. 5); and the arched undercroft of the mill can be seen in the side of the mound on which the dovecote stands.

Wind and water-mills were common features of the landscape of this region from the medieval period onwards. Although many mill sites have a range of date-stones, sometimes from as early as the 15th century, most of the surviving buildings are the result of comparatively recent remodelling resulting from improvements in machinery standards, demanded by insurance companies, in the late 19th century. Rather than improve them, however, many landowners simply abandoned mill sites or converted them to other purposes.

Agricultural improvement relied on the application of lime to the heavy boulder clay of the region. The largest of the commercial limekilns are to be found on the south coast of Fife where there was coal, limestone and easy transport. The disused limekilns at Charlestown (no. 6) are the most extensive but the limekilns at Boddin Point (NO 713533), on the north end of Lunan Bay, look like an old Moorish fort out on a rocky promontory. Angus had little limestone and the lime for improving the soil in Strathmore was mainly obtained by dredging marl from the shallow lochs, many of these being drained and the land reclaimed for agricultural purposes.

A final group of buildings related to agriculture are the rural smiddies. Of recent years many of these have developed into engineering workshops repairing expensive and complex agricultural machinery. In the past their role was much wider. They acted as farriers, shoeing the horses that drove most forms of agricultural machinery. They made and repaired the metal parts for all forms of agricultural machinery, including the metal tyres for cart wheels, and many types of household appliances including locks, hinges, catches, supports for cooking pots, girdles, bannock spades and decorative features.

FISHING

Inshore fishing for both whitefish and shellfish is carried on from a number of harbours along the coast. Arbroath is the principal fishing centre in Angus (NO 6440) and Pittenweem has the same status in Fife (NO 5402). Inshore fishing for whitefish followed the first successful sea fishery in

**Harbour at
Anstruther
Easter, c 1885**

Scotland, that for herring. Herring fishing developed in parallel with agricultural improvement but did not have the same impact in terms of building. At the time of the development of the herring fishing many of the ports on the east coast were in decline. This was the result of their earlier trade with Europe giving way to a west coast trade with the Americas. Empty or underused harbours were occupied by the herring fishermen and former warehouses were converted for use by coopers and fish merchants. The only harbour, in the region, to be enlarged to accommodate the herring fleet was at Anstruther Easter (NO 568033), now the home of the Scottish Fisheries Museum (no. 7).

Timber boat-building was carried out in the open air at most of the old ports but gradually the industry has moved indoors with the construction of large boat sheds. Open air boat-building yards still survive in Arbroath, although in age they are the most recently established in the region.

Arbroath boasts a unique form of fish curing carried on as a back-door industry on about forty sites close to the harbour. The cured fish are known as 'Arbroath smokies' and the method is a hot cure resulting in a cooked smoked fish which can be eaten either hot or cold. This is thought to be the only hot cured fish still produced in traditional kilns or 'smoke barrels' as they are referred to locally.

The boats involved in the fishing have varied considerably over the years and photographs of the harbours at various times from the mid-19th century onwards shows changes in boat types and variations in the numbers of boats using the harbours. The Scottish Fisheries Museum (no. 7) does much to explain the history and development of this interesting and colourful occupation. The Broughty Castle Museum (no. 55) continues this story with a history of local whaling carried on from Dundee. It was because of Dundee's expertise in whaling that Captain Scott's ship, *Discovery*, was built at a Dundee yard. This ship has recently returned to the city to be a focal point in a new riverfront development at Discovery Point.

The only fishing surviving from the medieval period is that for salmon. Salmon fishing stations survive round the entire coast of the region and along the banks of the major river estuaries, particularly the Firth of Tay. Today the whole trade is in fresh fish but some of the older stations show evidence of former 'kitting', 'pickling' and other curing processes. They also have large icehouses, dating from between 1765 and the middle of the 19th century, erected at the start of the fresh salmon trade (eg no. 8).

INDUSTRY

The principal industry of the region was the manufacture of textiles. The main fibre used was flax and individual towns became recognised centres for particular branches of the trade. Dunfermline was the centre of fine damask weaving and its surviving mill-buildings indicate this additional wealth (NT 0987). Arbroath was known for its sail canvas and Dundee (NO 4030) moved into a cheaper type of textile specialising in the weaving of jute, which required whale oil, hence to local whaling industry. Kirkcaldy was a world centre for linoleum manufacture using jute as a backing and linseed as a principal ingredient (NT 2791). Stanley (no. 11) in Perthshire was erected round a cotton mill in 1785, development continuing there until circa 1850. The first power-driven flax mill in Scotland was set up in the planned village of Douglastown, Angus (NO 416473) in 1787.

1* Angus Folk Museum, Glamis, Angus

AD 1793 and later.

NO 385468. In the Kirkwynd, in the centre of Glamis village.

NTS.

The Museum occupies a terrace of six cottages, which was erected by the Earl of Strathmore in 1793 and presented to the National Trust for Scotland in 1957. The Trust restored the buildings adapting them to house the Angus Folk Museum. The collection was already in existence, having been assembled by Jean, Lady Maitland, aided by her husband, Sir Ramsay Maitland of Burnside, and given into the Trust's care in 1974. The museum was extended in 1976 by the addition of an agricultural gallery situated on the other side of the Kirkwynd from the cottages. This has since been remodelled as a small agricultural steading.

The Kirkwynd cottages contain: Madge Taylor's kitchen from Craichie; a Victorian farmhouse parlour; a 19th-century laundry; a schoolhouse; handlooms for weaving damask linen; musical instruments; and household equipment. The agricultural annexe contains: a collection of agricultural implements and tools; a forge from Eassie Smiddy; a wheel-ringing stone, converted from a damaged whin millstone, from Whigstreet Smiddy; and a typical Angus farmworkers' bothy.

Glamis village is worthy of attention, forming a natural extension to the Folk Museum. The churchyard contains some fine 18th-century tradesmen's tombstones. There is a Pictish cross-slab in the garden of the manse between the museum and the church (no. 77). The ground to the east of the museum has been in use as an estate nursery since the early 18th century. The houses and hotel in the main street date mainly from the second half of the 18th century when the Earl of Strathmore carried out extensive rebuilding. These buildings carry some fine date-stones and mason's marks. The deserted watermill on the west bank of the Glamis Burn also dates from the 18th century. The materials used in the construction of these buildings were all produced locally. The estate had a number of freestone quarries, and many of the tenants paid part of their rents in grey slate for roofs, flagstones or roof ridge stones. Millstones and oven soles were quarried to the south of the village. The estate also had a small brickworks to the north of the castle near Haughs of Cossans. The estate influence was considerable and the village should be considered in relation to Glamis Castle (no. 40).

2 Cottown School and Schoolhouse, Perth and Kinross

AD 1745, 1766, 1818 and later.

NO 205210. Signposted Cottown off the B 958 Glencarse-Errol road. Leave A 90 for Glencarse if travelling from Perth and for Errol Station if travelling from Dundee.

NTS.

The thatched roofed mud-walled school and schoolhouse at Cottown was erected in 1745, the year of the Jacobite Rebellion. The schoolmaster had to flee from Jacobite supporters from Perth in 1746 but returned after the Battle of Culloden. The original building was damaged by fire in 1765, and a collection was organised for its repair in 1766 when 'as much of the schoolhouse as was necessary for the accommodation of the master and scholars was rebuilt'. Further alterations appear to have taken place in 1818 as the clay chimney hoods to the central fireplaces are dated 1818. The hood at the west gable partly covers an earlier window opening. The roof is of two or three phases. The west end is the earliest with pit-sawn timbers dressed with a side axe. The east end had slightly higher eaves and the timbers are circular sawn with an adze dressing. The earlier roof eaves then appear to have been heightened to run through with the east end and the roof timbers had a bell-cast added to accommodate the raised eaves.

The bulk of the wall is mud-wall construction, the Scottish version of Devon cob. Part of the south wall is constructed in very poor quality sandstone, apparently quarried on site and built using clay mortar. Some fragments of earth render survive at the east end of the south façade, although this was covered by later lime harl. The internal partitions and chimney flues are formed with timber standards and clay. The brick chimneyheads balance on top of this flimsy structure. The present roof is reed thatched, but in the 18th and 19th centuries it would have been straw thatched, possibly secured by timber pegs or stobbed into the sub-stratum. The building ceased to function as a school in the late 19th century and became a private house. The cottage garden associated with this house was spectacular for its type and is to be restored in the near future. The school and schoolhouse should be completely restored and open to the public by 1997.

3 Tealing Dovecote, Angus

AD 1595.

NO 412381. Signposted from the A 929 Dundee-Forfar road.

Historic Scotland.

As a class, dovecotes tend to be the oldest surviving agricultural buildings in this region. Pigeon farming was an important agricultural pursuit from the medieval period onwards, only declining after the introduction of fresh meat markets at the end of the 18th century. Dovecotes had a similar status to rabbit warrens and deer forests but, being buildings, they are easier to identify. In addition to providing fresh meat and eggs over the winter months, the dovecote also provided large quantities of valuable manure. The pigeon farmed in these structures was a type of rock-dove which gave a white meat similar to rabbit rather than the dark meat of the wood pigeon. The pigeons were eaten as fully grown birds, as squabs or young birds and as eggs.

The dovecote provided a habitat similar to the caves inhabited by rock-doves. The birds bred naturally, the strongest birds occupying the top nests, the weakest birds in the nests at ground level. Birds were collected in the dark as they would not fly when they could not see. The collector would work by touch, wringing the necks of suitable birds.

The Tealing dovecote is unusual in that it is not of the beehive or lectern type but takes the form of a single cell building with a conventional pitched roof. As with most dovecotes in this region, the nesting boxes are constructed from flagstone ledges and haffits. The chamfered doorway is surmounted by an inscribed lintel. The skewput carries the initials DM and the date 1595.

Inscribed lintel (Top Right)

Tealing dovecote (Below)

Decorated skewput (Bottom Right)

Barry Mill, Angus

---

4 Barry Mill, Angus

AD 1814 and later.

NO 534349. Signposted from the A 92 Dundee-Arbroath road and the A 930 Broughty Ferry-Carnoustie road in Barry village.

NTS.

Barry Mill is a typical 19th-century water-powered corn mill standing on a site documented as a mill stance from 1539. It was one of two corn mills occupying this section of the Barry Burn. When both were operating the present mill was known as the Upper Mill or Over Mill of Barry. The other, slightly further down stream, almost within the village of Barry, was the Nether Mill of Barry. Oats formed the corn crop in Scotland and the mill produced oatmeal. The form of the earlier mills on this site is not known, but the present mill originates from a rebuilding after a major fire in 1814. It also incorporates subsequent alterations resulting from increasing grain yields as agricultural practices improved.

The mill building is a three-storey sandstone rubble structure with basement (meal floor), ground floor (milling or store floor) and attic (hopper or bin floor). The building is roofed with Carmyllie grey slate. The kiln and mill were originally under a single roof but the kiln roof height was reduced about 1940 giving the roof line a stepped profile. The original stone built lean-too annex along the back of the mill was extended in brick about 1930 to accommodate the growing output from the local farms and to provide an office for the miller. The overshot water-wheel is contained in a wheel ark at the south end of the mill.

The lade, serving the water-wheel, runs from a natural rock shelf half-a-mile upstream from the mill. There the water was held in a dam which in itself represented a considerable outlay. The lade was damaged in a flood in 1984 and the cost implications of repair brought the milling to a halt. Mills of this type were by that time considered obsolete and any additional financial burden normally resulted in their closure. The Nether Mill of Barry was demolished in the 1960s when a great many of the other mills in the region also closed. Barry Mill was in fact the last water-powered corn mill to work in Angus, producing oatmeal until the late 1970s and animal feed until 1984. Aberfeldy Meal Mill (NO 855490) in the burgh of Aberfeldy held a similar distinction in Perthshire (it has also been restored and is open to the public). The Barry buildings deteriorated until 1988 when the NTS purchased them with the aid of a generous bequest. The original machinery has been fully restored and is working again (milling demonstrations normally take place on Saturday and Sunday afternoons and for pre-booked parties). Alas the product can only be used for animal feed as present hygiene regulations make it difficult to produce meal for human consumption.

---

5 Dunbarney Windmill, Perth and Kinross

17th century AD and later.

NO 107183. Approach by a farm track from the B 935 Bridge of Earn-Forgandenny road.

Dunbarney windmill is one of the few surviving ruins of the vaulted tower-mills once common in this region. It is sited on a low rise above the alluvial plain of the River Earn, and the ruin comprises a tapered circular roofless tower over a vaulted undercroft. The tower stands 5.8 m high and reduces in diameter from 6.8 m at ground level to 5.2 m at the top. The wall of the tower is 0.9 m thick at ground level and rises vertically on the inside face to a corbel course about 1.2 m above the floor level. This allows the wall to return to its original thickness and continue with parallel faces to the top.

This vertical face and corbel course would give the miller maximum use of the whole of the ground floor. There are two doorways at ground level, one to the east, the other to the west, from which stone steps in the thickness of the wall led down to the main floor of the mill where the grinding stones were located. This floor was carried on a stone scarcement.

There are small emblems, cut in a casual manner and sloping to the right, on the lintels of the doorways to the tower. The meaning of these emblems is difficult to explain but may be talismanic.

On the south side of the tower is evidence for an arched underground chamber which formerly acted as the receiving and dispatching room. This room opened into the basement of the tower under the main floor. Its vault was covered with soil to the level of the ground at the doorways, forming a terrace in front of the tower from which the sails could be adjusted. The drawing by Paul Sandby entitled *Distant View of Perth* shows a similar windmill and underground chamber.

Evidence from old records suggests an erection date in the middle or latter part of the 17th century, but it is likely that there was considerable rebuilding in the 18th century.

Distant view of Perth by P Sandby

Traditionally landowners had the sole right to build corn-mills and bind their tenants to have their corn ground at a particular mill, on payment of duties known as 'multures'. In Scotland such thirlage only applied to watermills and tenants were not legally bound to a laird's windmill. This law was not always observed and the tenants of Dunbarney, including the village of Kintillo, remained thirled to the mill well into the 19th century.

6 Charlestown Limekilns, Fife

18th century AD and later.

NT 064835. Off the A 985 along the N shore of the Firth of Forth. Take the loop to the S through Charlestown and Limekilns. The limekilns face Charlestown Harbour.

The Charlestown limekilns were part of an early industrial complex based on lime, limestone and coal production on the estate of the Earl of Elgin. The seam of limestone ran parallel to the north shore of the Firth of Forth; it was from 6 m to 15 m thick and produced a white durable freestone capable of taking a fine polish. In the mid 18th century the 5th Earl of Elgin decided to expand his undertakings by the construction of a new harbour, new draw kilns and a tramway between the quarry and the kilns.

Charlestown harbour was the first area to be considered and the existing inner basin was constructed about 1770. The outer basin was added later, the north-west pier from about 1840 and the

south-east pier at the end of the 19th century. The harbour was an immediate success and by the early 1790s it was handling 1,300 separate cargoes of manufactured lime in addition to its coal and freestone cargoes.

Charlestown limekilns, old pier

The Charlestown limekilns were the largest group of limekilns in Scotland and played an important role in the agricultural improvements of the 18th and 19th centuries in providing lime for the improvement of the soil and for the construction of new farm buildings.

The present range of kilns date from 1777 and 1778 when construction work was started on 9 of the 14 kilns. The limestone was carried to the kilns on a horse-drawn tramway known as the Elgin Railway. This was later replaced by a branch line of the North British Railway which has now been lifted. Of the original kilns, all but the three at the east end of the range have been refaced. They are all draw kilns and constructed of dressed ashlar.

Charlestown limekilns

7* Scottish Fisheries Museum, Anstruther, Fife

18th-19th centuries AD.

NO 568034. Situated at the E end of Shore Street, Anstruther.

The Scottish Fisheries Museum was opened in July 1969 in a group of old buildings known as 'St Ayles'. Its situation on this site is most appropriate as, in addition to overlooking the harbour, St Ayles Land has recorded connections with fishing and fisherfolk dating from 1318. In a charter of that date William de Candela, Laird of 'Anstroyir', gave the land and certain rights to the Abbey of Balmerino. The rights included the erection of booths for lease to local fishermen and permission to dry nets on the land. A community of fishermen, coopers and brewers settled on the land and St Ayles Chapel was built in the 15th century on the site of the north building of the museum. A double-sided window-head rebuilt into the present structure is the only visible evidence to survive.

The Abbot's lodging on the east side of the courtyard is reputedly the oldest building on St Ayles Land, dating from the 16th century. If this date is correct the building has obviously undergone a major remodelling at some subsequent date. Much more convincing is the 18th-century dwelling built by the brewer William Lumsden on the other side of the courtyard. Originally three storeys, it was reduced in height and used as a ships' chandlers until 1961. The marriage-lintel reading 'WL HD 1721' can still be seen over the doorway in Haddfoot Wynd. The whole group has an air of having been lived-in and altered over the years to suit changing requirements. The museum has recently purchased some further houses to the north-east, one of which has a good example of an Eyemouth kiln, which has been converted for use as a domestic laundry. This will eventually make a fine exhibit when the linking galleries are commissioned.

The museum buildings contain a number of galleries devoted to various themes. These include: boats, boat-building, coopering, fishing gear, fisheries protection, marine engineering, navigation, North Atlantic fishing grounds, sail making and whaling. There are also examples of fisher dress, paintings, ships' figureheads and tapestries. A salt-water aquarium and floor pool give an excellent view of a variety of fish and shellfish found in Scottish waters. Reconstructions of a net loft and a fisher family room of around AD 1900 show items in context. This approach is also taken in a number of other situations including a walk-through wheelhouse complete with ship's radio and radar in working condition. A small room is given over to a memorial to fishermen lost at sea.

The courtyard contains a fine collection of small boats but this is only part of the boat collection, the larger items being berthed in Anstruther and Tayport harbours. The large boats include: *Reaper* FR958, a 22 m Fifie herring drifter built by Forbes of Sandhaven in 1902; *Research* LK62, a 24 m Zulu herring drifter built by Slater's of Banff in 1901; *Radiation* A115, the largest wooden line-fishing vessel built in Britain, 29.5 m long, built by Smith and Hutton of Anstruther in 1957 (in Tayport harbour); and *Light* A395, smaller than the others at only 5.5 m long, a Moray Firth sma'line boat built at Rosehearty in 1906.

Scottish Fisheries Museum, Anstruther, with the *Reaper* in the foreground

8 Fishtown of Usan Icehouse and Saltpan, Angus

17th century and later.

NO 725545. On the coast 3.5 km S of Montrose. Leave car at ruined cottages and follow track at E end of village.

The Scottish salmon fishing industry dates back to the Middle Ages, the fish being kitted, pickled or kippered for export. With the opening up of the English market in the 18th century an increasing proportion of the fish was sold in Billingsgate Market, London. George Dempster of Dunnichen advocated sending the fish to London packed in ice, thereby allowing them to be sold as fresh salmon. John Richardson (later of Pitfour), a Perth merchant, began experimenting with ice in 1765 and quickly established the best way of storing ice and of packing the fish. Richardson's enterprise was based in two centres: Newburgh in Fife (NO 235182) and Tugnet on Speymouth, Morayshire (NJ 349653). Gradually more and more fishing stations were equipped with icehouses and a whole system of transportation developed using fast sailing packets to ferry the fish to Billingsgate.

The commercial icehouse used by the salmon fishing industry differed significantly from the icehouses attached to mansion houses. Domestic icehouses were designed to retain the ice pack for as long as possible, in some cases up to three years, the foodstuffs being laid out on clean straw on top of the ice. The salmon fisher's icehouse was designed to allow ready quarrying of the ice. The Fishtown of Usan icehouse is at first glance typical of this type of icehouse. It comprises a large vaulted structure utilising the fall of the ground to allow access to the roof openings where the ice was loaded and the doorway where the ice was quarried. The large vaulted structure at Fishtown of Usan was used as a commercial icehouse in the second half of the 19th century. Internally it was subdivided to take account of the closed season, the smaller portion being intended for use in the early part of the summer, the remainder of the ice being retained for the longer second part.

The icehouse was filled with broken ice taken from a nearby pond, usually when it was about 35 mm thick. It was pounded into small pieces and packed tightly in layers about 150 mm thick. The crevices were packed with snow and sprinkled with water to crate a solid pack of ice. It was warm work and the men stripped to the waist but wore long seaboots. Once the vault was filled it was sealed and the openings insulated until the beginning of the fishing season.

When the season started the ice chamber was opened and fish boxes were filled with ice and taken out to the individual fishing stations where they were stored in a cool place. As the fish were caught they were laid on the ice to cool and at the end of the day they were transferred to the icehouse for repacking in fresh ice and shipping to London. This took place every second day from a pre-appointed harbour.

At Fishtown of Usan the vaulted chamber was divided into two parts but whereas the normal proportion was one to two, this building was divided at one to three.

This was not the only difference between the icehouse at Fishtown of Usan and those listed at the end of this section and only recently has a study of the manufacture of Scottish sea salt provided the answers. It was found that Usan had a saltworks from the 17th century. When the vaulted structure was examined in this context it became clear that this building had been constructed as a saltpan.

Anstruther harbour light (Left)

The building has a masonry structure, formerly and erroneously described as a buttress, built against the seaward gable. This was flanked by blocked windows. There was also an inlet into the lower part of the gable below high water mark. The projecting feature was a factory-style chimney reduced to the same height as the gable. The blocked windows were probably ventilators and the inlet would have admitted salt water to be pumped into the evaporation pan.

The smaller chamber within the vault provided evidence of an intermediate floor. To the south of the vault were the ruins of a two-storey structure with both windows and fireplaces. This building was L-shaped on plan, one leg abutting the south wall of the vault, the other built on the east edge of the rock-shelf in line with the east gable of the vault. This created a courtyard, open to the south, protected on the north and east by the buildings and on the south and west by the grass cliff.

On the seaward side of these buildings is a man-made channel, constructed on the line of a natural fault, across the southern edge of a flat area of rock. This rock has a slight rim and retains 50 mm-100 mm of water over its entire surface. This water discharged into the channel close to the vault. The seaward end of the channel has grooves in its sides to take sluice gates or a permanent barrier. The rim that retains the water on the rock plateau was damaged in 1985 and the water no longer lies to the same depth, but it is thought that this acted as a first stage evaporation area used to increase the salt content of the water prior to pumping it into the saltpan. This corresponds to smaller shallow rock-cut areas below the wind-pump at the St Monans saltpans (NO 533018), now open to visitors.

The salt was exported from the small natural harbour to the south of the saltpan complex. The ruined buildings probably contained the salt girnal or store and the Customs House as this was a taxable product. Both the small harbour and the saltpan/icehouse structure are still in use by salmon fishermen.

Other good examples of commercial icehouses can still be seen at Boddin Point (NO 713534), Fisherhills Kinnaber (NO 729621), Lunan House (NO 689515), Tayport (NO 456291), Newburgh (NO 235181) and Tentsmuir (NO 500267).

9 Perth Waterworks, Perth and Kinross

AD 1832.

NO 120231. Situated on the corner of Tay Street and Marshall Place, facing the South Inch, Perth. Now known as the Ferguson Gallery, part of the Museum and Art Gallery Department.

In this region a number of local authorities built elaborate water-towers in the 19th century to house water cisterns intended to supply water to their respective burghs. Many of these had a comparatively short life being replaced by more efficient, if less picturesque, rural reservoirs. Notable examples of these water-towers survive at Arbroath (NO 635407) in the form of a Gothic folly, and Montrose (NO 715588) in an octagonal tower, now converted to a dwelling house.

The Perth Waterworks designed by Dr Adam Anderson in 1832 in a neo-Classical style is a particularly fine example of this type of building. It is interesting for the quality of the architectural

Perth waterworks

composition, its contribution to the townscape of Perth and for its early use of cast-iron as a cladding to the upper portion of the cistern-house.

The cistern-house has the appearance of a domed Roman rotunda and sits on the corner of the street terminating the classical terrace facing the South Inch. The pump house is partly concealed by the rotunda and the chimney of the pumping engine has the appearance of a Roman triumphal column. The upper portion of the rotunda, which originally housed the water cistern, is constructed of cast-iron painted to match the stonework of the rest of the building.

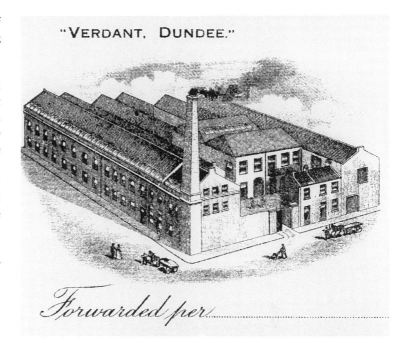

10 Verdant Works, Dundee

AD 1833.

NO 395303. The works are situated in West Henderson's Wynd, Dundee.

Dundee Heritage Trust.

Verdant Works is one of the best remaining examples of a typical Dundee jute works. The mill was constructed in 1833, in the heart of one of the earliest urban industrial areas in Scotland, centred round the Scouring Burn on what was then the western perimeter of Dundee. It is of average size for a Dundee mill and is one of the best surviving complete examples of a courtyard type mill. Originally built for David Lindsay, merchant and flaxspinner, by the 1850s it had been transferred to John Ewan, described as a manufacturer of canvas, sacking, bagging and hessian. The change from linen to jute had started the year before Verdant was built and the new mill may have played an important role in this change. By 1864 the mill had three engines driving seventy power looms with 2,800 spindles and had a workforce of 500. In terms of worker numbers Verdant ranked eighteenth out of the sixty-one spinning and power loom works in Dundee.

The jute was prepared and spun in the mill and the weaving was carried out in a small factory on the north side of Milne Street. By 1886 the owners were described as 'Merchants' rather than 'Manufacturers', their previous designation, and by 1899 the name Verdant had been removed from the list of mills and factories operating in the city.

The Milne Street factory was sold to D W Baxter and Sons in the 1880s as a carpet factory. The Verdant Works were occupied from 1899 by Alexander Thomson and Sons, china and waste merchants and flock manufacturers. In 1991, Dundee Heritage Trust announced that they had purchased the historic linen and jute mill known as Verdant Works and declared its intention to restore the mill as a heritage centre.

Verdant Works, Dundee

The history of linen and jute is a major part of the history of the development, people and character of Dundee. Verdant will tell that story through an important collection of original textile machinery, displayed in an authentic setting and supported by sophisticated displays and multi-media technology.

Dundee is rich in architectural monuments to the linen and jute industry. The massive classical façades of Tay Works and Dudhope Works face on to Lochee Road. Baxter Brothers were the worlds largest linen manufacturers between 1840 and 1890, and their two major complexes, the Upper Dens and the Lower Dens Mills still survive in part. At Cox's Stack, Lochee, the 86 m high campanile-style factory chimney is one of the few surviving fragments of what was the world's largest jute mill, Camperdown Works, employing 5,000 workers at its peak production period.

The Dundee tenement was developed to accommodate the large number of workers in the city and in 1911 about 70 percent of the dwellings in Dundee were single or two-room houses. At the other end of the social scale the jute barons were erecting huge mansion houses in West Ferry, the West End of Dundee and on the Dryburgh ridge above Camperdown Works, Lochee.

The jute industry was also linked to whaling, the whale oil being used to soften the fibres to allow the jute to be spun. A whaling museum is located in Broughty Castle (no. 55). Dundee's reputation as a whaling port with shipbuilding yards constructing whaling ships brought about the commissioning of the Antarctic exploration ship *Discovery*, now berthed at Discovery Point on the river front.

11* Stanley Cotton Mills, Perth and Kinross

18th century AD and later.

NO 114328. Situated on the N bank of the River Tay 3 km E of the A 9 Perth-Inverness trunk road.

Historic Scotland.

Stanley is one of the earliest examples of a model textile manufactory. The village and mills were designed as a unit to introduce cotton spinning and weaving to the area. This was the result of an initiative by George Dempster of Dunnichen in association with Sir Richard Arkwright, who were backed by a number of Perth merchants. The village and mills were founded in 1785, the same year as the more famous New Lanark.

The existing mill complex comprises an irregular courtyard containing a large free-standing chimney and bounded by: the Bell Mill, completed in 1790; the East Mill dating from about 1840; and the Mid Mill from about 1850. The six-storey Bell Mill is probably the best surviving Scottish example of a narrow body mill with timber floors and limited headroom. The building measures 27.4 m by 8.5 m internally and is amply provided with large regularly-spaced case and sash windows. The building is covered with a blue slated, gabled roof with a handsome belfry on the north gable. The walls are of masonry to first-floor level and of brick above. These bricks were made on site from local clays.

Originally the mills were powered by seven large waterwheels fed by some 244 m of conduit and producing a total of 400 horsepower. The village stands on a level area of high ground to the west of the mill complex and originally comprised a regular layout of two-storey terraced houses, some built of stone and others of brick. By 1828, the village also boasted a church, school, shops and a tenement block. Many of the houses in the village have been remodelled in recent years and, although they have their original massing, the materials, finish and scale have all been changed.

Stanley Mills

2 TRANSPORT

Aberfeldy Bridge

The great river estuaries of the Firth of Tay and Firth of Forth formed substantial barriers to road transport, which have only recently been overcome. Although car ferries did exist at the points where the two major road bridges were constructed, they were subject to delays and closed down overnight. The opening of Kincardine Bridge (NS 925871) in 1936, Forth Road Bridge (NT 125795) in 1964, Tay Road Bridge (NO 415294) in 1967, Friarton Bridge (NO 130215) in 1978 and the construction of sections of motorway and dual carriageway linking these bridges, have resulted in a transport revolution within the region. Travelling times to Aberdeen, Edinburgh and Glasgow have been reduced and towns such as St Andrews, Culross, Dunkeld and the burghs of the East Neuk of Fife have become accessible to the day tourist from Edinburgh, Glasgow and any part of our area.

The first comprehensive road system was established in the first quarter of the 19th century with the completion of the turnpike road system. This coincided with the completion of the first phase of agricultural improvements in the districts served by these roads: the new roads being used to get the increased produce to market. The turnpike road system made use of the recently drained and agriculturally improved valley bottoms to create a new road network avoiding, as far as possible, the steep hills and high ground encountered on the older road system. The new roads were constructed by trust companies who established toll barriers every six miles (9.6 km) along the length of the road. Toll houses were let to toll-keepers by offer, the prospective tenant being expected to calculate the possible income for the year and, after deducting his own salary, make an offer of rent, for the use of the house and the right to charge tolls.

Many toll-houses associated with this system still survive; they tend to have more architectural pretension than is usual in single-storey houses of this period and reflect the 'house-style' of the particular trust. Barnton Toll (NO 128220) still retains its tariff board and the remains of the toll bar. Other examples include: Clushford Toll (NO 355114) erected about 1820; Crieff (NN 868216); Cupar (NO 378146); Dunkeld Bridge Toll (no. 13); Invergowrie (NO 349303); Killiecrankie (NN 918623); Marykirk Bridge Toll (NO 685649); and the North Toll, Montrose (NO 716596).

Other features of the turnpike road system include: regular milestones, distance plates and directional signs, again designed according to the 'house-style' of the particular trust. The Dundee-Perth turnpike had stone mile-markers with a single letter, representing the town, and a number, representing the miles travelled. The upgrading of this road to dual carriageway has resulted in many of these milestones being moved to private ground or simply disappearing. Many of the Angus turnpikes had large sandstone blocks for milestones. These were deliberately defaced during World War II to obliterate the information inscribed thereon.

Marykirk Bridge in 1817 by J Steadman

A number of fine bridges were erected as part of the turnpike road system. These include: Marykirk Bridge (NO 685650) designed by John Smeaton in 1813 and incorporating a toll-house on the Angus bank of the river; and Perth Bridge (no. 14) also by Smeaton.

Military roads were constructed in the Highland areas of the region after the Jacobite rebellions of 1715 and 1745. The most impressive individual element in this considerable undertaking is the Aberfeldy Bridge (no. 16), designed by William Adam and completed in 1733 under the direction of General Wade.

Dairsie Bridge

Although there was no comprehensive road system in this region in the medieval period, a number of medieval stone bridges were erected and some still survive. The four major monuments in this class are: Brechin Bridge (NO 604592); Dairsie Bridge (no. 59); Guard Bridge (no. 17); and North Water Bridge (NO 652661) completed in 1539. Smaller bridges for foot or pack-horse traffic range from spindly, decorative, wrought-iron structures such as Glenisla Footbridge (no. 18) and Balhary footbridge (NO 263465), both typical of 19th-century engineering, or the earlier Chinese Bridge at Taymouth Castle (no. 19), to the light masonry pack-horse bridge of indeterminate age crossing the River Ore south of Coaltown of Balgonie, Fife (no. 20).

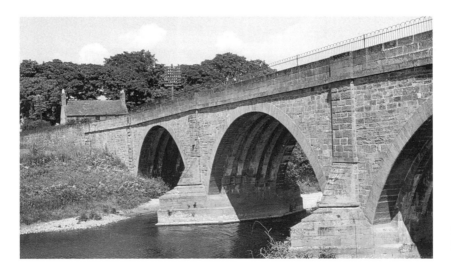

North Water Bridge

RAIL

The designers of the original rail network in eastern Scotland were quick to realise the need to bridge the two Firths. The Tay Rail Bridge (no. 12) was built between 1871 and 1878 but collapsed in 1879. A second Tay Rail Bridge was completed by 1887. The collapse of the first bridge caused a change of policy in designing the Forth Rail Bridge, resulting in a massively over-structured design which became one of the engineering wonders of the world.

As with the road network, connecting ferries were provided (in this case by the railway companies) prior to the construction of the major bridges. The ferry over the Firth of Tay ran between Tayport (NO 459290) and North Ferry, later Broughty Ferry (NO 464304) and some evidence of the former rail connections can still be traced.

The Tayside area was in the vanguard of rail travel in Scotland. The Dundee-Newtyle Railway opened in 1831 making it the earliest passenger railway in the country. It used three stationary engines to raise and lower the trains on the gradients. The line ran on the level between these inclines and included a tunnel through part of the Law Hill, Dundee. Parts of the line are still visible including the south entrance to the Law Tunnel (NO 395311) and the terminal building in Newtyle (NO 299413). Pieces of the track, with the sleepers running parallel to the rails, can be seen at the Angus Folk Museum, Glamis (no. 1).

WATER

Water transport has always been important in this region. The navigable waters of the Firth of Tay allow coastal shipping to penetrate to the centre of the land area, whilst those of the Firth of Forth give access to the whole southern boundary. Montrose, Dundee, Perth, Newburgh, Tayport, Leven, Methil, Kirkcaldy and Burntisland still function as ports for both coastal and international trade. Formerly the list of ports was much longer and included Arbroath, St Andrews, Crail, Cellardyke, Anstruther, Pittenweem, St Monans, Elie and Earlsferry, East and West Wemyss, Dysart, Charlestown and Culross. Many of the Fife ports were particularly small and lost importance as trading harbours by the end of the medieval period, although many continued to function in a limited way till the beginning of this century. Others have become fishing centres.

Concentrated seagoing traffic inevitably requires sophisticated navigational aids and the whole coast is liberally provided with harbour lights, buoys, warning lights, lighthouses, lightships and other navigational aids.

The North Carr lightship has now been replaced by a beacon and the ship is berthed in Victoria Dock in Dundee. The Bell Rock Lighthouse was erected on the Inchcape Rock (NO 762270) between 1808 and 1811, making it the oldest lit rock-tower still in use. The designer was Robert Stevenson and the stones were prepared in Arbroath and shipped to the site. The Bell Rock Signal Tower (no. 22) was built to accommodate the lighthouse keepers and their families and to provide communication with the keepers in the lighthouse prior to the provision of radio contact. The oldest lighthouse to survive, in part, is on the Isle of May in the Firth of Forth and dates from the 17th century (no. 23).

12 Tay Rail Bridge, Dundee and Fife

Late 19th century.

NO 391278. Can be seen at close quarters from Riverside Drive, Dundee or the main road through Wormit, Fife.

The original Tay Rail Bridge was designed for the North British Railway Company by Sir Thomas Bouch. It was an ambitious project to build a bridge over 3.2 km long across the exposed estuary of the Firth of Tay. Few of the problems associated with the construction of long bridges in exposed sites had been considered at that time. Bouch took advice on wind forces but was given a ridiculously low figure. Similarly the rolling-stock in use at that time was not tested for stability in exposed situations.

The bridge carried a single railway track for 3,261m across the Firth. Work was started in 1871 and the bridge was opened in 1878. It is not certain what caused the bridge to collapse but the slender nature of the design, the poor quality of the workmanship and the possibility that the train may have been exceeding the speed limit of twenty-five miles per hour or may have been derailed by the force of the wind may all have contributed to its failure. The bridge collapsed within nineteen months of its opening and Bouch was apportioned most of the blame. There are a great many books and articles on the subject and with hindsight Bouch appears to have been badly judged. The brick column bases used to support the cast-iron

Tay Rail Bridge

columns of the first bridge may still be seen on the east side of the second bridge.

In 1882 the North British Railway Company commenced work on the second bridge. The engineers were W H Barlow and Sons and the contractor was William Arrol and Company of Glasgow. The second bridge was sited 18 m upstream from the original. Since the regulations in force at that time did not allow the use of steel for bridge construction, many of the wrought-iron

The first Tay Bridge

girders from the Bouch design were re-used by Barlow. The new bridge was nearly 3.5 km long and had eighty-six piers, seventy-six of which were in the river.

Sir William Arrol also built the Victoria Bridge at Caputh (NO 088395) for William Cox of Snaigow and Foggyley. The bridge was started in 1887 and made use of girders of identical design to those used on the Tay Bridge.

13 Dunkeld Bridge, Dunkeld, Perth and Kinross

AD 1809.

NO 026424. Links Birnam and Dunkeld across the River Tay. Best viewed from the riverside walks on both sides of the river.

This bridge is one of Thomas Telford's outstanding monuments. Telford was an engineer of genius and one of the first to undertake road building on a massive scale. In 1803 he was appointed surveyor and engineer to the newly-created Commission for Highland Roads and Bridges. He held this post for eighteen years and during that time was responsible for 1,470 km of new road and over a thousand bridges. His roads set new standards in surfacing and the bridges varied in scale from mere culverts to some very large spans of iron or masonry.

Dunkeld Bridge is 208 m long and 8 m wide and was built in 1809 as a toll-bridge. The toll-house at the south end of the bridge brought objections from the townspeople of Dunkeld from its inception. The problem became even more acute after the opening of the Dunkeld and Perth Railway in 1856 as the station was on the south side of the river and the toll had to be added to the cost of rail travel. In 1868 there were 'toll riots' in Dunkeld and a detachment of Royal Highlanders were sent to keep the peace. On several occasions the toll-gates were removed and thrown into the river. The bridge was eventually taken over by the County Council in 1879. The toll-house still survives on the eastern side of the south abutment. The town lock-up occupied the chamber within the north abutment.

Telford employed a very distinctive toll-gate constructed of wrought-iron straps forming a double sunburst pattern, the straps radiating like the rays of the sun from two quadrants, one in each of the two hinged corners of the gate. A gate of this design can be seen at Cortachy Castle (NO 394592), but it is not known whether it is an original Telford gate or a later copy.

Dunkeld is now by-passed by the A 9 trunk road and the reduction in traffic within the town presents the opportunity to stop and examine this fine monument. Dunkeld Cathedral (no. 64) and the NTS restoration of the High Street and Cathedral Close are also worthy subjects.

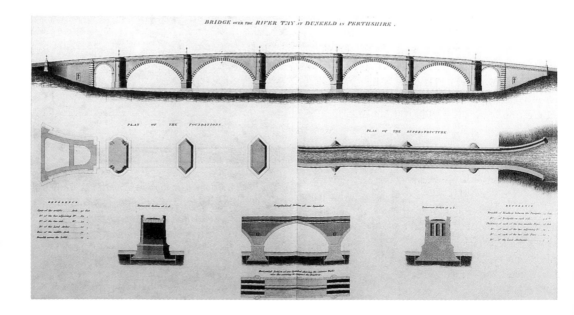

Dunkeld Bridge, drawing in Telford's *Atlas*, 1838

*View of Perth
from north by
A Rutherford,
1774*

---

14 Perth Bridge, Perth and Kinross

AD 1766-70 and later.

*NO 121238. Best viewed from Tay Street or from the
North Inch.*

Perth Bridge was designed by John Smeaton, better
known as the engineer of the Eddystone Lighthouse
and the Forth and Clyde Canal. The bridge
replaced an awkward and dangerous ferry which
had been in operation since the destruction of an
earlier Perth Bridge in 1621. The old bridge, built in
1616, had been a low structure with insufficient
room under the arches to accommodate flood
water and the first major flood after its erection
saw its destruction. Some idea of the problem can
be seen in the inscriptions on the west pier of
Smeaton's bridge. These inscriptions, facing the
North Inch, depict various flood levels since the
bridge's construction. The river level rose 4.5 m in
February 1950, 4 m in 1931, 5 m in June 1859 and
5.8 m in 1814. The problem is now reduced since
the erection of the Hydro-Electric dam at Pitlochry.

Smeaton was aware of these problems and, to
protect the foundations, he constructed the cut-
waters for the piers inside coffer dams. These can
still be seen when the river is low. The bridge has
nine arches with blind openings in the spandrels
and a total span of 268 m. On its completion there
were great celebrations in Perth: copper 'halfpenny'
tokens were struck depicting the bridge and the
dance tune 'The Bridge of Perth' was composed in
its honour.

By the mid 19th century the bridge was considered
to be too narrow for the traffic using it. In 1869 the
stone parapets were removed and iron brackets
were used to support new footpaths and cast iron
parapets on either side.

In 1859 this became the only bridge over the River
Tay to carry a public tramway system. The Perth-
Scone tramway used the bridge for thirty-four
years. Horse-drawn trams were used until 1905
when the service was electrified. The service closed
in January 1929.

There is an inscription cast into the iron panel of
the parapet at each end of the bridge. It reads:

> 'Bridge built 1766–
> William Stewart, Lord Provost
> John Smeaton, Engineer.
> Bridge widened 1869–
> John Pullar, Lord Provost
> A. D. Stewart, Engineer.'

---

15 Bridge of Dun, Angus

AD 1785-87.

*NO 662584. Bridge over the River South Esk to the
W of Montrose Basin. Approach from N by A 935
Brechin-Montrose road.*

Bridge of Dun was founded on 7 June 1785 and
completed on 27 January 1787. It is an elegant
Gothic design worthy of a major road, the policies
of a large house, or an urban setting, and its

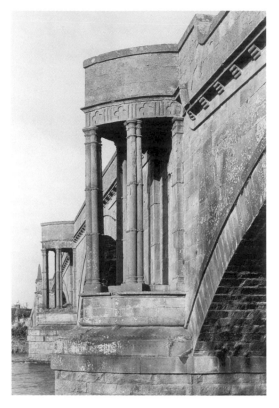

Bridge of Dun

Aberfeldy Bridge

16 Aberfeldy Bridge, Perth and Kinross

AD 1733.

NN 851492. Crosses the River Tay on the NW side of Aberfeldy on the B 846 to Weem and Kenmore. Best viewed from park SW of bridge.

General Wade was responsible for some 402 km of scientifically planned roads in the Highlands. They were constructed between 1726 and 1735 and included forty stone bridges, the best known being Aberfeldy Bridge (also known as Tay Bridge), built in 1733. At the time of its construction it was the only bridge spanning the River Tay, earlier bridges at Dunkeld and Perth having been destroyed.

The five-arched bridge is 112 m long and 4.5 m wide. It is hump-backed and still in use. The large central arch and stone obelisks at the ends of the level portion of the parapet give it a distinctive appearance.

The designer was William Adam, described by Wade as 'the best Architect in Scotland'. The stone was a chlorite schist from a quarry between Aberfeldy and Kenmore. It took two years to prepare the stones for its construction. At the quarry they were marked and numbered prior to being transported to the site of the bridge. The erection of the bridge was completed in a single year, the piers being supported on timber piles driven into the river-bed.

There are two inscriptions engraved in the parapet. The first in English reads:

> 'At the command of His Majesty King George the 2nd this bridge was erected in the year 1733: this with the roads and other military works for securing a safe and easy communication between the high lands and the trading towns of the low country was by His Majesty committed to the care of General George Wade, Commander-in-Chief of the Forces in Scotland who laid the first stone of this bridge on 23rd April and finished the work in the same year.'

The other inscription is in Latin and has been translated as:

location on a minor road of no importance is difficult to comprehend. It is a stone bridge of three arches with unusual columned supports to refuges over the cut-waters on either side of the main span. The parapets are detailed with castellated features.

'Admire this military road stretching on this side and that 250 miles beyond the limits of the Roman one, mocking moors and bogs, opened up through rocks and over mountains, and, as you see, crossing the indignant Tay. This difficult work G. Wade, Commander-in-Chief of the Forces in Scotland, accomplished by his own skill and ten years labour of his soldiers in the year of the Christian Era, 1733. Behold how much avail the Royal auspices of George 2nd.'

17 Guard Bridge, Guardbridge, Fife

15th-16th century AD.

NO 451188. Crosses the River Eden N of the A 91 NW of St Andrews. Best viewed from the car park of Guardbridge Hotel, Old St Andrews Road, Guardbridge.

The name 'Guard' appears to be a corruption of 'Gare' or 'Gaire', meaning a triangular piece of ground. This possibly reflects the Z-shaped course of the River Eden at this point. If this etymology is correct, 'Le gare-brig' was built at great expense by Bishop Wardlaw of St Andrews (1404-40), founder of the University. 'The Gair Bridge' was repaired in 1685 from the revenues of vacant stipends.

This is a good example of a Scottish medieval bridge. It has six arches, all unribbed and chamfered at the arris. The east arch is smaller and lower than the others. It carries a roadway 3.7 m wide with three parapet refuges at each side. These may date from the rebuilding of the parapets some time after the original construction. On either side

of the bridge there are panels bearing the initials and arms of James Beaton, Archbishop of St Andrews (1522-39). This could be interpreted as evidence of repairs carried out on the instruction of the Archbishop but could equally well be the date of the present structure.

18 Kirkton of Glenisla Footbridge, Angus

AD 1824.

NO 212603. Crosses the River Isla at Kirkton of Glenisla.

Built in 1824 to designs by John Justice (Junior) of Justice & Co, Dundee, this small metal suspension bridge carries a footpath across the River Isla. The bridge is important not only for its ingenious structure but as a prototype for the larger suspension bridge at Haughs of Drimmie, Perthshire (NO 170502) by the same designer.

The footpath of the Glenisla bridge is 1 m wide and the bridge has a clear span of 18.85 m between the stone abutments. The bridge is suspended from four short iron pylons, two on the edge of each abutment. Each pair of pylons is tied together at the head by a curved yoke and has decorative scroll brackets at the base of each pylon to increase the lateral stability. Each pylon is tied to the bank by three anchor stays. The deck of the bridge is suspended from the pylons by sixteen suspension rods, four from each pylon. These provide equally-spaced supports with the longest rods meeting in mid-span. These straight suspension rods are

Guard Bridge

Kirkton of Glenisla footbridge

Kirkton of Glenisla footbridge, detail of ironwork

The bridge is signed and dated 'Jn. Justice, Dundee, 1824' on the connecting yokes between the pylons.

19 Chinese Bridge, Taymouth Castle, Kenmore, Perth and Kinross

Mid 18th century AD.

NN 782467. About 1.6 km downstream from Kenmore Bridge in the grounds of, and close to, Taymouth Castle.

The Chinese Bridge was built by the 3rd Earl of Breadalbane in the mid 18th century as a private estate bridge to allow pedestrians, riders and light carriages to cross the River Tay without requiring to leave the park surrounding Taymouth Castle. It derives its name from supposed eastern qualities in the design, yet its general appearance and proportion owe more to the arches and window tracery of Tudor Gothic than to eastern bridge construction.

supplemented by four curved suspension members, two of which are incorporated within the depth of each handrail parapet and form the bottom two members of the parapet structure for about half of the total span. The straight stays and parapet rails are coupled together for additional stability.

The elegant cast-iron structure comprises three equal spans supported at each bank by stone abutments and in the river by two stone piers carefully designed to provide a cut-water whilst echoing the curves of the ironwork. The carriageway is only 2.7 m wide and is enclosed by elegant railings. In the description of Queen Victoria's visit to Taymouth Castle in 1842, there is an account of a drive taken by the Royal party via the Chinese Bridge and a more utilitarian wrought-iron structure, known as Newhall Bridge (NN 789469), situated about 1.2 km downstream.

Both bridges are now closed to traffic but a footbridge has been constructed within the original framework of Newhall Bridge for the convenience of anglers.

20 Packbridge near Coaltown of Balgonie, Fife

17th century AD or earlier.

NT 307983. Walk S from Coaltown of Balgonie along rough footpath leading to West Wemyss.

A narrow stone bridge of two arches and without parapets, crossing the River Ore to the south of Coaltown of Balgonie, this bridge of indeterminate age appears to have been used by the pack animals transporting coal from the Balgonie mines to the coast of the Firth of Forth for shipping.

21 Guideplates and Milestones, Fife

19th century AD.

NO 608082 Crail-St Andrews, guideplate no. 1 on A917

NO 524152 Crail-St Andrews, guideplate no. 2 on A917

NO 516159 Crail-St Andrews, guideplate no. 3 on A917

NO 604089 Crail-St Andrews, milestone no. 1 on A917

NO 600103 Crail-St Andrews, milestone no. 2 on A917

NO 517157 Crail-St Andrews, milestone no. 3 on A917

NO 545141 Crail-St Andrews, milestone no. 4 on A917

NO 531149 Crail-St Andrews, milestone no. 5 on A917

NO 593118 Crail-St Andrews, milestone no. 6 on A917

NO 586131 Crail-St Andrews, milestone no. 7 on A917

NO 572135 Crail-St Andrews, milestone no. 8 on A917

NO 559135 Crail-St Andrews, milestone no. 9 on A917

NO 441228 Dairsie-Newport, guideplate no. 1 on A92

NO 438233 Dairsie-Newport, guideplate no. 2 on A92

NO 420192 Dairsie-Newport, milestone no. 1 on A92

NO 427206 Dairsie-Newport, milestone no. 2 on A92

NO 435219 Dairsie-Newport, milestone no. 3 on A92

NO 439231 Dairsie-Newport, milestone no. 4 on A92

NO 436246 Dairsie-Newport, milestone no. 5 on A92

NO 431261 Dairsie-Newport, milestone no. 6 on A92

NO 436042 Largo, mileplate NE of Upper Largo on A915

NO 518047 Newton of Balcormo, guideplate at junction of B9171 and Arncroach road

NO 431186 St Andrews-Dairsie, milestone no. 1 on A91

NO 418177 St Andrews-Dairsie, milestone no. 2 on A91

NO 447189 St Andrews-Dairsie, milestone no. 3 on A91

NO 492175 St Andrews-Dairsie, milestone no. 4 on A91

NO 477181 St Andrews-Dairsie, milestone no. 5 on A91

NO 463188 St Andrews-Dairsie, milestone no. 6 on A91

NO 364125 Tarvit Mill, mileplate 350 m NE.

The turnpike roads of Fife are rich in terms of well-designed guideplates and milestones. These give a remarkable amount of information and are often attractively lettered, each road or turnpike trust having its own house style. In the majority of cases the lettering is raised in cast-iron, either on a plate

Milestone on A921 near Easter Pitcorthie Farm, two miles east of Colinsburgh (NO 506036)

attached to a stone or post or as a free-standing structure. In some cases these include the name of the manufacturer and/or the date of erection. The A 92 road between Cupar and St Michaels has a particularly attractive form of milestone signed and dated: 'Alexr. Russell 1824 Kirkcaldy Foundry'.

The examples given above are all scheduled monuments and are identified as they appear on official lists. It should be noted that the A 91 and A 92 roads are marked at mile intervals from Cupar rather than from Dairsie. The A 92 branches from the A 91 just beyond Dairsie, travelling from Cupar. Many other fine examples exist in addition to those listed above.

Bell Rock Signal Tower, Arbroath

22* Bell Rock Signal Tower, Arbroath, Angus

AD 1807-11 and later.

NO 640404. On A 92 in Arbroath, now the Signal Tower Museum.

The building of the Bell Rock Lighthouse 19.2 km south-east of Arbroath was one of the major engineering feats of the early 19th century. The lighthouse is of the 'lit rock-tower' type, that is, it is a wave-washed structure with the entire accommodation provided within the tower that supports the light. The site was submerged every high tide. The working season was limited to four months per year, yet the building took only four seasons to complete, coming into service in 1811. The story is a remarkable one that says a great deal for Robert Stevenson, the engineer in charge of the whole operation, and for the men who worked under him. Full details of the history can be had at the Signal Tower Museum.

The lighthouse tower was constructed of four separate types of stone. The eighteen irregular foundation stones were of granite from Cairngall Quarry near Peterhead. These were formed to fit holes cut in the bedrock to provide a level foundation. The main tower had an outer skin of granite from Rubislaw Quarry near Aberdeen and a core of old red sandstone from Mylnefield Quarry, Kingoodie. The cornice and parapet wall round the light were cut from sandstone from Craigleith Quarry near Edinburgh.

The quarry blocks were transported to Arbroath by sea and taken to a yard in Ladyloan, due north of the Signal Tower and half-way between it and the harbour. The yard contained a circular masonry platform corresponding in size to the base of the lighthouse tower. Each course of masonry was tested on this before being marked with oil paint and stacked ready for shipping to the site. The yard had workmen's shades round three sides. The fourth side contained the barracks which backed onto Hannah Street. During the building season the stones were returned to the harbour and shipped to the site. Each ship had its own mooring near the rock and the stones were transferred the short distance from the moorings to the landing stage by a form of small boat known as a praam. The stones were unloaded from the praams onto a raised railway to be carried across to the base of the tower. They were then twisted into position by a series of cranes, the last of which was a balance crane used for the final placement. It was the forerunner to present-day tower cranes but had a double jib and a mobile balance weight to counteract the weight of the stone. The men working on the rock were quartered in one of the tenders but, as work was speeded up, they were moved, first into the temporary lightship, the *Pharos*, then into the *Sir Joseph Banks*, a ship purchased specifically to fulfil this function. Work was carried on at any time of the night or day when the site was accessible. Bad weather created most of the major problems and, as large waves are capable of moving enormous weights, all stones landed had to be properly positioned and clamped before the end of that particular shift.

As soon as the lighthouse tower was complete the platform in the Bell Rock Yard was dismantled and the stones built into the Signal Tower.

The Signal Tower occupies a seafront site so close to the sea that the keepers' drying greens were retained by the sea wall. The accommodation provided was intended to house the Principal Lightkeeper, the Principal Assistant Lightkeeper, the Master of the Lighthouse Tender and three other assistant Lightkeepers and their families.

The tower had a 1.5 m achromatic telescope housed in a small observatory. Over this was a flagstaff on which was mounted a 46 cm copper sphere. This was used for communication between the lighthouse and the shore. The ball on the lighthouse was raised at a particular time each day if all was well, but if there were problems the ball was left unraised. In this event the tender put to sea immediately. A pair of carrier pigeons was also used to transport messages. The pigeons were presented by Captain Samuel Brown, RM, who built the suspension bridge at Montrose, now demolished. The pigeons took an average time of only eleven minutes to fly the 19.2 km between the lighthouse and the Signal Tower. Both floors of the building are stone flagged and originally the windows were fitted with storm shutters. The houses had a detached garden in Millgate Loan

now occupied by the Mount Zion Brae. The keepers' accommodation was moved to Salvesen Crescent, Edinburgh, in the 1950s and Arbroath's link with the Bell Rock was broken.

This building presently houses the Signal Tower Museum, administered by Angus Council. There are seven exhibition rooms covering various facets of Arbroath's rich history: the early history of man in the area; the medieval period when the Abbey was built; the design and construction of the Bell Rock Lighthouse; the Arbroath fishing community; the natural environment; civic history and local public services; local industries including flax spinning and weaving, shoemaking, clockmaking, agricultural machinery and mechanical engineering; there is also a gallery of everyday life. The museum was opened in 1974 and was the Scottish Museum of the Year in 1975.

23* Isle of May, Old Lighthouse, Fife

AD 1636.

NT 655993. Approach by boat from Anstruther.

The old lighthouse on the Isle of May was erected in 1636 as a direct response to a request by mariners on the understanding that they would have to pay a toll according to their tonnage. A Thomas Bikkertoun instigated the development in 1635, asking that the dues be similar to those charged by the English lights. The patent was granted to John Cunningham and Charles Geddes on the understanding that they would be allowed a reasonable and constant duty. This was set at four shillings Scots per ton for foreign vessels, including English, and two shillings per ton for Scottish ships. All ships entering Scottish waters between Dunnottar and St Abb's Head were subject to this tax.

This provided a substantial income in the 1630s. In 1790 the collections rose from £280 to £980. The fire was then burning 400 tons of coal per year and on a long windy night could use up to three tons. Mariners were no longer satisfied with the brightness of the light and discussions began as to its possible replacement.

This was the principal Scottish lighthouse in the 17th century and is today the most notable survival of this class of building anywhere in Britain. The original building took the form of a three-storey tower with a square plan. The ground floor and second floor were vaulted, the upper vault carrying a plinth on which the brazier stood. Coal was hoisted up the face of the building using a simple derrick.

Robert Stevenson built the replacement light in 1816 using the Bell Rock Yard at Arbroath as a base for his masons. The old lighthouse obscured the new light and Stevenson truncated the building, adding a pitched roof over the ground-floor vault. This was done on the intervention of Sir Walter Scott who persuaded Stevenson to 'ruin it a la picturesque' rather than demolish it completely.

24 Crail Harbour, Fife

16th century AD or earlier.

NO 611074. Signposted from the crossroads at the Tolbooth in Crail. Suggest leaving car in the Marketgate and walking.

Crail was created a Royal Burgh in 1310 and is likely to have had some form of protecting bulwark from an early period. The date of the construction of the south quay of the existing harbour is uncertain but the vertically-jointed masonry suggests a late 15th- or early 16th-century structure. By 1593 the harbour was considered to be too small and a supplication was made to the Convention of Royal Burghs asking that an area of ground called 'Pinkertoun' be purchased for the founding and erecting of a harbour to the town. The position of this harbour to the east of the burgh would appear to be a large natural haven later referred to as Roome Harbour (NO 619078).

The petition was continued for many years but without success, the last attempt being in 1610 when the old harbour was in need of repair. Many of the harbours of Scotland were destroyed or badly damaged in the storms of the 1650s and, with trade and commerce at a low ebb, any development was unlikely. At the beginning of the 18th century Crail was again enjoying a period of prosperity and

was granted the sum of £20 sterling to repair the ruinous harbour.

No further development took place until the early years of the 19th century. Ainslie's map for 1775 shows Crail harbour as comprising a single dog-leg quay. In 1821, Robert Stevenson produced a plan for the improvement of the old harbour. This work appears to have been carried out as Dower's map of 1828 suggests the building of the west quay which still survives.

With the return of herring to the Firth of Forth in the 1830s and 1840s, Crail again attempted to have a harbour built at Roome. James Leslie, the Dundee Harbour Board engineer, prepared a plan in 1846. This consisted of two proposals for an 'Asylum Harbour' in Roome Bay. The first plan enclosed an area of 6.48 hectares of water at low tide and 9.3 hectares between the low and high watermark. He also suggested a wet dock and repairing dock or slip between high and low water. The smaller plan was similar but with a reduced area of deep water. This proposal was prepared in the light of a Government plan to create a 'Harbour of Refuge' on the east coast of Scotland. Crail's claim for this harbour included lists of recent wrecks on the Carr Rocks. They also proposed that the Cellardyke fishermen could 'emigrate' to Crail. Wick in Caithness was, however, selected as the site for this harbour in 1858.

Crail abandoned the 'Roome' project and effected improvements to the old harbour. These were completed in January 1862 with the erection of a crane to place booms at the entrance. The 19th-century work at the entrance to the harbour is very obvious as it is built with horizontal masonry and mortar joints. The boom was intended to protect boats in the harbour in stormy weather, but fishermen complained that it obstructed free access and egress for their boats.

There has been no further development since that period other than general repairs and the harbour is now used by only a few very small boats working lobster pots. It is an attractive place and does much to put the scale of medieval trading vessels in perspective.

TOWNS AND TOWNSCAPE

Dundee, High Street

The largest centre of population in the region is the City of Dundee (NO 4030), closely followed by the combined populations of the group of industrial towns in south Fife which includes Dunfermline (NT 0987), Glenrothes (NO 2701), Kirkcaldy (NT 2791), Leven (NO 3800) and a host of smaller units often physically attached to the larger centres. Glenrothes is the only New Town in this group, the rest developing naturally from old established burghs. This is the situation over the remainder of the region where there is a reasonably even spread of small burghs all developing from medieval foundations.

All the towns have considerable suburban areas in which it is possible to find attractive houses or small groups of houses but, on the whole, these suburbs lack overall townscape quality. The same can be said of recent town centre developments and even the new town of Glenrothes lacks an overall pattern in the design of its central area.

The last period of comprehensive townscape design took place in the central area of Dundee in the second half of the 19th century. Dundee was the only centre in the region large enough to accommodate a development on this scale. The development resulted from an area of congestion to the north and east of the High Street which impeded access to the town. The Town Council appointed William Mackison as Burgh Engineer and Surveyor in 1868. After some initial consultation with John Lessels of Edinburgh, Mackison demolished most of the pre-Georgian area of the City Centre and rebuilt to a concept based on the work of Baron Haussman in

Paris. He exercised rigid control over the facades of his new streets, particularly the upper section of Commercial Street, Whitehall Street and Whitehall Crescent. He insisted on a tall ground storey with a cast-iron structure to allow larger areas of glass than had been possible with traditional masonry construction. Over this he asked for three complete storeys and an attic. This gave a height and sense of urbanism lacking in the earlier Georgian developments. Early photographs of these streets show the original design to have been much livelier and more elegant than that which now survives. The original shops were designed with elaborate sign boards and window patterns but subsequent modernisation in the 20th century has resulted in the removal of many of these features to the detriment of the whole area.

Large areas of tenement accommodation were developed in all the larger burghs of the region in the 1870s. Many architectural firms were set up to specialise in this form of development. These early tenements were still ill-designed and poorly appointed and improving standards came only after the lull in building activity in the 1880s, the highest standards being reached in those buildings erected at the turn of the century. The superficial appearance of those tenement developments owed much to early 19th-century Georgian street façades and the gridiron plans that accompanied them.

Dundee was alone in the major Scottish cities in that it had no early 19th-century new town or even large scale development of Georgian terraced houses. The other towns in the region tended to follow the pattern in Edinburgh and Glasgow but were too small to produce new town areas of any significance. They did however develop a neo-Classical character both within and immediately surrounding their medieval core. The best examples are undoubtedly Cupar (NO 3714), Montrose (NO 7157), Perth (NO 1123) and St Andrews (NO 5116), and the most complete street façades are the terraces and crescents fronting the North and South Inch in Perth.

The majority of important townscape monuments are linked to the chain of medieval burghs along the East Neuk and south coast of Fife. These formed an important group of burghs in the medieval period which tended to mark time in the 18th and early 19th centuries to be revived by the success of the herring and white fish industry in the second half of the 19th century. Burghs such as Culross (NS 9885) and Dysart (NT 3093) had all but died when the National Trust for Scotland began to show an interest and to purchase properties for redevelopment. Most of this redevelopment took the form of conservation and rehabilitation work to convert the former town houses into flats and houses for merchants and industrialists from the nearby industrial areas. The exercise was successful in that it attracted new inhabitants, prevented buildings from disappearing entirely and generally created areas which are extremely pleasant to visit or to live in.

Many Scottish burghs comprised a single street widening towards the centre to accommodate the market stance. Here stood: the burgh cross, the symbol of the burgh's right to trade; the tolbooth or 'Town House'; and the

St Andrews, West
Port, c 1870

luckenbooths, a row of shops or buildings where items of considerable value
were sold. On either side of the street stood the burgess 'lands'—large
multiple occupancy buildings; in the larger burghs, the principal owner
occupied the first and occasionally also the second floor, with tenants
above. The tenants diminished in social status the further up the building
they lived. Behind the 'lands' was a 'tenement' of ground in the form of a
long strip which stopped against a somewhat enlarged garden wall known
as the 'back dikes'. Outwith this wall was a lane which often took its name
from its position in relation to the market and the boundary wall: hence
'North Back Dikes' and 'South Back Dikes'. At the points where the back
dykes turned along the last tenement to meet the main street stood the town
'port' or entrance. Only two such 'ports' survive in Scotland: the East Port
or Wishart Arch, Dundee (NO 406307), now situated in the Cowgate but
formerly thought to have stood at the end of the Murraygate or Seagate;
and the West Port, St Andrews (NO 505165), now heavily restored.
Montrose and Newburgh (NO 2318), are particularly well-preserved
examples of this type of single street planning.

Many burghs had a second street, sometimes parallel to the first and
sometimes at right angles. This type of layout can be seen in Arbroath,
Crail, and Perth.

Dundee and St Andrews had two of the most ambitious medieval plans of
any of the burghs of Scotland. Dundee had four large medieval streets
radiating from the corners of a generous market stance. Nethergate,
Murraygate and Seagate still retain their relationship with the High Street
or market area but the narrows which formerly defined these areas were
swept away in the central area development already discussed. The
Overgate has now disappeared under a modern shopping development. St
Andrews was only slightly less impressive in its layout with three large
medieval streets forming an almost wedge-shaped burgh. This plan lacks a
focal point and it has been argued that there should be a square between
North Street and South Street, the Cathedral precinct and Castle Street; a
considerable amount of urban archaeological excavation and reassessment
of documentary evidence would be required before this could be proved.

Townscape of Crail

The 'tenement' system on either side of these main thoroughfares led to the cross circulation in these towns being by way of lanes, pends, wynds and vennels. In St Andrews these are used as pedestrian routes between various University buildings.

The tolbooth or 'Town House' stood within, or faced, the market place. This was the medieval equivalent of today's municipal buildings. Tolls or market dues were paid there, the town weights and measures were stored, the town council and burgh court met, prisoners were held, the town guard assembled, the town arsenal was located, burgh records were stored and any other function required for the running of the town was carried out there. The buildings fulfilling this function range in form from simple 16th-century tower-houses to highly complex classical mansions.

One aspect of medieval life to survive is the provision of bull-baiting stones where the beast was tied. Two of these are still visible. The example at Leslie (no. 32) is more or less complete and heavily grooved where the ropes have been attached. The second example is less obvious as it now lies on its side against a dyke on the north side of an old roadway to the south of Crook of Devon, Perth and Kinross (NT 033997). There is some doubt as to its association with bull-baiting and it may simply be a form of boundary marker. A similar stone to that at Leslie, but more phallic in shape, was found on a hilltop on the farm of Bolshan (pronounced 'bough-shun' and derived from 'Beau Champs') in Angus (NO 620520). Similar stones in Ireland are associated with the fertility of animals.

25 Crail Market Cross, Fife

17th century AD and later.

NO 613078. Situated on E side of Marketgate. Approaching from St Andrews, turn left at tolbooth: from Anstruther, continue past tolbooth.

Crail is an old burgh with three medieval streets: High Street, Marketgate and Nethergate. Looking at the air photograph it can be seen that High Street and Marketgate may in the past have formed one large market stance. The Golf Hotel and surrounding buildings break the building line immediately to the west of the tolbooth. This may indicate the original boundary of the High Street or the position of former luckenbooths—an area of the market, close to the tolbooth or guard-house, where permanent stalls were erected to accommodate those merchants, such as goldsmiths, whose wares were highly priced and easily stolen.

The market cross was the symbol of the Burgh's authority and was normally situated close to the tolbooth in a prominent position in relation to the whole market area. It is not known where the original cross stood in Crail but the present cross was re-erected in 1887 on the Marketgate site. The cross utilises a 17th-century shaft with 19th-century unicorn and base. The design is probably faithful to the original appearance. When considering the cross in relation to the Marketgate as a whole, one must ignore the avenue of trees that cut across this space on the line of the present road.

The Marketgate is comparable in size to the High Street and the tolbooth acts as a focal point to both streets. It sits at a rather odd angle to the present building lines. The tolbooth is a quaintly attractive building with a belfry of 1776 surmounting the massive tower.

The lower part of this tower probably dates from the late 16th century and may have looked like a tower-house or like Dysart Tolbooth (no. 29) without its belfry. The 1814 'Town House' and council chamber replace a building of the early 17th century.

The Marketgate has a number of fine townhouses of 17th and 18th-century dates. Unlike their counterparts in some neighbouring burghs, many of these have been restored without resorting to the use of harl. There is a small town museum to the south of the tolbooth and the Crail Preservation Society has published a good guide to the buildings of the burgh.

Crail market cross

26 Culross Market Cross, Fife

16th century AD and later.

NS 986859. In the centre of the burgh. Leave car at the NTS car park at the W end of the Sandhaven.

Culross presents one of the most visually exciting but chronologically confused series of buildings in Scotland. The value of these monuments was recognised in the 1930s when the Fife *Inventory* was produced and the National Trust for Scotland set up its 'Little Houses Scheme' in an effort to save the most interesting buildings. The project was a great success and the town is now largely NTS property. It attracts large numbers of tourists and has been used as a backdrop to many historical films and television programmes.

Culross, Town House

medieval street are older than the 17th century, although one or two of them incorporate earlier datestones, while buildings on other medieval streets are all of late 17th century date or, in many cases, even later. The base of the market cross, situated at the head of Back and Mid Causeway, dates from the late 16th century, but the shaft and head are modern.

The street pattern suggested above does much to relate the Culross burgh plan to those of other prosperous medieval burghs, and the later abandonment of the medieval plan reflects the changing fortunes of the town in the late 19th and early 20th centuries. The depressed nature of this community in the recent past is also reflected in the roof coverings as the pantiled roof coverings appear as late replacements for formerly thatched roofs. The fact that the pantile was, in Fife, considered an inferior roofing material can be confirmed both visually and through documentary sources. The visual evidence is the lack of pantiles in those burghs remaining prosperous in the 19th century, where the common roofing material is slate, whereas those burghs which were depressed have pantiled roofs. See also no. 41 for Culross Palace.

27* Inverkeithing Tolbooth, Fife

18th century AD.

NT 130829. In Tolbooth Street, Inverkeithing.

Inverkeithing is an ancient Royal burgh with charters from William the Lion in 1139 and Robert III in 1399. The Dutch bell within the present tolbooth is a remnant from a former building and is inscribed, partly in Latin:

> JOHN BURGERHUYS MADE ME SOLELY FOR GODS GLORY' 'GIFTED BY CAPTAIN JAMES BENNET & JOHN DICKSON, BAILIES, FOR THE USE OF THE TOWN COUNCIL OF INVERKEITHING, 1667'.

The form of the earlier building is not known but in 1550 a rent of twenty shillings accrued from the shops or booths on the ground floor of the Town House. The council chamber was situated on the first floor. The Renaissance tower at the western end of the present building is the oldest part, the

Careful study of the town plan appears to reveal three wide medieval streets now built over; later road improvements have cut through the burgess' feus to disguise further the original planning intention. The original medieval street appears to run from the cross to the Sandhaven, the northern building line being the north side of Back Causeway, the southern, the south side of Mid Causeway. This assumption is based on the pattern of the burgess' feus but appears to be confirmed by a town plan in the *Report on the Parliamentary Boundaries of Scotland* 1832. The Sandhaven appears to have been the second medieval street perhaps originally running behind the tolbooth (Town House) and terminating at Culross Palace. The third street is at the bottom of the Little Causeway running parallel to the shoreline of the Firth of Forth and continuing into the Dunfermline road.

It should be noted, however, that few if any of the surviving buildings in the area of the original second stage being erected in 1754 and the third stage in 1755. The remainder of the building was rebuilt in 1770 with the debtors' prison on the top floor, the Court Room in the middle storey and the black hole or prison on the ground floor.

The 16th-century market cross formerly stood in front of the tolbooth but is now farther down the street. The octagonal shaft, rising from a graduated base, supports a unicorn with a shield depicting the saltire. The unicorn was placed on the cross in 1688.

Inverkeithing tolbooth (photographed before the market cross was moved)

28* West Wemyss Tolbooth, Fife

18th century AD.

NT 325946. Situated on S side of Main Street.

The West Wemyss tolbooth is a modest rectangular structure dating from the beginning of the 18th century. It is two storeys in height with a proportionately lofty bell-tower projecting into the street. A forestair built against the tower gives access to the upper storey, whilst a vaulted pend passes through the western side of the building. In the pend are the blocked openings of the former prison cells. The building is constructed of harled rubble with a slated roof to the belfry and pantiles to the main block.

Two panels face the street but are now defaced. The upper one read:

> 'THIS FABRIC WAS BUILT BY EARL DAVID WEMYSS AND TOWN FOR THE CRIBBING OF VICE AND SERVICE TO CROWN'.

The lower panel contained a coat of arms with the initials D.E.W. for David, 4th Earl of Wemyss (1678-1720).

This building replaced an earlier structure built between 1511, when West Wemyss became a burgh of barony, and 1592, when it was reported as having a tolbooth and market cross.

West Wemyss tolbooth (Left)

Dysart tolbooth

The upper part of the tower was reconstructed in 1743-4 to provide an ashlar bell-chamber covered with an ogival roof in stone.

In the 1840s the 17th-century prison was still in use and described as 'two rooms in Town House . . . dry, but not very secure . . . quite unsuitable as a prison'. The hall-range to the east was rebuilt and enlarged in 1885.

30* Ceres Weigh-house, Fife

Early 18th century AD.

NO 400114. In the centre of the burgh of Ceres. Follow the sign for the Fife Folk Museum.

Ceres was a burgh of barony under the control of the Hopes of Craighall. The weigh-house served as a burgh tolbooth and as a venue for the Barony Courts. The building is a plain, two-storey, single-bay unit similar in form to an urban counting house. The roof is finished with scrolled skewputs. At the entrance are the burgh jougs for the retention of wrong-doers during market day. They comprise an iron collar attached to a short length of chain stapled to the wall and served a similar purpose to the pillory in England. Over the door is a panel depicting scales with a weight on one side and a bale on the other. This is superscribed: 'God bless the just'.

29* Dysart Tolbooth, Fife

16th century AD and later.

NT 304931. On the E side of the High Street, Dysart.

Dysart became a burgh of barony in 1549 and the tolbooth appears to have been erected in 1576. It took the form of a square-plan tower-house with a stair-turret projecting from the north-east angle. Ten years later the tolbooth charter was deposited in the Kirk of Dysart. By 1606 the building was in need of major repairs and masons were consulted as to ways of providing an adequate prison. Taxes were imposed to meet the costs but the work does not appear to have been completed until 1617 and this date appears in a panel on the forestair built against the south side of the tower.

The building was gifted to the Central and North Fife Preservation Society who opened the Fife Folk Museum in this and the adjoining premises in 1968. The weigh-house now serves as the entrance to the museum complex. The collection is based on the economic and social life of Fife with special emphasis on rural activities. Items of everyday life are displayed in a cottar's living room of the last century and fine gowns, lace and linen have their place in the Costume Room. The garden gallery overlooks the Ceres Burn and the Bishop Bridge (NO 400114) dating from the 17th century. Buildings on the other side of High Street provide a venue for agricultural and countryside interpretation. The museum has a comprehensive collection of tools associated with the crafts and trades common in the small burghs and landward areas of Fife. These include the tools of a stonemason, blacksmith, cartwright, cobbler, reed thatcher, tinsmith, baker and weaver.

There are a number of 17th-century and 18th-century houses in the vicinity of the museum, one having a lintel inscribed M.M. 1669, another 1707 A.P. M.B.

---

31 Bay Horse Inn, Pan Ha', Dysart, Fife

AD 1583 and later.

NT 303929. On the shore close to Dysart harbour.

NTS (but privately occupied, not open to the public).

The Bay Horse Inn was famous in the 19th century as a centre for ship sales for the east coast of Scotland. It is not certain when this activity started or when the building became an inn, but advertisements for the ship sales appeared in the *Dundee Advertiser* from its inception in the early years of the 19th century.

The property was purchased by the National Trust for Scotland as part of its Little Houses Scheme and they commenced alterations. Ceilings with traces of painted decoration were found after the roof had been removed.

The building comprises two separate parallel blocks on either side of a courtyard. The south block facing the shore is a two-storey, three-bay structure. Each of the ground-floor apartments had direct access to the courtyard and was also interconnected.

Although the building has been altered internally and is not open to the public, a description of the interior may help in understanding the external expression.

The east room on the ground floor contained a former kitchen fireplace. On the upper floor the end rooms had attics. The central room was open to the collars. This room was entered from a gallery at the top of the forestair. There was an exceptionally large fireplace flanked by windows in the south wall. This was accommodated in a chimney corbelled from the face of the building.

The painted ceilings were found in the end apartments and were of slightly different dates. Boarded linings and ceilings were carried up into the roof space of the central room. One of the

ceilings had two sets of initials which helped identify this building as the house occupied by Patrick Sinclair, son of Henry, 5th Lord Sinclair, in 1585. At that time the house was described as 'new biggit'. The date over the doorway was 1583 confirming that the house had been recently built.

The Pan Ha' area contains some fine 18th-century houses, many restored as part of the NTS Little Houses Scheme. These are linked by 19th- and 20th-century buildings to create an attractive environment.

---

32 The Bull Stone, Leslie, Fife

18th century AD or earlier.

NO 255020. Situated on the Green in Leslie.

The Bull Stone comprises a roughly shaped granite boulder, 1 m high, 0.3 m diameter at the top and 0.7 m square at the base. It is deeply grooved with rope or chain marks and is the stone to which the bull was secured in the ancient rural pastime of bull-baiting.

Bull-baiting took various forms but basically it consisted of the setting of specially trained dogs, one at a time, on a bull chained to a stake by the neck or leg. The dog attempted to seize the tethered animal's nose. The only protection offered the bull was a hole in the ground into which the bull might thrust this vulnerable part. This was not always provided and in some areas the bull's nose was blown full of pepper to further annoy it. A successful dog was said to have 'pinned the bull'.

This pastime was popular from the 12th to the 19th century when it was banned by Act of Parliament in 1835. Baiting and its variations declined, although very slowly, from the late 17th century onwards, having been banned by the Puritans during the Civil Wars and Commonwealth (1642-60). It is interesting to note that the only account of this stone appears in the New Statistical Account of Scotland, prepared the same year as the Act banning this activity, the writer stressing that bull-baiting in this area had occurred in the distant past. Bull-baiting is synonymous with bear-baiting, bears being substituted on special occasions.

STATELY 4 HOMES

**Blair Castle,
design drawing for
restoration by
D Bryce, 1869**

Fife and Tayside form an area with many natural advantages. Its rich farmland, abundant quarries, considerable forests, stocks of both saltwater and freshwater fish, abundant game, industries and other attributes were situated close to the centre of Scottish culture. This is nowhere better illustrated than in its palaces, stately homes and country mansions.

The existence of these great houses depended to a large extent on a considerable labour force being available. Labour was required for their erection, maintenance, servicing, supply and support. Practically all the inhabitants of the region, apart from the gentry, professional and merchant classes, were tenants to the owner of one of these houses. Rents were often paid partly in service or in produce. Even rich farmers did not own the land they farmed. This explains the relatively modest farmhouses compared with the size of the farms and the considerable numbers of large mansion-houses, as rents paid by the tenants supported the life style enjoyed in the 'big house'.

The era of the stately home came to an end with the peace after World War I. Many of these large houses still survive but in reduced circumstances. Former 'public rooms' intended for the reception and entertainment of guests are now being opened to the general public on payment of an entrance fee. In some cases the family still occupy the family section of the house whilst in others they have withdrawn to former service quarters. Service areas of houses stand empty or are only in partial use.

There are several distinct phases in the development of this type of dwelling. The early 19th century saw the development of the highly organised plan with public, private and service suites. Public areas were designed to impress and to accommodate the pomp and splendour of lavish entertainment. The private suite was the family home. The service suite accommodated the household servants and the service rooms. Servants were segregated according to both sex and position. The service rooms were also organised in suites according to function. These estates were almost entirely self-supporting and each formed an independent community, the only interaction between the entire group taking place when they attended the family chapel. Morality was a prime factor in the planning of these houses. Male and female servants were segregated. Bachelor guests were allocated secure quarters as were visiting personal servants. The principal servants who served the family were in their turn served by lower servants, senior servants having a separate hall from the juniors. Women servants ate with the men but withdrew to the housekeeper's pantry at the end of the meal just as the women withdrew from the main dining-room.

Stracathro House, Angus, 1827-30

Late 17th- and 18th-century houses were much simpler in their conception. Plans were less complex and the service areas were more basic in both accommodation and concept. But the organisation was still present. It is interesting to note that these buildings are Palladian in concept and that the agricultural system adopted by Scottish estates appears to be based on that existing in the vicinity of Venice in the 16th century. Copies of Palladio's books are to be found in a great many libraries of this period either in the original Italian or in French or English translations.

The 17th-century houses were for the most part based on former tower-houses but do incorporate many Renaissance concepts and details. The change from the tower-house to the Renaissance palace is particularly interesting in this region. The 16th-century royal palaces of Dunfermline (NT 089872) and Falkland set the pattern. The courtyard facade at Falkland Palace, 1537-41 (no. 42) is the earliest coherently designed Renaissance facade in Britain, while the Royal Tennis Court of 1539 heralded a change in attitude to a more civilised way of life.

The Abbot's House at Arbroath Abbey (nos 43, 66), around 1500, gives some impression of the form of a great ecclesiastical residence immediately prior to the introduction of Renaissance principles.

In some cases early houses were reused as part of the mansion house organisation. For example, when Mountquhanie Castle (no. 34) was vacated and the family occupied the new Mountquhanie House, the castle was deliberately ruined to form a decorative feature in the park surrounding the house.

Kinross House

33* Hill of Tarvit, Fife

AD 1907-8 and earlier.

NO 378118. Situated 3 km S of Cupar on the A 916.

NTS.

When the site of Hill of Tarvit was purchased by a new owner in 1904, it was occupied by Wemyss Hall, a small house, dating from 1696 and attributed to Sir William Bruce (see no. 39), with two 19th-century wings to the rear. Sir Robert Lorimer was commissioned to build a new house of similar character to Wemyss Hall but larger, with well-windowed lofty rooms capable of accommodating the new owner's collection of French furniture. There was no conflict of interests in these requirements as most 17th-century Scottish architecture, particularly that produced by Bruce, was influenced by French styles.

Lorimer chose to retain the two 19th-century wings and, by roofing the space between them with glass, was able to create a compact service unit incorporating the kitchen and servants' hall. The new house was wrapped around this core on the south and west. The south front formed the principal facade with the main rooms facing a splendid view. The west faced the approach to the house and contained the entrance.

The interiors of Hill of Tarvit were devised as a series of settings for the client's collection of antique furniture. This included Flemish tapestries, Louis XV and Louis XVI furniture, Scottish and English 18th- and 19th-century furniture, a collection of paintings, and a fireplace from Scotstarvit Tower (no. 49). The diversity of these pieces results in some very imaginative designs and shows Lorimer at his best.

One of the most interesting aspects of this house is the service accommodation which shows the range of rooms and equipment necessary for the smooth running of a well-to-do household immediately prior to World War I.

34* Mountquhanie Castle, Fife

16th and 19th centuries AD.

NO 347212. Some 7 km NNW of Cupar on the Cupar-Hazelton Walls road. Approach by Mountquhanie farm road by appointment only.

The ruin of this 16th-century fortified house comprises an oblong tower-house, formerly of three storeys. There is a courtyard to the west, open to the north and walled to the south. There are two-storey buildings on the west side of the courtyard, the corner tower of which has a conical roof. The courtyard buildings are now occupied as a house known as Feather Cottage.

The castle was deliberately ruined after the completion of Mountquhanie (or Mountquhannie) House in the 1830s. A small single-storey 'Gothic' laundry was constructed to the east of the tower-house. Feather Cottage was used for estate workers' housing and the upper portion of the circular tower was converted to a dovecote. The vaulted ground-floor chambers were converted to an estate slaughterhouse and butcher shop. The slaughterhouse occupied the east chamber and had a large tree trunk built into the walls to support it just under the vault. This was used to hoist the carcases during the slaughtering process. The west chamber contained the butcher shop and two of the blocked window recesses were converted to smoke kilns for the curing of meat.

The cattle were driven from Balquhidder to Mountquhanie each Martinmas and a butcher was brought from Cupar to slaughter the animals and cure the meat. This practice continued into the first half of this century when the slaughterhouse was abandoned.

There is also a small domestic icehouse a little to the west of the farm buildings.

To complete the romantic image the ruin was planted with ivy. Its position on the brow of a hill helped to achieve its utilitarian function of disguising these estate buildings and screening the farmstead from the mansion house.

Hospitalfield House

35* Hospitalfield House, Arbroath, Angus

19th century AD and earlier.

NO 625404. Situated off the Westway, close to the A92 trunk road between Elliot and Arbroath.

Hospitalfield is interesting on several counts. The former house provided the model for 'Monkbarns' in *The Antiquary* by Sir Walter Scott. The present house, which still contains remnants of the former, was the private residence of the artist/educator, Patrick Allan Fraser who acted as his own architect. He also intended the house to act as a school of art, which it still does.

Fraser was far from orthodox in his approach to the design of the house. The building was erected in stages without the benefit of an overall plan. His inspiration was drawn from medieval domestic architecture, many of the elements being used entirely out of context. He based the art gallery on a medieval hall. English, Scottish and European elements are used indiscriminately. The entrance hall, staircase and upper hall are finished in polished ashlar, hung with paintings and using mirrors to create the impression of additional corridors. Subsequent additions to the gallery wing incorporate the foundations and lower wall of the previous house.

The whole building is romantic in concept yet functional in its internal organisation. The intrinsic art-work is the work of local craftsmen working under Fraser's direction, whereas the art objects displayed in the house represent the work of the fashionable Scottish artists of the period.

36* Blair Castle, Blair Atholl, Perth and Kinross

Late 19th century AD and earlier.

NN 865661. The entrance gates are situated on the Blair Atholl service loop off the A 9 Perth-Inverness road.

The imposing white-harled Scots-Baronial exterior of Blair Castle dates from the 1870s when David Bryce of Edinburgh was commissioned by the 7th Duke of Atholl to remodel and extend the early Georgian mansion known as Atholl House. This building in its turn incorporated the truncated remains of an earlier Blair Castle. The whole history of the building appears to follow this pattern back to the earliest building reference of 1269. Fortunately many of the interiors survived one or more of these remodellings leaving a rich legacy of period interiors from the 18th and 19th centuries. The most magnificent of these are the classical interiors from the 1747 to 1758 remodelling. These were designed and executed by craftsmen of the highest order. The plasterwork in the principal apartments is the work of Thomas Clayton of Edinburgh. The woodwork is by Abraham Swan and the stone chimney-pieces are the work of Thomas Carter of London. Much of the 18th century and Regency furniture is of English manufacture, although some fine French pieces are in evidence.

Blair Castle has had many Royal connections. Queen Victoria visited Atholl House in 1844. In 1745, Prince Charles Edward Stuart stayed for a few days in the earlier Blair Castle. Mary Queen of Scots visited and was entertained with a hunt during which three hundred and sixty red deer and five wolves were killed. Edward III of England stayed at Blair in 1336 and in the years after the Wars of Independence, Blair was owned by Robert II and his son Walter.

The present Duke of Atholl boasts the only surviving private army in Europe, the Atholl Highlanders, who regularly parade in the castle grounds. The last siege of the building took place early in 1746 making this the last house on the British mainland to withstand a siege.

In addition to the architectural and historic interest of the buildings, Blair Castle also houses a number of excellent collections ranging from antique furniture, paintings, china, valuable books, documents, embroidery and lace to Atholl family trophies, mementos and a natural history collection.

The village of Blair Atholl houses a working corn (oats) mill and country museum.

Possibly Bryce did more than any other Scottish architect to break down the refinement of the late Georgian era. His boldness of concept and brashness of detail produced some very exciting buildings. On the whole these buildings have suffered badly, being constructed on such a grand scale that they have proved almost impossible to maintain on any but the largest estates. Many were demolished in the post-war period at a time when their architectural value was not fully appreciated. At Kinnaird Castle (NO 634571), 1854-56, Bryce reconstructed a Classical house as a French Gothic chateau to create one of the most splendid houses in the region. Unfortunately a fire in 1921 resulted in the loss of its romantic roof-line and splendid interiors. Otherwise the house survives and remains the seat of the Earl of Southesk.

Blair Castle

37* Scone Palace, Perth and Kinross

AD 1803-12.

NO 113265. Situated on the E bank of the River Tay, 3 km N of Perth on the A 93 Perth-Blairgowrie road.

Scone Palace is one of the earliest of the asymmetrically planned Georgian houses in Scotland. This early neo-Gothic building is the work of William Atkinson, an English architect of considerable ability and pupil of James Wyatt. Work started in 1803 and the designs were exhibited in the Royal Academy in 1808 and 1811. The building was completed in 1812. James Claudius Loudon of Edinburgh, author of various encyclopaedias on architecture, agriculture, horticulture, interior design, and landscape gardening, produced a manuscript proposal for the 100 acre park surrounding the house. Many of the ideas in this proposal were put into effect, including the demolition and re-location of the Burgh of Scone. Some features of the old burgh were retained in their original position, including the old market cross, the Scone gateway, chapel and graveyard. A replica market cross was erected at the replacement village of New Scone some 2 km to the east.

The house, interiors and gardens are all of one period and represent the avant-garde of the early 19th century. The building is the seat of the Earl of Mansfield but is open to the public on a regular basis. The family collections include rare porcelain, needlework, furniture, clocks, ivories, six generations of family photographs and the Vernis Martin collection. There is also a collection of veteran agricultural machinery to the east of the castle.

Scone was one of a group of houses erected in the region at the beginning of the 19th century. Rossie Priory (NO 285308), 1810, was another of Atkinson's designs although this house is now much reduced by the demolition of the principal rooms. Sir Robert Smirke designed Kinfauns Castle (NO 150226), 1820-24, in the castellated style, even extending the romantic composition to include two 'ruined watch-tower' follies on the crags above the main house. James Gillespie Graham was possibly the most successful designer of these houses in the

region, his best house being Dunninald (NO 703542), 1823-24. The houses listed above are all in private ownership and occupied as family houses and are seldom open to the public. The exception is Kinfauns Castle which is occupied by a holiday co-operative.

38* House of Dun, Angus

AD 1730.

NO 670598. Situated on the A 935 Brechin-Montrose road.

NTS.

House of Dun is one of the most original houses designed by William Adam, the father of the Adam brothers: John, Robert, James and William. The plans were prepared in 1723 for the Erskines of Dun but construction was delayed for a number of years, a modified design being erected in 1730. The house is somewhat severe and heavy; its composition is based on a simple rectangular block with a giant order running through two storeys to form a 'triumphal arch' entrance portico, which results in scale problems. The idea appears to be based on a Vanbrugh device but in this case the result is clumsy.

House of Dun

(Right)

House of Dun

Nothing in the grey heavy external expression prepares the visitor for the ornate Baroque plasterwork in the principal rooms. This is similar in character and execution to the Thomas Clayton plasterwork at Blair Castle (no. 36). This creates an entirely different mood and these rooms form a series of rich flamboyant interior spaces.

The offices are particularly complete and include a full complement of walled gardens, icehouses, stables, and so on, the whole layout being compact and easy to comprehend. The house is small enough to have remained in domestic use until the recent past when it was converted to a hotel. It has now been taken over and restored by NTS.

William Adam was the most successful of the second generation Classical architects in Scotland. He was the son of a Kirkcaldy stonemason whose forebears were small lairds in Angus, first at Fanno (NO 517511) then at Queen's Manor (NO 452506). He ran a number of commercial enterprises from the family home at Blair Adam (NT 129956). After his death the estate supported Robert and James on their Grand Tour and later met the debts of their ill-fated Adelphi project in London. Blair Adam still remains the Adam family home.

39* Kinross House, Kinross, Perth and Kinross

AD 1675-93.

NO 126020. Entrance gates situated on the E side of Kinross High Street.

Kinross House is one of the most important houses in Scotland as it is the finest and best preserved example of a group of houses designed by Sir William Bruce according to Palladian principles.

Bruce bought Kinross Estate in 1675 and had the house built for his own use. From 1675 until the house was completed in 1693 he occupied Loch Leven Castle (no. 52). The house was planned on an axis drawn between the tower of Loch Leven Castle and the Tolbooth Steeple of Kinross, the house being sited about half-way between these features. Bruce utilised a 'double-pile' plan similar to that used by Sir Roger Pratt at Coleshill, England, but combined this with massing and detailing which is obviously French in origin. The exterior of the house is expressed as a two-storey structure over a semi-basement. There is an attic storey suppressed in external appearance by locating the windows above the cornice and below the steeply pitched roof. Similarly there are mezzanine floors at each end of the building providing servants' rooms, lit from the gables.

The interior decoration is in the Anglo-Dutch style that Bruce had introduced into Scotland, but shortage of funds prevented the finishing of the upper floor to the same standard as that of the lower. Externally this shortage is not evident and a well-integrated series of forecourts, gardens and policies demonstrates Bruce's talent for formal planning on a grand scale.

Bruce's other houses in Tayside and Fife have fared badly, most being demolished or destroyed by fire. Only his former house of Balcaskie near Anstruther (NO 524035) has survived intact but this was a conversion from a former tower-house to an approximately symmetrical house. The formal garden at Balcaskie is a worthy forerunner to the gardens at Kinross.

40* Glamis Castle, Glamis, Angus

17th century AD and earlier.

NO 386480. Entrance to the policies is at the W end of Glamis village on the A 928 Glamis-Kirriemuir road. This entrance is 350 m N of the A 94 Perth-Aberdeen trunk road.

Glamis Castle is one of the finest examples of a large medieval tower-house extended and remodelled to the proportion and general appearance of a palace. It is the hereditary seat of the Earl of Strathmore and Kinghorne, the birthplace of Princess Margaret, and a favourite holiday home of Princess Elizabeth prior to her becoming Queen.

The early history of Glamis Castle is somewhat obscure, but at the end of the 16th century it took the form of a four-storey L-plan tower-house in which three of the four floors were vaulted. In 1606, Lord Glamis was created Earl of Kinghorne and immediately began the remodelling of the Castle. A large square wing was erected on the south-east angle of the original tower-house. The original building was heightened and enriched, and a large stair tower was constructed in the re-entrant angle of the old tower giving it a new scale and presence.

The architect for this work may have been William Schaw, Master of the King's Works. The 1st Earl died in 1615, leaving the work incomplete but it was continued by the 2nd Earl who acted as his own architect. He built the wing on the north-west angle in 1620 thereby giving the building a superficial appearance of symmetry.

Later the Earl took a commission in the Covenanting Army under the Marquis of Montrose and spent his fortune purchasing arms to the extent that he eventually borrowed against most of his holdings. On his death, the estate was fined £1,000 by Oliver Cromwell for the Earl's activities with the Covenanters. He had also been inclined to lend money to his friends without security and when the four year old Patrick Lyon succeeded as 3rd Earl of Kinghorne in 1646, the estate was in very poor condition. This state of affairs continued until Lord Kinghorne completed his studies at St Andrews University in 1660 and set about restoring the family fortunes. Glamis Castle was at that time almost denuded of furniture and the family's second home, Castle Lyon, formerly and now Castle Huntly (NO 301290), was uninhabitable. He began the restoration of Castle Lyon immediately, living there until 1670 when he moved to Glamis. The Glamis restorations began in 1671 and were completed in 1689. The story of this remarkable achievement is recorded in a diary known as the Glamis Book of Record.

In 1677, Lord Kinghorne was granted the present family title of Earl of Strathmore and Kinghorne, Viscount Lyon, Baron Glamis, Tannadice, Sidlaw and Strath Dichty.

Work on the castle continued through the following centuries and a letter from James Menzies, Lindertis, gives an account of the building work carried out on the estate in the year 1774. The work includes: re-roofing two courts at the castle; plastering the servants' rooms and the stair between the kitchen and the great hall; taking down the west wing of the castle; inserting a new drain under that wing and rebuilding to first-floor level; levelling the ground in front of the castle; building a gatehouse at the head of the approach; putting up an old gate near the church; rebuilding the Gladiator Gate at the Kirriemuir road entrance; defending the Glamis Burn; building three large

Glamis Castle

houses at the west end of the town of Glamis. The rest of the list deals with agricultural buildings, but it gives some impression of the constant activity on a large estate.

41* Culross Palace, Culross, Fife

AD 1597-1611 and later.

NS 985859. Situated at the west end of the Sandhaven, Culross, close to the NTS car park. Approach by the B 9037 road.

NTS.

Culross Palace was built between 1597 and 1611 as the town mansion of George Bruce (later Sir George) of Culross, later of Carnock. Bruce, the third son of Edward Bruce of Blairhall, acquired a fortune about this time from his interests in commerce, coal mining and salt manufacture. The house was built in stages but, after its completion, remained comparatively unaltered. The title 'Palace' is somewhat pretentious but it is described in the title-deeds as 'the Palace or Great Lodging in the Sand Haven of Culross'. The layout of the house is difficult to understand when considered in relation to the present courtyard but the site appears to have been purchased piecemeal, as ground became available, and the house and courtyard developed accordingly. The detached north range of domestic accommodation over a byre-stable is difficult to interpret, particularly since it has the same high quality painted

decoration as the main house, yet lacks kitchen accommodation. The house on the other hand has the remains of a kitchen at the east end of the 1597 range and a kitchen and bakehouse in the vaulted north range. Perhaps the north range was an independent house, with a detached kitchen or a kitchen in the basement, purchased by Bruce and converted to his requirements.

Whilst the buildings of Culross Palace are of considerable interest and encourage speculation, they are not the only features of interest. The internal paintwork of tempera and oil on the timber lining to the walls, ceilings and roof beams gives it additional importance.

Culross Palace

Falkland Palace

When looking at this picturesque house with its yellow-ochre lime-washed walls and red pantiled roofs, it should be remembered that the external appearance may have changed many times since the 17th century. At that time the timberwork may have been silvery coloured oak and the roofs, dark thatch. Change in buildings is inevitable and buildings of quality accept this change with little loss of character, indeed they sometimes gain from each successive change.

See also no. 26 for the market cross and discussion of the medieval street plan of Culross.

42* Falkland Palace, Falkland, Fife

16th century AD and earlier.

NO 253074. In the centre of Falkland.

NTS.

The present Palace of Falkland was erected by the Stuarts as a royal hunting seat and was the product of two main building programmes, the first extending from about 1500 to 1513 and the second from 1537 to 1541. The property had been forfeited to the Crown by the Earl of Atholl in 1437 and the existing quadrangle may have replaced an earlier steading. The former Castle of Falkland which

stood to the north of the quadrangle was abandoned as the new buildings were completed. The date of its final destruction is not known but it had been erected between 1337, when the earlier castle was levelled by English invaders, and 1401, when the replacement was first mentioned. The excavated ruins of this building date from the 13th century. A 17th-century house was erected on this site but has now entirely disappeared.

Only the south quarter of the quadrangle remains intact, but a substantial fragment also survives of the east quarter, which contained the royal lodgings. The courtyard facades, with their buttresses modelled as classical columns and incorporating medallion busts, are attributed to two French master masons, Nicholas Roy and Moses Martin. Their work contrasts sharply with the gatehouse, constructed under the direction of a mason who had previously worked at Holyroodhouse, Edinburgh.

The 'catchpole' or Royal Tennis Court adjoins the stable towards the north end of the palace grounds. The Falkland court is unique, being the only surviving *jeu quarre* court in the world. It was built in 1539 for James V and is still in regular use. There were originally two types of court in France, where the game originated: the *jeu quarre* and the '*jeu à dedans*'. All the surviving courts, apart from Falkland, are '*jeu à dedan*s' courts. The '*jeu quarre*' court has penthouses on only two sides, rather than three, and four window-like apertures in the wall at the service end. The game was originally played in monastery courtyards without rackets, and rackets had still to be invented when the Falkland court was built. It is one of the most difficult ball games and has been likened to chess in its subtleties and complexities. There is an active playing group still associated with the court.

There are many fine 17th- and 18th-century houses to be seen in the Burgh of Falkland, one of the most interesting being Moncrief House, opposite the Palace and dating from 1610. This two-and-a-half storey townhouse retains a thatched roof but has lost a row of wallhead dormer windows, the remains of which can be seen at the eaves.

The collection in the Falkland Palace museum includes two fragments of Pictish symbol stones (see chapter 8), both found when part of the steading at Westfield Farm (NO 238073) was demolished in 1971. Each has been cut into a rectangular block in modern times, and the small square hollows are also modern. One stone has a sharply incised double disc symbol and the so-called 'mirror-case' symbol, while the other shows part of a circular design and the symbol known as the 'notched rectangle'. There are also three prehistoric carved stones (see no. 92 and chapter 10).

43* Abbot's House, Arbroath Abbey, Angus

AD 1300 and 1500.

NO 642412.

Historic Scotland.

The Abbot's House at Arbroath Abbey is by far the most extensive and complete abbot's house in Scotland. It was erected around 1500 and incorporates in the basement the sub-croft of the western extension of the south range of the great cloister. This was erected in the late 12th or early 13th century. The sub-croft is a rib-vaulted chamber of two aisles of three bays. The large fireplace in this chamber was inserted at the time the Abbot's House was erected, allowing the undercroft to be used as the kitchen. Little is known of the organisation of these large houses. The survival of this particular example is due to its continued occupation after the Reformation when the remainder of the abbey was being used as a quarry for the rebuilding of the older areas of the town. Indeed, when Dr Johnson visited the abbey on 20th August 1773 and established its extent 'by following the walls among the grass and weeds', he failed to notice the Abbot's House among 'these fragments of magnificence', possibly because it was still occupied. During most of this period it served as a dwelling or number of dwellings but for a time it also acted as a thread manufactory. Continued and changing occupation was also responsible for a number of alterations carried out over the same period. These alterations have the effect of making the building very difficult to interpret. Notwithstanding the alterations of four or five centuries, this is an exceedingly important building illustrating the splendid manner in which a great ecclesiastical dignitary of the later Middle Ages was housed. It was acquired by the Office of Works in 1905 and opened as a museum in 1934.

Abbot's House, Arbroath Abbey

The house now contains a collection of relics from both the abbey and the Abbot's House. Those from the house include two 16th-century carved timber panels, part of a series originally mounted in a timber frame. One depicts the Angel of the Annunciation, the other a stylised thistle motif.

See also no. 66 for the Abbey.

FORTIFIED 5 HOUSES

**Edzell Castle
and pleasance**

This group of monuments often appears under the collective title of 'tower-houses', yet some are quite horizontal in their general appearance, others are constructed round courtyards and some, although having a tower-like appearance, are only two to two-and-a-half storeys in height. What is certain is their reflection of the troubled nature of Scottish society from the 14th to the early 17th centuries, when all classes of 'gentry' appear to have occupied this type of building, from royalty to bonnet lairds. Equally important is their association with the ownership of cultivable land and the fact that, when originally constructed, most of these fortified houses would have been linked to one or more courts of offices or to a loosely formed group of agricultural buildings, possibly housing tenants and even sub-tenants in addition to livestock and draught animals.

It should also be borne in mind that tower-houses are not simply a Scottish/Irish phenomenon and that they did at some time exist in all areas of Europe from the 11th century onwards. Indeed Europe appears to have many more early examples than survive in Scotland. This may reflect the fact that many early Scottish towers appear to have been constructed of timber rather than stone, a fact that explains many of the decorative features that have become part of Scottish building tradition.

One division that has not yet been established in Scotland is that between the urban and rural tower-house. In West Germany, for example, there is a class of tower-house dating to the early medieval period which is found in the backlands of medieval burghs. These were attached to the inner wing of an L-plan timber building which fronted the street. These appear to have been used for the storage of household goods and valuables in times of strife or when the burgh was threatened by fire. This may explain the curious situation of Gardyne Land in the backlands of the High Street, Dundee, or the similar structure which stood immediately across the pend and yielded some fine painted ceilings when demolished at the end of the 19th century. Other possible examples have been located in Anstruther, St Andrews and other parts of Scotland.

It should be noted that although many of these houses are known by the name 'castle', they are not castles in the true sense of the word, and 'tower' or simply 'house' would be more accurate.

The fortified houses of the 16th and 17th centuries tend to be quite complex in their organisation and external expression. By this time Scottish society was more settled. The King had erected the great palaces at Dunfermline and Falkland and new ideas on architecture, clothes, food, games and sport were being brought from Europe and were changing the expectations of all levels of society. Domestic arrangements were becoming more sophisticated and houses began to reflect this change both in their architectural expression and in the planning and provision of specialist features. Some of the new ideas brought superficial change such as the method of painting ceilings and walls, richly decorated plasterwork, and changes in furnishings. Others involved organisation from the planning stage: the move towards symmetrical facades; the provision of smoke chambers for the curing of meats and fish; the provision of guardrobes and slop sinks; increased window sizes; ground-floor halls; the eviction of animals from the basement; Aberdour Castle (no. 45); Elcho Castle (NO 164210; Historic Scotland); Huntingtower (no. 47); Kellie Castle (NO 520052); Mains Castle, Dundee (NO 410330); and Powrie Castle (NO 421345), all fall within this category although Powrie is considerably smaller than the rest. Perhaps the most complete example of a tower designed to include a degree of domestic comfort whilst still remaining a fortified dwelling is the small Z-plan tower at Claypotts Castle (no. 46).

The Fife tower-houses of Lochore Castle (NT 175958), Monimail Tower (NO 298140) and Newark Castle (NO 518012) all incorporate smoke chambers in the kitchen flues with access to the smoke chamber from an upper floor. These would be used in the curing of meat and fish.

A number of sites have more than one tower of similar date. The reason for this is not fully understood but it appears likely that both towers were inhabited at the same time. Examples of twin towers survive at Auchterhouse (NO 331372), Huntingtower (no. 47) and Powrie Castle.

In any form of stacked accommodation, a kitchen on the ground floor, close to the only stair, would have constituted a considerable fire hazard especially when meat was roasted beside an open fire. The simple solution was to locate the kitchen elsewhere and have the servants carry the food an extra few yards. A number of towers in the region made use of this arrangement. These include Auchterhouse, Earlshall (NO 464210), Kinnaird Tower (NO 241289), Murroes House (NO 461350) and Scotstarvit Tower (no. 49).

The Scotstarvit kitchen has been demolished but was possibly located in the single-storey wing which formerly stood against the west facade. Although dated 1627, Scotstarvit appears to be a late 15th- or early 16th-century tower altered at that date.

Braikie Castle, Angus

There are a large number of 15th-century towers in the region. These present a severe countenance. The few windows are set high in the walls and are often covered with metal grilles. Affleck Castle (no. 50) is one of the best preserved examples and is reckoned to be one of the most interesting towers of this period in Scotland.

Small towers survive on a number of sites. It is uncertain who the occupants were as towers often appear on estates already having a major house. Younger sons, superior tenants or dowagers appear to be the most likely inhabitants but as yet there is no substantiated explanation. Ballinshoe Tower, Angus (no. 51) is typical of this class, having an overall plan dimension similar to the six-storey Scotstarvit Tower but only rising to two-and-a-half storeys. Other examples may be seen at: Easter Fordel (NO 141125), two storeys with later additions; Hynd Castle (NO 504415), a very small ruin which caused doubts until some Welsh examples were examined; and Murroes House (NO 461350), two storeys, later extended by the addition of a ground-floor hall with laterally placed hearth. It is possible that buildings of this type were to be found in considerable numbers at the beginning of the agricultural improvements but that they were considered to be too small to be worth retaining and were demolished, any interesting stones being built into the new farmhouse or steading. This is documented in the case of Cossans Castle (NO 391498), which was demolished in 1771, dormer stones being built into Haughs of Cossans (NO 402495) and Meikle Cossans (NO 392498) farmhouses. Unfortunately there is no indication of size given with this documentation but with demolition costs of only 6/6d (32.5p) the building does not appear to have been extensive.

Aberdour Castle

**Edzell Castle,
aerial view**

44* Edzell Castle, Angus

16th-17th centuries AD.

NO 584691. Situated 1.6 km W of the village of Edzell.

Historic Scotland.

Edzell Castle, perhaps more than any other fortified house in Scotland, illustrates the impact of the change in attitude towards domestic comfort and architectural grandeur that took place in the late 16th and early 17th centuries in Scotland. The simple L-plan tower-house was extended to provide a courtyard house with formal pleasure garden or pleasance, incorporating a summer house and bath house, and at a short distance to the east a dovecote and the home farm, all executed with a degree of intellectual and architectural flair. The tower and courtyard house are now ruined and the farm steading has been replaced and altered during successive agricultural improvements, but the most significant element in the composition and the one that lifts Edzell beyond its contemporaries is the pleasance. This comprises a walled, parterre garden incorporating within its classical framework various heraldic and symbolic sculptured panels and architectural devices which are unique in Scotland and give Edzell Castle a distinctive place in the history of European Renaissance art.

The original manorial centre of Edzell is represented by an earthwork castle close to the site of the original parish church 350 m south of the present castle (NO 583687). This old castle was the seat of the Stirlings of Glenesk who, about 1357, gave place to the Crawford Lindsays. In the first half of the 16th century the Lindsays built the fine tower-house that forms the core of the present castle. The courtyard house was added to this tower around 1580 and the pleasance added in 1604. The 'lichtsome Lindsays' were a gay, gifted, gallant, turbulent and tragic family who retained possession of Edzell until 1715 when the estate was sold to the Earl of Panmure. The man responsible for the expansion of the original tower-house was Sir David Lindsay, Lord Edzell. He was the eldest son of the 9th Earl of Crawford by his second wife. David succeeded his father as the laird of Edzell in

1558 when only seven or eight years old. He was educated by James Lawson, a colleague of John Knox, and travelled widely with him on the continent. There he developed his taste and scholarship and displayed an enlightened approach far in advance of his time. He was knighted in 1581, became a Lord of Session in 1593 and a member of the Privy Council in 1598. In addition to his scholarship and magnificent taste he demonstrated boundless energy and carried out a number of estate projects including a large scale afforestation policy and mining operations in Glenesk. There he used his overseas contacts to obtain the services of Bernard Fechtenburg and Hans Ziegler, mining engineers of considerable standing, from Germany. It was also from Germany that he obtained the prints from which the sculptured panels of the pleasance were copied. He died in 1610 leaving the family in extraordinary debt.

After the estate passed to the Earl of Panmure in 1715, the lands were almost immediately forfeited owing to his involvement in the Jacobite rising that year. The York Buildings Company obtained possession and began the process of despoiling the mansion and its policies. The final ruin came in 1764 after the Company was declared bankrupt. The beech avenue was felled and the floors and roofs stripped out and sold on behalf of the creditors. In the same year the forfeited Panmure Estates were repurchased by William Maule, Earl Panmure of Forth. On his death in 1782 the estates passed to his nephew, the 8th Earl of Dalhousie. In 1932 Lord Dalhousie placed the pleasance under the custody of HM Office of Works (now Historic Scotland). The remainder of the ruins were also placed in custody in 1935. Since then the structure has been consolidated and the garden reconstituted.

45* Aberdour Castle, Fife

13th-17th centuries AD.

NT 192854. Clearly signposted from the centre of Aberdour on the A 921 Forth Bridge-Kirkcaldy road.

Historic Scotland.

Aberdour Castle presents a complex of buildings and gardens representing four distinct building periods dating from about the 13th century to the 17th century. This complex has been constructed on the site of an earlier castle which formed the capital messuage of the Barony of Aberdour granted by Robert Bruce to his nephew, Thomas Randolph, Earl of Moray, about 1325. The Morays granted a charter of the barony to William Douglas, Knight, in 1342 and the property has remained in the possession of successive branches of the Douglas family ever since. In 1386 the baronies of Aberdour and Dalkeith were united into a single barony of regality known as the Regality of Dalkeith, an arrangement which lasted until 1642.

The site of the castle was originally one of considerable strength but this has been diminished at various times. The construction of the garden terraces to the south of the castle, thought to be by Regent Morton in the 16th century, and the construction of the railway embankment on the north side in the 19th century were the two most influential factors in changing the site. Various other alterations have taken place over the years to make the building more domestic in character, particularly the reduction of the inner courtyard wall to its foundations. When viewed as a whole the castle expresses this long process of alteration and expansion.

The oldest part of the castle is the tower which forms the west range of the present layout. The plan-form of this tower is a parallelogram measuring approximately 16 m by 11 m overall. The walls are finished with flat clasped buttresses at the north and east corners. The foundation is stepped except for part of the south-east wall which is built on a splayed base course. The walls are 1.8m thick. These remains and some internal fragments suggest that the tower may have started as an early 13th-century hall-house, which was later heightened as a tower-house in the 15th century. The angle buttresses, splayed base course and cubical masonry are characteristic of 12th-century structures and the double lancet window at first-floor level is typical of 13th-century work.

Rebuilding of the upper part of the tower probably took place in the 15th century. The accommodation provided in the reconstructed tower, although adequate when built, was less than adequate for the requirements of a 16th-century laird's household and a new range was added to the south-east. This forms the central range of the present layout and is roughly rectangular on plan with a projecting stair at the south corner. The new building is linked to the old by a stair which serves them both at all principal levels. Internally the accommodation comprises two rooms per floor connected by a passage along the north side. On the ground floor the vaulted kitchen contains a large arched fireplace into which an oven was inserted in 1674. East and west of the castle are courtyards which were added in the 16th century but which may reflect an earlier layout repeated on a larger scale. In the west courtyard is a range of outbuildings built against the courtyard wall, including a brewery and bakehouse with two large ovens. The east courtyard contains a well house which may also have served as a laundry.

The existing east range was added to the north-east of the 16th-century building by Earl William Morton who succeeded to the title in 1606 and died in 1648. This extension is L-shaped on plan with a projecting wing at the south corner and the principal stair in the re-entrant angle. One of the two small towers projecting from the north front is original, the other an early addition. The whole of the first floor of this range formed a picture gallery and it is possible that the ceilings were painted in tempera, as was popular in Scotland in the early 17th century. Certainly the entresol has such a ceiling. The walls were panelled in timber.

The gardens are situated to the east and south of the castle. The east walled garden encloses half a hectare within walls 3.7 m high in characteristic 17th-century style, with enriched pediments on the two gateways, one with the Douglas heart and the other with the date 1632 and the monogram of William, Earl of Morton and his wife Countess Anne. The courtyard gate was inserted in 1740. The garden also contained a summer house and bridge to the kitchen garden but only slight evidence of these features survives.

To the south of the castle are the restored terraces recorded as existing in 1745. Beyond them is a large beehive-shaped dovecote containing about 600 nests. Beyond the dovecote was the orchard or 'wilderness' situated on land that was drained and laid out in 1690.

46* Claypotts Castle, Dundee

AD 1569-88.

NO 452319. On A 92 Arbroath-Dundee road. Turn towards Broughty Ferry at Claypotts road junction. Enter from Claypotts Road (B 978).

Historic Scotland (Interior by appointment).

The 'Tower Fortalice and Mannor Place' of Claypotts was erected between 1569 and 1588. The lands are referred to in documents from 1247 when they were described as belonging to the Abbey of Lindores (NO 243184) on the south side of the Firth of Tay. This fortified house is one of the most complete examples of the type of planning found in a number of other 16th-century buildings. It was erected by John Strachan or Strathauchin, a cadet branch of Strachan of Angus and Thornton in the Mearns.

The adoption of a Z-shaped plan form for a house of three storeys and attic provides a greater number of rooms and a higher degree of domestic comfort than had hitherto been the norm. The staggered, three-unit plan not only provided more rooms but better defensive coverage as the shot-holes in the end units allowed defenders to fire across the faces of the main building. The end units were treated as drums on diagonally opposite corners of the main building and these were capped with square penthouses with pitched roofs and crowstepped gables. This gave the building a richly modelled form and a complex and dramatic skyline. All of the richness was concentrated in the upper floor, the lower portion depending on the juxtaposition of flat to curved walls for its interest. It should be remembered that this fortified house, like all the others in the region, would have been situated in a fermtoun and would have had its own farm steading around it. The layout for this is not known but the improved steading, built in the 19th century, stood to the west of the house on the ground now occupied by a small housing development. This steading was demolished in the early 1960s.

Little is known of the estate organisation or the day-to-day life in the house when it was first erected, but the will of John Strachan, the feuar who had the castle built, gives some clues. Four tenants of Claypotts lands were listed as witnesses, suggesting that at least four families lived in the fermtoun in addition to the Strachans. The estate livestock amounted to: fourteen working oxen, five cows, seven bullocks, two workhorses, nineteen ewes with their lambs, and sixty ewes with their wethers (lambs in the second year). The sown crops amounted to: eight bolls of oats (expected return thirty-two bolls plus fodder), fifty bolls of oats (to return one hundred and fifty bolls plus fodder), fourteen bolls of bere, a form of barley (to return fifty-six bolls plus fodder), and six bolls of pease (to return twenty-four bolls). The house contents and utensils were valued at 100 marks. The total inventory of stock and utensils amounted to £1,118-6s-8d Scots on 27th April 1593.

At the beginning of the 17th century the superiority of Claypotts passed to the newly-created Barony of Lindores. The Strachans moved north to Balhousie, a farm adjacent to their lands at Scryne. They sold Claypotts to Sir William Graham of Ballunie in 1601. Graham took the title 'of Claypotts' and transferred the lands to his son David in 1616. David was the last owner to occupy the house and in 1620 sold the estate to Sir William Graham of Claverhouse for 12,000 marks. The Claverhouse lands were declared forfeit after the Battle of Killiecrankie in 1689 and reverted to the Crown. They were granted by Royal Charter in 1694 to James, 2nd Marquis of Douglas. It still forms part of the Douglas and Angus estates under Sir Alex Douglas Home. The house was placed under the guardianship of the Commissioners of Works in 1926.

47* Huntingtower Castle, Perth and Kinross

15th-16th centuries AD.

NO 082251. Situated 3.2 km W of Perth on the A 85 Perth-Crieff road.

Historic Scotland.

Huntingtower comprises two medieval tower-houses standing close together on an east-west line and linked by a single volume of late 17th-century date. The towers were originally connected by a curtain wall on the line of the south wall of the eastern tower. On the north side the courtyard buildings have disappeared but as late as 1790 the ruins of a great hall were still visible. This was a

single-storey building with large windows and a 16th-century style fireplace at the north end. This range abutted the north wall of the western tower and terminated at the north end in a two-storey building.

The oldest part of Huntingtower is the eastern tower. In its present form it dates from the late 15th or early 16th century and is remodelled from an early 15th-century structure. The original hall was on the first floor of the eastern tower. It was remodelled when the underlying vault was introduced and again in the 17th century. These successive alterations resulted in the preservation of a painted wooden ceiling from about 1540. This may be the earliest tempera-painted ceiling surviving in a Scottish dwelling. The ceilings in the main are decorated with a knotwork pattern in black on a white ground. One shows a tendril and leaf pattern. The joists between these panels are decorated in three simple patterns in: black and white on yellow; black and white on red; and white on black. The main beams are more ornamental with leaf-work, fruit, scrolls and zoomorphic patterns. The painted decoration on the wall plaster is probably slightly earlier but less complete.

The western tower of three storeys and an attic is of similar height and width to the eastern tower but is

Huntingtower Castle, drawing by J Drummond, 1849

much longer in total volume as it has its long axis running north and south. There are traces of mural painting on the plaster of the first-floor room. There has been more alteration to this tower with enlarged windows and fireplace insertions. This possibly dates from the period when the buildings were linked.

The linked fortified houses of Huntingtower make an impressive building. The original organisation of the site when the towers were independently occupied is still unclear. Perhaps if the outer defensive works, the garden, and the orchard had survived they might have shed more light on this aspect of medieval life.

48 Burleigh Castle, Milnathort, Perth and Kinross

16th century AD.

NO 128045. Situated on the E side of Milnathort on the A 911.

Historic Scotland.

Burleigh Castle

(Right)

Burleigh Castle presents a series of interesting elements which in themselves are unusual and which, when considered as a group, are not satisfactorily explained. The oldest part of the castle is the tower at the northern end of the site. This dates from the early 16th century. It has a simple rectangular plan rising to four storeys and an attic. In 1582, a second range was built, in alignment with the west wall of the original tower, running southwards to form the western boundary of a courtyard layout. This range terminates in a small tower at the south-west angle of the courtyard. This small tower is complete but the rest of the extension including a south range has all but disappeared leaving only the west wall of the west range. These demolished buildings hold the key to the domestic arrangements of the entire building. The remaining evidence is slight and can only give an indication of the size of these buildings. The raggle in the south wall of the original tower suggests that the west range was of three storeys and the surviving two-storey west wall, with no evidence of tusking for the third storey, suggests that the upper storey was constructed of timber. The south range is also known to have been three storeys, but was reduced in height prior to its final

demolition. The south-west tower appears to have been entered from within the angle of the south and west ranges.

49* Scotstarvit Tower, Fife

Early 17th century AD.

NO 370112. Situated 4.8 km S of Cupar on the A916 Cupar-Leven road.

Historic Scotland (key kept at Hill of Tarvit, no. 33).

Scotstarvit is a well-preserved simple L-plan tower-house of five storeys and an attic. It is thought to date from the early 16th or even later 15th century and was altered in 1627 for Sir John Scot and his first wife, Lady Anne Drummond. A charter of 1579 mentions a tower on the barony of Tarvet.

Sir John purchased 'Tarvett' from Alexander Inglis in 1611, and in 1612 his lands in Fife were incorporated as the Barony of Scotstarvit. He was Director to the Chancery, the author of *The Staggering State of the Scots Statesman* and a keen antiquary. This last interest may explain the antiquated appearance of the building. The apparent existence of an earlier tower does raise some doubts, but Scotstarvit does not have the appearance of an early building converted at a later period but rather a late tower built to give the appearance of being older. It has a number of unorthodox features including a garret fireplace of extraordinary quality and incorporating the monogram of Sir John and Lady Anne with the date 1627. This same date and initials appear on the panel over the cap-house door. These date-stones are both linked to the attic storey and it may be assumed that Sir John used this as his private study affording him a degree of privacy and pleasant views on all four sides. Another unusual feature is the slender proportion of the chimney stalks.

There is no evidence for a kitchen within the house but a number of raggles in the east, south and west walls show that other buildings abutted the tower at some time in its history.

50 Affleck Castle, Monikie, Angus

15th century AD.

NO 494388. Enter from the road between Luckyslap Garage and Monikie.

The tower-house known as Affleck Castle is situated on the gentle south-facing slope of the declining range of the Sidlaw Hills known as the Downie Hills. The house commanded views of the whole coastal plain from Dundee to Carnoustie and looked over the Firth of Tay to Fife and St Andrews. It is recorded that before the house was surrounded by trees it was used as a landmark by mariners entering the Firth of Tay.

Affleck was the seat of the family of Auchinleck, or Affleck, of that Ilk. The lands were held in chief from the Crown for an annual rent of one silver penny. The house appears to date from the late 15th century and, in 1471, James III confirmed a deed subscribed at Auchinleck on 16th March 1466 by David, Earl of Crawford. The first record of the existence of the tower-house is in 1501.

The accommodation provided in Affleck Castle is that normally found in a small medieval house: cellarage, common hall, lord's hall, solar and chapel. There is no kitchen and cooking must have been done in an outbuilding, possibly within the barmkin wall. The accommodation is provided in a tower of four storeys and an attic. It is described as an L-plan structure, although the secondary wing is very small and occupied by the principal staircase for most of its height. There is a small mezzanine floor, entered from a mural stair from the lord's hall, above the second- floor landing, and the chapel occupies this space on the third floor.

The arched doorway is situated in the re-entrant angle. The cellars are ceiled with the floor of the common hall above. The common hall is vaulted, has three good-sized windows but lacks a fireplace or any other feature to improve the level of comfort. Above this all the floors are of wood and

Scotstarvit Tower in 1866 (Left)

the rooms are well-appointed. The lord's hall has provision for a dais at the north end and behind this is a handsome fireplace. It is also provided with a latrine and a large wall press. The solar, on the third floor, is a room of exceptional distinction and of such excellent proportions that despite its small size it has few equals in Scotland. It has a good fireplace, latrine, large mural closets which may have contained bunks, a wall press and a beautiful chapel situated behind a miniature chancel arch in the wing over the principal stair. The chapel is vaulted in fine ashlar and has an octagonal stoop corbelled out from the wall. The accommodation is completed by an attic over the solar and two cap-houses, one over the chapel, the other over the secondary stair.

51 Ballinshoe Tower, Angus

16th century AD.

NO 417531. Approach from A 926 Forfar-Kirriemuir road.

Ballinshoe (pronounced Benshee) is an example of a class of fortified house much smaller than is presently considered the norm. Whatever their function, these small towers probably existed in considerable numbers and may account for many of the decorative dormer stones built into the walls of improved farmhouses and steadings.

Ballinshoe was at one time part of the Glamis Estate (no. 40), as was the neighbouring Fletcherfield (NO 403522) and the nearby Cossans (NO 392498). All had 'castles' prior to agricultural improvement supporting the theory that these buildings were occupied by rich tenants or younger sons.

The building comprises a simple rectangular plan with a projecting turnpike stair tower at the north-east corner (now demolished), and the accommodation is provided on two storeys and an attic. The missing floors were of timber, and the attic floor gave access to a small circular turret in the south-west corner. There are only two fireplaces, one at first-floor level, the other in the attic. The building probably had a detached kitchen but no evidence of this survives, although a similar tower at Murroes had a kitchen 10.7m from

the house across a small courtyard. Ballinshoe has an enclosure to the south which appears to be part of the original lay-out.

52* Loch Leven Castle, Kinross, Perth and Kinross

14th century AD and later.

NO 137017. Access by boat from the S end of the burgh of Kinross.

Historic Scotland.

Loch Leven Castle stands on a small island in Loch Leven. Originally the castle and its garden occupied almost the whole island, but the water-level was lowered between 1826 and 1836, increasing the area from about 0.7 hectares to 3.2 hectares. This increase in available land allowed the planting of the trees that now give the castle its romantic aspect. The castle comprises a rectangular tower-house with a barmkin or courtyard containing the ruins or foundations of a number of buildings including the former great hall, kitchen, bakery and women's house.

The tower probably dates from the 14th century and, although roofless, is one of the best-preserved examples of an early Scottish tower-house. The building is rectangular in plan and measures 11.2 m by 9.7 m externally with walls up to 2.5 m thick at ground level. Although roofless by the end of the 17th century, the tower is structurally complete. The top storey is thought to be an addition behind an existing parapet. It contained five storeys and a garret and was entered at second-floor level, 5 m above ground level. The walls are intaken at a string course 5.5 m above ground level and carried out again over a row of evenly spaced single stone corbels at the parapet, 12.3 m from the ground.

The ground floor consists of one small chamber provided with loop-holes, for ventilation and defence, in its north and east walls. Access is through the barrel vault via a trap-door in the first floor. The vaulted chamber on the first floor with its large fireplace and salt-box is likely to have served as a kitchen. The first floor also contains a latrine, slop sink and wall cupboards. Access was by turnpike stair from the floor above. There was also a hatch through the vault above the fireplace.

The hall was situated on the second floor. Originally the entrance area was partitioned off by a wooden screen, and the sockets to take its timbers can still be seen above the door to the turnpike and in the opposite wall. The fireplace at the upper end of the hall in the west wall was reduced in size in the 17th century but was originally of similar size and detail to that surviving on the third floor. Above this level all the floors were of timber.

The third floor was the laird's hall and this was the chamber occupied by Mary, Queen of Scots, during her imprisonment. The conversion of the east window embrasure to serve as a small oratory or private chapel possibly dates from this period. On the floor above was another chamber surmounted by the cap-house or garret.

The barmkin wall dates from the later 14th and later 15th centuries and for the most part reflects the line of the earlier polygonal curtain wall of around 1300, much of which still survives. The north wall is considerably thinner than the other sides and is probably later. Opposite the tower-house is the Glassin Tower, one of two such additions to the curtain wall. These were erected in the 16th century to provide protective fire along the face of the curtain wall.

During the First War of Independence the castle was held by the English. During this period it was possibly stormed by Sir William Wallace and was later visited by King Robert Bruce. In 1335 Loch Leven Castle was one of only five strongholds held for David II after the English overran Scotland. It was besieged by Sir John Stirling and an English force but was successfully defended by Alan Vipont. It remained a Royal Castle until 1390 when it was granted to the Douglas family who held it until the 17th century.

Mary, Queen of Scots, was held prisoner in the castle from June 1567 prior to her escape in the following year, her defeat at Langside and final imprisonment in England.

Sir William Bruce utilised the castle to terminate a formal vista from Kinross House which is planned on an axis from the castle to the tolbooth steeple at Kinross (see no. 39).

Tulliallan Castle, ribbed vaulting in undercroft

53 Tulliallan Castle, Fife

13th-14th centuries AD.

NS 926887. Situated about 1 km NW of Kincardine-on-Forth.

Tulliallan Castle is one of the best preserved examples of a comparatively rare building type, the Scottish hall-house or, more accurately, upper-hall-house. It is also unusual in having the principal doorway and a number of dwelling rooms in the vaulted undercroft. The doorway is defended by a drawbridge, portcullis and sliding draw-bars. It gives access to the stair to the hall and to a storage chamber or ante-room in the western part of the undercroft. At the east end, the undercroft contains a handsome apartment with a fireplace and stepped window seats. A row of piers down the centre of the undercroft supports quadripartite ribbed vaulting. The upper floor or hall has been remodelled and little comment can be made on the former arrangements; if it was occupied as a single room, it would have measured fully 18 m in length. It has been suggested that the wings to the north are later additions.

The building has been conserved by the Mitchell Foundation.

MILITARY ARCHITECTURE 6

Broughty Castle

Tayside and Fife have a large number of existing and former military installations from the recent past. These include: the nuclear bunker (no. 54) at Crail; the Royal Naval Dockyard, Rosyth (NT 102821); a fighter base at RAF Leuchars (NO 470205); the Royal Marine Commando base at Arbroath (NO 620430); a former US Navy base at RAF Edzell (NO 630690); and so on. Dozens of other 1st and 2nd World War bases lie neglected or have been partially returned to agricultural purposes. Others have become industrial estates or private air-strips. Hangars have been absorbed into agricultural or rural industrial use. It is not that these structures are without interest to today's public, it is simply that there are so many buildings of this class that it is difficult to recognise their worth on a national scale.

To give some impression of the potential it is worth considering a few isolated examples. An extremely large World War I timber aircraft-hangar was recently removed from the former Montrose airfield (NO 719595) to be re-erected at a Museum of Flight in England, yet this building was known by local experts and had stood empty since the airfield was abandoned after World War II. In this instance the building was recognised as being important and has been saved, unfortunately not in a local context. A World War I seaplane hangar on the harbour front in Dundee, which appears in one of the first German air reconnaissance photographs, was used from the end of World War II by a food packaging company and then as an engineering workshop connected with North Sea oil exploration service work. It was demolished in 1986, just as the regulations for its protection were being processed. A derelict but almost complete P.O.W. camp still exists to the south-east of Balhary House, Perth and Kinross (NO 266464). Dozens of these camps existed at the end of the last war but most were removed as soon as the prisoners were repatriated.

It is recognised that not every monument can be taken into the nation's care and that many more buildings may be destroyed before sufficient work is done to establish their importance on a national scale. In a number of cases this is not a criterion and buildings capable of serving some utilitarian function are often safe, as are buildings considered to be a local landmark or buildings on sites which are generally inaccessible. A monument such as Broughty Castle (no. 55) satisfies the first two criteria. This mid 19th-century structure was obsolete almost as soon as it was completed yet it fulfilled various military functions until 1969 when Dundee Museums moved into the building and laid out the tower as a local fishing and whaling museum. Its site on a peninsula projecting into the Firth of Tay ensures its protection by local amenity societies who have in the past objected to proposed developments on the shoreline of Broughty Ferry which threatened to interrupt the dramatic silhouette of the castle. The fortifications on Inchkeith in the Firth of Forth (NT 2982) satisfy the third criteria in being generally inaccessible and only altered or occupied in periods of national emergency.

There are remarkably few major fortifications surviving from earlier periods. In the 18th century Fife and Tayside were too far south to be of strategic importance in controlling the Jacobite clans, although there was a major Black Watch regimental barracks at Perth and two of the major military roads into the Highlands started at Coupar Angus and another passed through Crieff and Aberfeldy.

Ravenscraig Castle (no. 57) sited on a cliff on the north shore of the Firth of Forth, is a fine example of castles which form a link between ordinary keeps and castles built round a courtyard. Built in the mid 15th century the construction shows a higher quality of workmanship than is normally associated with earlier keeps.

A number of castles have 13th-century foundations, but most of these show substantial rebuilding and remodelling in later periods: St Andrews Castle (no. 56) for instance has considerable new work erected in the 15th and 16th centuries. Again this castle occupies a cliff-top site, a site more dramatic today than when the castle was first erected as a number of major rock-falls have been recorded over the centuries which have removed areas of land formerly let for agricultural purposes. Fragments of a few other early stone castles survive. Redcastle (NO 687510) on the shores of Lunan Bay was erected by King William the Lion as a royal hunting seat. It is possible that the fragment of the massive wall of enceinte is part of his original fortress. Similarly the ruins of Panmure Castle (NO 544376) can still be seen. This castle was erected in the 12th century and was reputedly demolished by 1336.

Prior to these large masonry castles, motte and bailey castles with timber keeps were the norm. Monuments of this class abound in the region, possibly reflecting their local significance, more akin to that of the tower-house than to the regionally or nationally important fortified sites of later centuries. A particularly fine example of a motte may be seen at Maiden Castle, near Windygates (NO 349015).

Broughty Castle from the air

54 Secret Bunker, Crail, Fife

1950s AD and later.

NO 568088. Signposted from the B 9131 Anstruther to St Andrews road. Open April to October inclusive. Phone 01333 310 301 for details and party bookings.

Scotcrown Ltd.

The Secret Bunker has only recently been de-classified. It is a former Underground Nuclear Command Centre constructed at the onset of the Cold War. Built in great secrecy, the main command centre is 100 feet below ground level and is entered via a ramped entrance passageway over 500 feet long. The passageway connects the Guardhouse, built on the surface to look like the pump house of a water reservoir with pantiled roof and columned veranda, with the top of the bunker staircase. The bunker is encased in 15 feet thick reinforced concrete and provided a base from where central government and military commanders would have run the country had the UK been attacked and nuclear war declared.

Built to withstand aerial attack, the Bunker could accommodate 300 personnel working and sleeping in safety whilst organising all facets of communication, medical assistance, police and fire-fighting services, military and NATO retaliation above ground. The bunker has its own water supply, electricity generators and can handle 52,000 cubic feet of air every minute including filtering against radioactive particles, gas and biological warfare providing 56 air changes per hour. This could be stepped up even further in case of fire.

Visitors can examine the areas used for the full range of functions, all furnished with authentic equipment, furnishings, files and papers. The functional areas include: the Security Command Control rooms including the Secretary of State suite and the Minister of State office/bedroom: the Nuclear Command Control Centre: RAF Operations and Radar room: the Royal Observer Corps suite: the Civil Defence Control rooms: the Police and Emergency Services Control rooms: the BBC suite: Meteorological Communications suite: telephone exchange: offices: dormitory: cinemas: chapel: and plant rooms. The original refectory is open as a cafe and there is an exhibition gallery, a display of Russian uniforms: an electronic games area for children and a gift shop. The cinemas show authentic Cold War film.

The Bunker provides a fascinating glimpse into recent history and its already outdated equipment illustrates the speed of development of the communications industry over the last 40 years. There is a great deal to see and visitors should allow time to explore the complex in detail.

55* Broughty Castle, Dundee

AD 1860-1 and earlier.

NO 465304. Situated on a promontory adjoining the harbour of Broughty Ferry.

Historic Scotland.

Broughty Castle

Broughty Castle, gun emplacement

barracks, apart from the vaulted ground floor which became the only magazine. Two 68-pound guns were placed behind the west curtain to engage ships in the river. Two 10-inch guns covered the channel and three more faced the approach from the open sea. Between the two groups of 10-inch guns was a third 68-pound gun which could cover the sea approach or the channel. A fourth 68-pound gun was positioned at the landward end of the battery to cover the sea approach and the beaches to the east. A guardhouse was constructed to the east of the tower, controlling the drawbridge entrance. An enclosure was constructed at the south-west of the west curtain to cover the harbour area in case of land attack. This is considered to be the site of the hospital.

The tower-house and guardhouse were treated as an essay in historical architecture and contrast with the stark simplicity of the rest of the works which are unadorned military engineering.

Broughty Castle dates back to the 15th century but by the mid 19th century it comprised a ruined shell. The site had obvious strategic importance and it was purchased by the Government in 1855 to protect the Firth of Tay from Russian warships. The Crimean War ended without any further action on the Government's part. The site stood derelict until the next war scare in 1860-1, when it was decided to reconstruct the castle as a small self-defensible coastal battery. The work was carried out by a young Royal Engineer, Robert Rowand Anderson, who was later knighted and received the RIBA Gold Medal for Architecture.

The project was ill-conceived in that the limitations imposed by this exposed and restricted site were not fully appreciated or considered, especially in the light of the recent introduction of built-up rifled guns. The brief called for a battery to control the entrance to the Firth of Tay and to be self-defensible from a possible surprise land attack. The Tay is only 335 m wide at this point and any problems in the siting of the guns were created partly by the shape of the site and partly by Anderson's decision to utilise the ruined tower-house and enclosing wall.

The tower was increased in size by the sensitive addition of another wing and was used as the

Twenty-five years after the building of this fort, it was decided to make provision for laying a minefield in the Tay. An addition was made to the north-east of the fort to accommodate the Tay Division Submarine Miners RE (Volunteers) raised 17th March 1888. That same year Captain J G Grant lectured on 'The Defence of the Tay' describing Broughty Castle as:

> 'badly built, badly designed, and utterly useless for the purpose for which it was constructed . . . A fort such as this could never defend our river, for its total demolition would only afford an enemy an hour's pleasant and agreeable recreation, unharassed by any thoughts of possible danger to themselves.'

This brought out a number of compromise alterations. More alterations were made during both World Wars. In 1935 it passed into the care of the Office of Works.

Broughty Castle was opened as a museum in 1969. This is a branch of Dundee Museum and has galleries depicting: the history and development of Broughty Ferry; the local fishing community; and the Dundee whaling museum.

St Andrews
Castle from the
air

Gatehouse (Below)

56* St Andrews Castle, Fife

16th century AD and earlier.

NO 512169. Situated on a cliff-top site on the N side of the town of St Andrews. The entrance is from The Scores.

Historic Scotland.

St Andrews Castle is a dramatically-sited ruin of a courtyard castle apparently utilising the cliffs to the north and east as part of the defences. Originally the building was sited at some distance from the cliff edge but over the years erosion has increased the dramatic effect. The castle has strong ecclesiastical connections, having been the residence of the bishops and, later, archbishops of St Andrews, who used it as a palace, fortress and prison. It has a long history of demolition and rebuilding since its first erection around 1200.

Detail of carving above the gateway

The existing ruin dates mainly from the last rebuilding undertaken by Archbishop John Hamilton between 1549 and 1571. Hamilton's work has a strong Renaissance character more in keeping with the building's function as a palace than with a military fortress. The building declined in importance after the Reformation and in 1654 the St Andrews Town Council ordered part of the building fabric to be used for the repair of the harbour walls.

One of the most interesting features of the castle is a very rare survival of a medieval siege technique. This comprises a mine and counter-mine dating from the siege of 1546-7. The Earl of Arran's forces established the mine with the intention of undermining the walls to the castle courtyard. A gallery, 1.8 m wide and 2.1 m high, was cut through the solid rock from the side of the ditch, south-east of the Fore Tower, to a minehead 8.2 m from the tower from which branches could run to breach the wall foundations at a number of places. This gallery had to slope down to pass under the ditch. The attempt was foiled by the defenders who drove a counter-mine from the east of the Fore Tower to intercept the mine and broke through into the minehead from a higher level. The counter mine follows an uncertain route possibly resulting from trying to estimate the course being taken by the enemy sappers in the mine by calculation and sound. Visitors can traverse both the mine and counter-mine in safety as these are now lit by electricity.

Inside the mine

Ravenscraig Castle, inner end of entrance passage

57* Ravenscraig Castle, Fife

15th and 16th centuries AD.

NT 290924. On a promontory on the seafront to the E of the town centre of Kirkcaldy.

Ravenscraig occupies a dramatic cliff-top site on the north shore of the Firth of Forth. From the A 92 Kirkcaldy-Dundee road the castle has the appearance of a somewhat unorthodox tower-house but, when viewed from the land to the east or from the beach to the south, the true scale and form of the building can be appreciated.

Built as a royal castle for Mary of Gueldres, Queen to James II, the castle was designed by the Royal Master Mason, Henry Merlzioun, assisted by Friar Andrew Lesouris as master carpenter. Work was begun in 1460 and continued despite the death of the king the same year. The work on the main defences, comprising two round-fronted towers linked by a range containing the entrance gate, continued until the death of Mary of Gueldres in December 1463. Although the two towers are of similar plan and height, the nature of the landform gives prominence to the west tower. The massive wall thickness, regularly placed shot-holes and deep rock-cut ditch show Ravenscraig to be one of the earliest castles to attempt to provide for defence by and from artillery.

In 1470, James III granted the castle to William, Lord Sinclair, in exchange for the lands of the Earldom of Orkney. The building work at Ravenscraig was temporarily abandoned to be completed to a modified and reduced plan in the 16th century. The Sinclairs occupied the building on a regular basis until the 17th century, when it probably declined in favour, although the building remained in their possession until 1896.

7 RELIGIOUS BUILDINGS

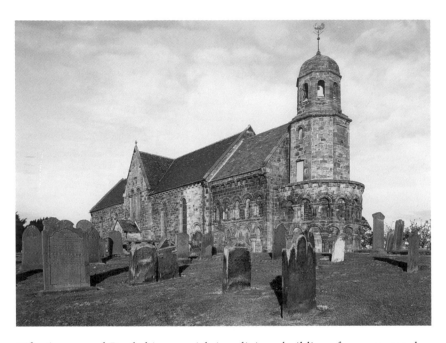

Leuchars Church

Fife, Angus and Perthshire are rich in religious buildings from present day examples back to the prehistoric period. The attitude of society to these buildings is constantly changing, and at present many churches are under threat. The move from urban to suburban living since World War II has resulted in failing attendances in town centre churches, amalgamation of congregations and closure of church buildings. New churches are being built in the new towns and housing estates. Other Christian groups, social groups and ethnic minorities are making use of some of the abandoned churches but others are being demolished or used for commercial and other purposes. Some ethnic groups are erecting new religious buildings: in Dundee, for instance, there is a Jewish synagogue, a Sikh temple and a Muslim mosque.

POST-REFORMATION CHURCHES

20th-century church building has been somewhat utilitarian especially since World War I, but some new ideas have evolved. St Paul's RC Church and priest's house at Glenrothes (NO 280004), by Gillespie, Kidd and Coia of Glasgow, utilises inexpensive materials in strong simple shapes, questioning the then (1957) accepted image of a church. Somewhat earlier Dr Reginald Fairlie, a local architect working from Edinburgh, carried out a similar exercise as building economics forced a change of approach after World War I. Fairlie's ideas evolved gradually in a series of buildings erected in the region. The final building in the series is the RC Church of Our Lady Star

of the Sea, Tayport (NO 456283), completed in 1939: the first is St James'
RC Church, St Andrews (NO 507170), completed in 1910. The Tayport
building is simple and restrained using rendered brickwork which is painted
white. The St Andrews building has strong, richly decorated natural
stonework in a Gothic revival style reminiscent of 14th century Scottish
churches. Both buildings show quality in their design and, although very
different in conception, are unmistakably Scottish in character. This is not
surprising considering Fairlie's background, being the son of a local
landowner, raised in Myres Castle (NO 241109) on the outskirts of
Auchtermuchty and only 3.5 km from Falkland Palace (no. 42).

**Arbroath
Western
Cemetery,
Patrick Allan
Fraser
Mausoleum**

The quality of church design in the Edwardian era evolved from a period of
extravagant eclecticism in the second half of the 19th century. This
eclecticism is best illustrated by one of the strangest buildings in the region:
the Patrick Allan Fraser Mausoleum in the Western Cemetery, Arbroath
(NO 625417). This building incorporates architectural details collected
from buildings all over Europe, used freely without any regard to scale or
context. It is the work of the designer-owner of Hospitalfield (no. 35) and
was erected as a family tomb. This period of eclecticism involving a
multitude of individual, hybrid and free- styles followed the 'battle of the
styles' between the exponents of neo-Classical and Gothic revival designs.
A few neo-Classical churches were erected but the Gothic revival was always
more popular for church buildings.

One of the finest Gothic-revival designs in this area of Scotland is the
splendid spire added to the Auld Kirk, Montrose (NO 714577) by James
Gillespie Graham in 1834. Graham was a friend of Augustus W N Pugin of
London, who may have had a hand in the design.

The churches of the Georgian period are well described by George Hay, who also includes a short history of the Presbyterian Church in Scotland, including the various secessions and re-unions. One of the most picturesque sects to emerge during this period was the Glasites, named after their founder, John Glas who was deposed as minister of Tealing, Angus in 1730. The Glasite Chapel, Dundee, is now incorporated in the church halls of St Andrew's Church, Dundee (no. 58). It was built about 1777 to a simple octagonal plan similar to that used for the Methodist Church, Arbroath (NO 645410) in 1772.

Scottish churches of the second half of the 18th century are mainly Renaissance in character. They are organised to accommodate a church service based on the preaching of a sermon. Wide bodied churches developed about this time as imported timber allowed the use of larger scantlings which in turn allowed longer spans. In these churches the preacher was positioned in the centre of the south wall with the congregation facing him from the other three sides. This results in a characteristic elevational treatment of the south wall, involving a change of scale between the fenestration of the double volume preaching space and that of the double storey where the galleries abut the south wall. St Andrew's Church, Dundee, is a good example of this type. Kettins Church, Angus (NO 237390), 1809, by the same architect, shows this elevational treatment applied to a small rural church.

Many churches originally built with narrow bodied medieval style plans have been converted to this new form by adding a wing in the middle of the north wall to form a T-plan. The pulpit is situated against the south wall at the interception of the three wings. Elie Church (NO 491001), 1726, incorporates two 17th-century doorways in a T-plan layout. It also has a tower in the centre of the south wall which is now surmounted by a 19th-century cupola.

Some rural churches were laid out on the T-plan principle from the outset. This was probably for economic reasons as they do not require the large scantlings used to roof wide bodied churches. Aberlemno Church (NO 522555) and Aberdargie Church (NO 079202), 1773, are good examples. Monimail Church (NO 302141), 1796, also takes this form but has unusual fenestration, a semi-octagonal gallery and Adam-type plaster enrichments. James Gillespie Graham added a small Gothic tower in 1811.

One of the most sophisticated Classical buildings is the small mausoleum in Methven churchyard (NO 025260). The building takes the form of a Greek temple embedded in elaborately rusticated masonry. This is a remarkable structure both in terms of its scale and its massing, showing a quality of detailing almost impossible to convey in drawings. This building was designed by James Playfair in 1793, the year before his untimely death at the age of 39. A local man, Playfair had started his career in London as an orthodox neo-Classical architect producing finely proportioned buildings such as the Kirriemuir Parish Church (NO 386539), 1786-90. About this time he developed an interest in the works of Sir John Soane and Claude Ledoux and this mausoleum represents one of the few opportunities Playfair had to put his new ideas into practice. On his death, Soane purchased his entire collection of architectural drawings.

Few churches were built in the century and a half after the Reformation and those tended to be simple oblong types of T-plan variants, all following their medieval precedents in their narrow plan form and in style. Tulliallan Parish Church (NS 933880), built in 1675, and Anstruther Easter Parish Church (NO 569036), 1634, are good examples of 17th-century T-plan churches.

Dairsie Parish Church

Dairsie Parish Church (no. 59) built in 1621 is a model church designed by Bishop Spotiswoode for worship under an Episcopal regime. Unfortunately the original layout, which included a choir screen, has disappeared making this impossible to assess.

Burntisland Parish Church (no. 60) is unique on a number of counts: plan form, layout, section, structure and appearance. It is one of the few churches built by the first generation of Reformers, being completed in 1592. The square plan appears to be a direct response to the requirements of a preaching church yet on detailed analysis it is an uneconomic structure, the triangular space behind the pulpit being of little use for seating the congregation. When a T-plan or wide bodied church plan is superimposed it can be clearly seen to be influenced by this layout but achieving similar accommodation in a much more economic manner.

PRE-REFORMATION CHURCHES

Fife and Tayside contained no fewer than three medieval cathedrals, including that of the wealthy and extensive diocese of St Andrews, whose bishops held metropolitan authority over the other Scottish sees from 1472 onwards. The cathedral of St Andrews (no. 67), greatest of all Scottish medieval churches, was allowed to fall into decay after the Reformation and now survives only as an impressive ruin. Brechin (no. 69) and Dunkeld (no. 64) have continued in ecclesiastical use up to the present day and retain substantial portions of their medieval fabric, the nave at Dunkeld (now roofless) being a particularly remarkable example of Scottish late Gothic design.

The majority of Scottish medieval parish churches failed to develop after their initial erection and, of those that did develop, few survived the Reformation. The result is a number of unrelated building fragments which can only suggest the range and quality of ecclesiastical buildings during this period.

The late 15th-century Old Steeple, Dundee (NO 401301) is one of these fragments, being all that remains of the largest medieval parish church in Scotland. The original church was founded in the late 12th century by David, Earl of Huntingdon. The choir and possibly the nave and lower storeys of the tower were rebuilt after 1442. The nave was destroyed in the 16th century and the remainder of the medieval church, excepting the tower, burnt down in 1841. The upper storeys of the tower probably date from 1495 and stands 47.5 m, making it the highest surviving medieval tower in Scotland. It was originally topped by an open crown and therefore the stair turret stopped short of the roof. A cap-house replaced the intended crown in 1590 and the stair turret was raised by two rounds in 1644-5 by John Mylne. The tower was restored and many parts recased in 1872 by Sir G G Scott and retooled with considerable loss of detail in the 1960s.

The 12th-century parish church of St John's, Perth (NO 119235) suffered a different fate. At the Reformation the church was split into three conventicles as also happened at Dundee. The partitions, pews and galleries of these three units interrupted internal views of the original church and it was decided to commission Sir Robert Lorimer to restore the building. Unfortunately Lorimer was somewhat over zealous in this task, obliterating much of the primary evidence in his search for the building's original beauty of form and texture. The work involved cleaning out the whole interior, rebuilding a number of piers and the south wall of the nave, providing new and larger windows, raising the tower over the north porch to its original height, converting a chapel adjoining the north transept into a War Memorial, providing a barrel vault roof of fumed oak with painted panels over the nave, exposing the roof of the choir, and providing new stalls, organ, organcase and pulpit. The result is attractive, but as a 1920s design rather than as an authentic medieval church.

The incomplete parish church of St Monans or St Monance, Fife (NO 522014) with its steep-roofed chancel and transepts, stumpy square tower and octagonal steeple, gives some impression of the form of smaller 15th-century Gothic churches. It was built as a votive chapel by David II and granted to the Dominicans by James III.

Another form of church popular in the later Middle Ages was the collegiate church. These were non-monastic communities of secular clergy owing

St Monans Parish Church

their existence to endowments from the Scottish nobility, from Burgh Councils, or from the higher clergy, as at St Salvator's. Collegiate churches took two main forms. The smaller examples retained the simple oblong plan of the smaller parish church. The more typical plan was cruciform, with well defined unaisled choir having a square or polygonal eastern end. These were more common in the Lothians and the best preserved collegiate churches in Tayside and Fife were of the oblong type: Fowlis Easter, (NO 322334), is one of the best examples. Built in 1453, probably by Andrew, Lord Gray, Fowlis Easter may have replaced an earlier parish church. The church retains part of its original timber rood-screen and has an elaborate sacrament house and some interesting painted decoration. Other collegiate churches in this area include: Abernethy, Perth and Kinross, founded before 1345 but now demolished; Crail, Fife, 1517 (NO 613079); Guthrie, Angus, c 1479 (NO 567504); Methven, Perth and Kinross, 1433 (NO 025260); St Mary of the Rock, St Andrews, Fife, c 1250 (NO 515166, Historic Scotland); St Salvator's, St Andrews, Fife, 1450 (NO 509168); Strathmiglo, Fife, c 1527 (now demolished). It is interesting that, with a few notable exceptions, including St Mary of the Rock, collegiate churches survived the Reformation and continued, in many cases, to function as parish churches, only being replaced when structurally unsound or when too small for their function.

Leuchars Church (no. 62) is undoubtedly the most interesting surviving example of an early medieval church, the small Romanesque chancel and apse being richly decorated externally with two tiers of blind arcading.

MEDIEVAL MONASTERIES

During the medieval period there were at least thirty-four monastic houses in Tayside and Fife. This figure includes abbeys, priories, friaries and convents but excludes monastic hospitals and outlying chapels. The majority of these were small foundations, their minimum incomes, in 1561, ranging from £16 to £750. By considering the 1561 minimum incomes of some of the larger foundations an impression of relative importance can be obtained.

The three largest monasteries in the region had incomes considerably in excess of the largest foundations in other regions. St Andrews Priory, an Augustinian foundation attached to the Cathedral church (no. 67) had an income of £12,500: Arbroath Abbey (no. 66, Tironensian), £10,924; and Dunfermline Abbey (no. 65, Benedictine), £9,630. These figures should be compared with: Paisley Abbey with an income of £6,100; Holyrood Abbey, Edinburgh with £5,600; Melrose Abbey with £5,180; and Kelso Abbey with £4,830. Far from rivalling the great abbeys of Tayside and Fife, these abbeys are closer in income to the second tier of foundations in this area, namely: Coupar Angus (NO 223398) (Cistercian), £5,590; Scone Abbey (Augustinian), £5,350; and Lindores Abbey (NO 243184) (Tironensian), £4,790.

The third tier of monastic foundations in the region comprises: Balmerino Abbey (NO 358246; NTS) (Cistercian), £1,793; Perth Priory (Carthusian), £1,680; Culross Abbey (NS 989862; Historic Scotland) (Cistercian), £1,600; and Inchcolm Abbey (no. 63) (Augustinian), £1,240(?).

All of the monastic foundations listed in the top three tiers, apart from Perth Priory, were established in either the 12th or 13th century. Smaller foundations of Dominican Friars (Blackfriars), Franciscan Friars (Greyfriars and Observant Friars), Carmelite Friars, Cistercian Nuns and Franciscan Nuns are later, dating from the 13th to the 15th century.

Innerpeffray, early 18th-century graveslab (now under cover)

EARLY FOUNDATIONS

Fife and Tayside contained a proportionately large number of early ecclesiastical foundations. Among those that survived into, or reappeared in, the Middle Ages were Abernethy (no. 70); Brechin (no. 69); Dunkeld (no. 64); Inchaffray, Perth and Kinross; Lochleven, Perth and Kinross; Monifieth, Angus; Muthill, Perth and Kinross; Restenneth (no. 68); St Andrews (no. 67). The most important of the surviving remains are the round towers at Abernethy and Brechin and the fragment of a square tower at Restenneth.

58 St Andrew's Church and Glasite Chapel, Dundee

AD 1774 and 1777.

NO 404306. Situated at the junction of King Street, Cowgate and St Andrews Street adjoining the Wellgate Centre.

St Andrew's Church is a fine example of the wide rectangular preaching churches built in Scotland in the second half of the 18th century. It was built in 1774 by the Incorporated Trades of the burgh to a design by Samuel Bell. The Palladian elements of the facade reflect the organisation of the interior. The two large tripartite windows flank the pulpit in the middle of the south wall. The two-storey treatment of the end bays shows the position of the south ends of the U-shaped gallery and the twin doors lead into the aisle round the communion table. The church has an elegant steeple surmounted by a lively gilded dragon as a weather-vane. There is a formal garden to the south with contemporary gates and railings to the street.

The Glasite Chapel of 1777 is situated on the eastern boundary of the garden. This is a small octagonal building with the usual pyramidal roof and two storeys of round leaded windows. The interior was gutted some years ago when the building was used for commercial purposes. The refectory where the members ate between Sunday services stood to the north-east. This building has been demolished and the octagonal chapel has been incorporated into the St Andrew's Church halls which link the two structures.

Although the Glasite or Sandemanian sect is almost extinct, being reduced to two chapels in Britain, John Glas remains an important figure in other non-conformist sects. Many of these sects consider his writings as fundamental to their beliefs, and, although he did not live to see the octagonal chapel described here, these writings were produced in the city.

59 Dairsie Parish Church, Fife

AD 1621 and later.

NO 414160. Situated 1.5 km S of Dairsie village.

The church shares the brow of a hill with Dairsie Castle and overlooks Dairsie Bridge which crosses the River Eden.

The building is a peculiar hybrid of Gothic and Renaissance features. The overall form is Gothic. The simple oblong plan is divided by buttresses into bays, each containing a pointed arch window decorated with 'plate' tracery. The window-sills extend into a string course which breaks upwards at doorways. The wall and buttresses in the south-west corner support an octagonal turret surmounted by a stone spire. The Renaissance door piece, dated 1621, occupies the west end of the building. Above it a panel contains the arms and initials of Archbishop Spottiswood who built the church. Below the shield are the initials 'IS' and the text 'IEHOVAH. DILEXI. DE/COREM.DOMVS TVAE'. This is executed in metal and translates as: Jehovah, I have loved the beauty of thy house'. The existing slate roof dates from the 18th century and replaced the original flat lead roof which was contained within a small parapet. It is uncertain whether the parapet supported finials over the buttresses but the composition could imply this. Rain-water from the flat roof was carried through the parapet to outlets in the form of grotesque masks. The church is now in private use.

Dairsie Castle stands about 45 m south-south-west of the church. The castle, now being restored, consists of a three-storey oblong block with two circular towers on diagonally opposite corners. The south-west tower was converted to a dovecote after the castle was ruined.

The fine medieval bridge below the church carries the initials and arms of James Beaton, Archbishop of St Andrews 1522-39, as on Guard Bridge (no. 17). The bridge is 29.5 m long and has three arches, each with four stout chamfered cut-waters, one of which is carried up as a refuge. The parapets and approach at either end have been renewed but otherwise the bridge appears to be in its original condition.

Burntisland Parish Church

Painted panel

60* Burntisland Parish Church, Fife

AD 1592 and later.

NT 233857. On a hilltop to the S of the High Street, Burntisland.

This church replaced the former parish church, the ruins of which still stand at the Kirkton, north of the town (NT 230863). Burntisland had grown considerably in the 16th century and achieved Royal Burgh status in 1568. To symbolise this prosperity the inhabitants of the burgh decided to build a new church. Permission was obtained from the heritors and the townsfolk raised the funds. The design made a considerable contribution to the development of the architectural traditions of the

Reformed church, producing a plan form and method of construction unparalleled in Scotland. The church was erected in 1592 and local tradition suggests that it was copied from Noorderkerk, Amsterdam. It does not resemble that building but is closer in planning terms to the Oosterkerk in Amsterdam, the Nieuwe Kerk in Haarlem and the Scot's Kirk in Rotterdam (now destroyed), although all four churches are later than Burntisland. The idea may indeed have come from the continent but, until a model is found there, it must be regarded as a Scottish design.

The building is approximately 18 m square internally and four piers enclose a 6 m square in the centre. The piers are connected by semi-circular arches, whilst rampant arches spring from external angled buttresses to abut the piers on the diagonal. The tower and buttresses are constructed of ashlar, and the walls are harled rubble. The four lower courses of the tower are original, but the top section dates from 1749. A stone above the west door has the date '1592' and an inverted anchor.

The gallery is entered from the east by means of a forestair with a good moulded balustrade. The moulded doorway architrave is inscribed on the lower member of the cornice: 'GODS. PROVIDENCE. IS. OUR. INHERITANCE. JUNE 6 1679.' and has an inverted anchor on a cushioned frieze.

Internally, the church has a wooden gallery on each wall. The fronts of these galleries are panelled and painted. The panels bear a number of dates, mottoes and representations of ships, seamen and nautical instruments. There are also a number of craft or guild symbols.

The pulpit is sited against the south-west pier leaving an entrance area, vestry and stair to the gallery in that corner. The minister could then preach diagonally across the church. This was an important break with the traditions of the Roman Catholic churches and expressed the Presbyterian requirement to hear the spoken word. Directly opposite the pulpit is a fine 17th-century canopied pew, constructed of oak inlaid with other woods. The front and back are panelled and the canopy is supported on moulded and reeded shafts. It bears the date 1606, the initials S.R.M. and the arms of Sir Robert Melville.

Although this church was not copied in its entirety by any of the other Scottish burghs, its seating arrangement with pews facing the pulpit from three sides may well have inspired the T-plan and wide rectangular forms with the pulpit in the centre of the long wall.

61 St Mary's Church, Grandtully, Perth and Kinross

16th and 17th centuries AD.

NN 886506. Signposted from the A 827 Aberfeldy-Grandtully road.

Historic Scotland.

The church is a simple building with lime-washed rubble walls and blue slate roof. It gives the appearance of a long low 18th-century farm steading, whose walls and roof are not quite straight. It is believed to have been constructed prior to the Reformation and is known to have been repaired in 1636. At that time there were doors and windows in both the south and east walls, but those in the south wall are now blocked. The approach is by a fenced path on the east side of a farm steading and the exterior lacks any interesting qualities. This makes the interior all the more breathtaking. The simple rectangular shell has a 17th-century painted timber wagon ceiling extending one-third of the length of the interior and possibly covering the laird's pew. The remainder of the roof is exposed timbers. The Renaissance-style painting combines family heraldry with biblical illustration. The central panel shows death about to claim the occupant of a canopy bed.

On leaving the church many visitors fail to realise that the graveyard lies to the west of the building and that to gain access one must continue up the path to the north gable and round to the other side of the church. There is a strange feeling of antiquity in this small space, particularly when the lime-washed walls of the church show signs of weathering.

There is an excellent view of Grandtully Castle from the track as one returns to the main road.

62 Leuchars Church, Fife

12th century AD.

NO 455215. In the centre of Leuchars village. Car park on the N side.

Leuchars Church is possibly the finest Romanesque church in Scotland, dramatically sited on a mound in the centre of the village. It has been suggested that the church was erected between 1183 and 1187 and was dedicated by Bishop Bernham in 1244, but it could date to about 1150. Only the chancel and apse survive of the original building, a new nave having been added in the 19th century. The chancel is almost square and the chancel arch is off-centre. This is further accentuated by the nave being off-set to the north. The apse is vaulted and the original timber roof was removed in the 17th century and replaced by an octagonal bell-turret surmounted by a lead weather-vane. The wall-heads are brought forward on corbels carved with heads of monsters, oxen, rams and human grotesques.

The church was rather crudely altered in the 17th century when new windows were slapped through the blind arcading of the chancel. The wall-head of the nave of the 17th century was lower than the wall-head of the chancel. These alterations were recorded in a sketch by David Roberts, RA, in 1831. The restoration of the church was carried out by Dr Reginald Fairlie. He also appears to have heightened the belfry, changing the plan form of the upper section and reforming the vault. There has been considerable discussion as to whether the bell-turret should be removed and replaced by a more conventional timber roof. This would be counter-productive as much of the charm of this small building is derived from the unorthodox juxtaposition of elements from various periods.

There are some fine 16th-century tombstones in the graveyard.

63* Inchcolm Abbey, Fife

12th-16th centuries AD.

NT 189826. Inchcolm Abbey is situated on the island of Inchcolm in the Firth of Forth opposite Aberdour, Fife. A regular ferry service operates from South Queensferry and North Queensferry. Details of tides and availability of boats may be obtained from the Abbey Custodian (Dalgety Bay 823332) or from the Custodian at Aberdour Castle (Aberdour 860519).

Historic Scotland.

Inchcolm housed a religious community long before the establishment of a monastery in the early 12th century. The early inhabitants were hermits devoted to the guardianship of a holy place whose reputation for sanctity stemmed from its links with St Colm, identified with St Columba, the 6th-century abbot of Iona. The hermits probably lived in the simple stone cell which survives to the west of the medieval monastery but in an apparently 14th or 15th century restored form. In the visitor centre there is a fine, though weathered, example of a hogback tombstone; four rows of tegulae, or roof-tiles, are carved along the sides and a great beast's head adorns either end. Dating to the mid 10th century, this is probably the earliest hogback to survive in Scotland. It lay originally on a knoll beyond the hermits' cell.

The Inchcolm hermitage received regal recognition in 1123 when Alexander I and some of his courtiers were storm-bound on the island for three days. During this enforced visit the hermit sheltered them and shared his scanty provisions. Alexander made plans to establish a monastic settlement but these were interrupted by the King's death the following year. It is not known when the first Augustinian canons settled there but the earliest surviving charter relating to the monastery dates from about 1162-9. The mid 13th century saw a period of relative prosperity although it did come under periodic attack during the Wars of Independence. After the Reformation, no new canons were admitted and the last document relating to the monastery dates to 1578. The isolated position of the island is largely responsible for the fine state of preservation of the buildings.

Inchcolm creates in the mind of the visitor an unusually clear and vivid impression of monastic life, despite the fact that the surviving structures belong to several periods of building and modification. The polygonal chapter-house was built in the 13th century and represents a design fashionable in England but used only three times in Scotland (another example may be seen at Elgin, Moray, and the third was at Holyrood in Edinburgh but no longer exists). It has a fine ribbed and vaulted ceiling, and the stone seating for the monks still lines the walls. The chapter-house is incorporated into one side of a 15th-century cloister (incorporating 16th-century alterations), with its open court, covered cloister walk and seats for the monks in the window recesses in which they worked. The upper floor contains their living quarters, including a warming house with a fireplace over the chapter-house. The original church was founded in the 12th century, and a new church was built to the east of it, probably in the early 15th century. A rare feature is the fragment of 13th-century wall-painting with clerical figures outlined in black, red and yellow, preserved by having been sealed behind masonry during a later extension of the church.

64 Dunkeld Cathedral, Perth and Kinross

Mid 13th century and later.

NO 024425. Signposted from the A 9 Perth-Inverness trunk road and situated to the west of the square in the centre of Dunkeld.

Historic Scotland (church in use).

The cathedral church of Dunkeld was built over a 250 year period commencing in the mid 13th century and completed by the end of the 15th century. At that time it was surrounded by the ancient burgh of Dunkeld but after the Reformation only the choir and sacristy of the church was retained for use by the local community. The nave was un-roofed soon afterwards. The burgh centre was moved eastwards to its present position after the destruction of Dunkeld in the battle of 1689 and the cathedral grounds were incorporated in the vista of the house of the Dukes of Atholl, resulting in the pleasant landscaped grounds that surround the cathedral today.

The roofed eastern portion of the church has particularly fine decorative arcading, dating from the mid 13th century, on the north wall and an early 14th-century *sedilia* (seating) in the south wall. The window tracery dates from a restoration in 1814-15 and the finishings to a restoration of 1908.

The un-roofed west portion comprising the original nave was constructed in the first half of the 15th century. The sacristy to the north of the roofed east portion dates from the same period. The tower is slightly later.

The Sacristy contains some interesting carved stones. The Apostles Stone appears to be a fragment of 9th-century cross-slab, and it is a reminder of the earlier church that was sacked by Vikings in the 9th century. The tomb of the Wolf of Badenoch, more correctly Alexander Stewart, Earl of Buchan who died in 1405, is an extremely fine example of this type of monument.

The upper part of the tower has surviving wall paintings of the judgement of Solomon and of the woman taken in adultery.

65* Dunfermline Abbey, Fife

12th century AD and later.

NT 089873. From carpark in Chalmers Street (beside Tourist Information Office), walk along High Street, turn right along Kirkgate to Abbey.

Historic Scotland.

The great monastic church of Dunfermline was commenced in 1128 and completed in 1250. It was built over the foundations of an earlier church and took the form of a fully-developed cruciform structure similar, in lay-out and detail, to Durham Cathedral. The church measured 64.5 m from west to east and 32.5 m from north to south transept gables. Unfortunately only the nave of the medieval church survives, incomplete and somewhat modified, but this remains one of the finest examples of Scoto-Norman monastic architecture.

During the 13th century there was a major enlargement to the eastern end of the building, including the addition of a chapel to St Margaret at the east end. This work was completed in 1250. The choir was extended on the north side in the 14th century, probably by the addition of the Lady Aisle which was later demolished. In the nave three of the aisle windows and all the triforium windows were changed from Romanesque to Gothic. At this time the wall-head of the aisle appears to have been lowered. Towards the end of the 14th century the west gable was reconstructed from above the doorway. In the mid 15th century the north-west tower and the two adjoining bays of the nave were rebuilt. The upper part of this tower, as it survives, appears to be the work of William Shaw, Master of Works to James VI from 1583 to his death in 1602.

The main body of the church appears to have been unsafe in 1563; in 1620 parts of the vault of the south aisle were rebuilt and a few years later the aisle walls of the nave were strengthened by the introduction of the heavy buttresses which now form a major element in the composition.

During the 17th and 18th centuries the church suffered major damage. In 1672 the east part of the choir and the Lady Chapel were blown down and in 1716 the crossing fell. This remained ruinous for the next century and in 1819 the transepts were removed leaving only the nave of the medieval church. The south-west tower was damaged by lightning in 1807 and rebuilt in 1810.

The church should be considered as part of the whole monastic complex of which the Palace pends and Frater range survive in St Catherine's Wynd and Monastery Street and the Abbot's House in Maygate and Abbot Street.

Arbroath Abbey

Arbroath Abbey

66* Arbroath Abbey, Angus

12th-16th centuries AD.

NO 642413. Situated at the head of the High Street, Arbroath. Enter by W doorway off Hamilton Green.

Historic Scotland.

The Abbey of Arbroath was founded by King William the Lion in 1178 and dedicated to St Thomas Becket of Canterbury. It was a Tironensian house established by monks from Kelso but independent of the parent monastery from the outset. William heaped endowments on the new foundation: the tithes and patronage of twenty-four parish churches; a toft of land in each of the Scottish Royal burghs; lands, fisheries, ferries and salt-pans in various parts of Scotland; Arbroath

St Andrews Cathedral

and the whole region about it with the right to establish a burgh, the burgesses to be toll-free in any part of Scotland, to hold a market every Saturday, to build a harbour and to exact customs. This was augmented by gifts of lands, fisheries, ferries and churches from other Scottish nobles, particularly the Earl of Angus. Even King John of England granted a charter allowing the monks of Arbroath to trade, toll-free, in any part of England except the City of London. The new abbey buildings reflected this wealth and William obviously intended it to become the principal monastery in Scotland. On his death at Stirling on 4 December 1214, King William's body was carried to Arbroath to be buried at the high altar of the then incomplete church. Royal patronage continued and it was at Arbroath that the Scottish nobles met on 6 April 1320 to sign the Scottish Declaration of Independence which was sent to Pope John XXII in Avignon.

After the reformation the abbey suffered from neglect and vandalism, being used as a quarry to obtain stones for the building of much of the older parts of Arbroath. The most interesting portions to have survived are: the south transept with its bold but simple fenestration; the west front, massively proportioned and containing an arcaded gallery over the deeply recessed west doorway (a similar arrangement formerly existed at St Andrews Cathedral (no. 67)); the Abbot's House (no. 43), now containing a small museum; and the Gatehouse range.

67* St Andrews Cathedral, Fife

12th to 15th centuries AD.

NO 513166. At the E end of North Street and South Street, St Andrews.

Historic Scotland.

St Andrews Cathedral was an Augustinian foundation, the original community being brought to the Church of St Rule, St Andrews, about 1127. The building of the present cathedral began in 1160 on a site adjoining St Rule's Church. The cathedral church was set on a grand scale with an internal east-west dimension of over 109 m. It was planned to have an unusually large number of bays, but these were relatively narrow and, although there are many longer English churches, it was by far the greatest church in Scotland. Unfortunately very little now survives apart from the ruined gables and parts of the south wall. The monastic buildings to the south of the church are even more ruinous apart from a remarkably well-preserved precinct wall; it encloses about 12.14 hectares and is 1.6 km long, 6.1 m high and 0.8 m thick, fortified by a series of attached towers, some round and others rectangular.

After the foundation of the cathedral and priory in 1160, building work followed the usual sequence, building in height from the east end towards the west front. The choir was completed prior to 1238 when Bishop Malvoisine was buried there. The great west front was destroyed in a storm and rebuilt between 1273 and 1279. Work may have been delayed by the Wars of Independence but the 'new kyrk cathedralle' was consecrated by Bishop Lamberton in 1318 in the presence of King Robert Bruce.

The second half of the 14th century saw the greater part of the cathedral destroyed by fire. The timber work of the choir and transepts had to be renewed as did a number of piers in the nave and transepts. The urgent work of consolidation took seven years to complete and the total damage was not remedied until 1440. From then until the Reformation the church required only minor repairs. After the Reformation, when it suffered the burning of images and mass-books and the breaking of altars, it was allowed to fall into decay. In 1826 the Barons of the Exchequer took possession of the ruins and in 1946 it was given to the State.

The museum in the undercroft of the monastic block houses sculpture, including an important example of late 8th or early 9th-century work known as the St Andrews Sarcophagus, although its function is more likely to have been that of a shrine or reliquary rather than a normal coffin. It is a stone box, composed of slabs slotted into corner-posts, and its reconstructed gabled roof is conjectural. This is the earliest sculpture surviving from St Andrews, despite its formidable ecclesiastical history; perhaps all trace of an earlier Dark Age ecclesiastical establishment was destroyed at the Reformation.

St Andrews Sarcophagus
(Above)

St Andrews Cathedral, St Rule's Tower

The Sarcophagus consisted originally of four thin sandstone panels fitting into the grooved sides of four substantial corner-posts, but only two panels and three posts have survived. Much of the carving has been carried out in remarkably high relief, and the main long panel represents a major work of David iconography: the human figures depict scenes from the biblical life of David, and their treatment shows strong Mediterranean influence. The large figure represents David rending the jaws of the lion, the figure on horseback wields a sword in his right hand and a falcon on his left and is under attack from a lion, while the standing figure has shield and sword. All three figures are dressed in elaborately draped clothing quite unlike the normal Pictish tunics. Exotic elements include the griffon devouring a mule to the left of the large figure of David and the pairs of monkeys depicted on the end-panel. The sculptor's mastery of interlace ranges from the animal interlace on the corner posts to the intricate patterning of the cross on the end-panel.

This skill in carving interlace can also be seen on the great cross-shaft (no. 14 in the museum), where all four sides of the shaft are covered in beautifully executed woven ribbons, and on the shaft of another free-standing cross (no. 19 in the museum), both of which may have been created in the 9th century. They reflect, together with other sculptural fragments in the museum, the importance of St Andrews in the early medieval period.

St Rule's Church stands to the south-east of the cathedral. The narrow proportions of the church, its solid walls and minimal windows, suggest similarities to Northumbrian building practice of pre-Norman Conquest date, although it most probably dates to between 1120 and 1150. The tall square tower with round headed two-light windows also belongs to the late Anglo-Saxon or early Anglo-Norman period. There are similarities between this tower and the tower at Restenneth Priory (no. 68). The church towers at Dunning (NO 019144), Markinch (NO 297019) and Muthill (NN 867170) have similar two-light windows.

The foundations of the 12th-century Culdee church of St Mary of the Rock (NO 515166) can be seen to the east of the cathedral and St Rule's Church, between the perimeter wall and the harbour.

Restenneth Priory

68* Restenneth Priory, Angus

11th to 13th centuries AD and later.

NO 482515. Situated on the B 9113 Forfar-Montrose road, 2 km E of Forfar.

Historic Scotland.

The ruined priory of Restenneth stands in the heart of the ancient kingdom of the Picts and its foundation dates to the Pictish period. In the year 710, Nechtan, King of the Picts, wrote to Ceolfrid, Abbot of Wearmouth, asking for advice on differences that had developed between the Celtic and Roman Church and for masons to build a stone church. This request was granted and the mission of St Boniface founded a series of churches in Pictland, all dedicated to St Peter. One of these churches was Restenneth. It has been suggested that the lower portion of the central tower may embody a remnant of St Boniface's church.

The present tower appears to date from about the turn of the 11th and 12th centuries. Later in the 12th century Restenneth is recorded as a small priory of Augustinian canons. The priory continued to prosper and King Robert Bruce was a generous patron and chose this as the burial place for his young son, Prince John.

After the Reformation, Restenneth had a number of owners—one of them, George Dempster of Dunnichen (nos 8 and 11), made part of the choir into a family burial place. In 1919 the ruins were placed in the custody of the State.

The most outstanding feature of the priory is the tower which rises to a height of about 14 m excluding the spire. It has a number of similarities to the tower of St Rule's Church, St Andrews (no. 67) and appears to date from about the same period. However the lowest 3 m appears to be much older and its character indicates that it is likely to have served as a porch prior to being heightened into a tower. The octagonal broach spire probably dates from the 15th century. The walls of the choir are reasonably intact and are a good example of early 13th-century ecclesiastical architecture.

The old font of Restenneth Priory is preserved in the Episcopal Church at Forfar.

69 Brechin Cathedral, Round Tower and Carved Stones, Angus

Late 8th-13th centuries AD.

NO 596601. In the centre of Brechin; an archway in the High Street opens into Bishop's Close, leading to the Cathedral.

Historic Scotland, tower only.

The round tower and some of the sculptures preserved within the cathedral are all that survive of an early monastery; the tower was originally free-standing, and its contemporary church probably lay beneath the later cathedral. The tower is likely to date to the late 11th century, while the earliest parts of the cathedral belong to the 13th century (the aisle now joining the tower to the cathedral is modern).

The tower rises gracefully to a height of just over 26 m at the wall-head, and the present roof was added in the 14th century. The windows are mostly in the upper part of the tower, and the entrance is fully 2.1 m above ground-level so that a portable ladder was needed to reach it. Inside, the tower was divided into seven storeys by wooden floors, each reached by a wooden ladder, but the interior is not open to visitors. The entrance is thickly framed by carved stonework, including a crucifix, clerical figures and animals (the blank panels flanking the head of the doorway are thought to be unfinished, their decoration for some reason left uncarved).

Inside the cathedral, the portion of the tower incorporated into an aisle displays another, unframed doorway cut and subsequently blocked up again in modern times. This corner of the cathedral houses a small collection of carved stones, including architectural fragments and a 17th-century tombstone, a fine late 8th- or early 9th-century cross-slab and a superb hogback tombstone of the early 11th century. One end of the hogback is damaged, but the rest is entirely covered by elaborate carving in relief, including clerical figures and intertwining animals along the sides, foliage along the top and a magnificent beast's head with prominent eyes forming the intact end of the monument. Similar clerical figures, gazing out full-face from the stone, are carved on the cross-slab alongside, which came originally from Aldbar,

some 3 km south-west of Brechin. This stone has the theme of David the shepherd and psalmist, showing David rending the jaws of the lion, together with a sheep and a harp. The highly decorative cross rises from a socketed base, shown in plan on the stone.

At the east end of the nave are a medieval graveslab and part of an important cross-slab of late 9th-century date. Both this cross-slab and the hogback must have embellished the graveyard at a period contemporary with the use of the round tower. Only the front position of the head of the cross has survived, but it shows very clearly, as does the hogback, that the Brechin sculptors were familiar with the fashions and tastes current in northern England. The centre of the cross depicts the Virgin and Child, encircled by a Latin inscription reading 'St Mary, the mother of Christ', and the scale and sophistication of this fragment imply a free-standing cross-slab of which the Brechin monastery would have been very proud. The choir of the present church is a shortened restoration of the original 13th-century building.

70* Abernethy Round Tower and Symbol Stone, Perth and Kinross

7th-11th centuries AD.

NO 189164. Situated off Main Street, Abernethy.

Historic Scotland. (Key to tower may be obtained from the Tower Restaurant opposite.)

Abernethy Round Tower

The round tower at Abernethy is probably broadly contemporary with its counterpart at Brechin (no. 69), dating from the 11th century. It stands approximately 22 m high, and access to the top, from which there is a superb view, is by means of a modern spiral stair. The internal diameter remains constant at 2.515 m but externally the wall batters from 4.648 m at the base to 4.267 m at the top. The bottom twelve courses are built in a different stonework to the remainder, but the entrance door is constructed of the same stonework as the upper section of the tower. This suggests that there may have been an earlier tower and that, on rebuilding it, a new doorway was slapped in the existing base. The stone used for the bottom courses is remarkably similar to that used for St Rule's Church, St Andrews (see no. 67), and both may come from the same source, possibly by sea as land transport from a common quarry is highly unlikely at this early date.

Abernethy Pictish symbol stone

(Right)

It is probable that Abernethy was a place of some importance throughout the Dark Ages. It is mentioned in the margin of one of the surviving copies of the Pictish king-list and some scholars believe that the king-list may have been compiled here in some vanished Pictish monastery, perhaps related to the tower. Several early carved stones have been found in the vicinity, including the Pictish symbol stone now set against the wall of the tower, beside the gate into the churchyard. This is a 7th-century stone, incomplete but bearing four sharply incised symbols: a 'tuning fork' flanked on either side by a hammer and anvil, and below a crescent and V-rod. Alongside is a metal collar, or jougs, by which offenders were chained as punishment in medieval times.

South-west of Abernethy, on a flank of Castle Law, there is a ruinous but still impressive hillfort (NO 182153). Its situation allows a clear view over the Tay and Earn rivers to the north and over Abernethy Glen to the south-east, a minor routeway into the interior of Fife. The fort was defended by a massive stone wall, some 6 m thick, which has collapsed into a broad band of rubble; excavation revealed that the stonework had been strengthened by transverse and longitudinal wooden beams. There is an outer wall at the west end of the fort, and a rock-cut cistern inside the fort on its south side.

PICTISH MONUMENTS

Glamis cross-slab

The Picts have left a startling heritage of stone-carving, highly distinctive and prolific and yet tantalisingly enigmatic. The stones depict scenes that we cannot identify, people whose names are unknown to us, symbols whose significance can only be the subject of speculation. All this because, in a literate age, the only Pictish document to survive, copied in Latin by later scribes, is a list of their kings. Apart from that, all that we know of Pictish history, political and social, derives from scanty references in the records of contemporary monks writing from a distance, from Iona or Northumbria, not one of whom mentions the aspect that has dominated Pictish studies in the 20th century: the symbols inscribed on stones throughout Pictland, from the Firth of Forth to Shetland. Some symbols are more common than others, and the fact that they recur over such a large area during the 7th, 8th and 9th centuries implies that they were not simply decorative but that they bore a meaning as intelligible to the Picts as it is baffling to us.

The symbols range from apparently straightforward pictograms of animals, birds and fish to abstract designs based on geometric figures, often executed with a peculiarly satisfying beauty. Many theories have been put forward to explain the meaning of the symbols and the function of the stones: tribal, family or personal emblems used to convey information on memorial stones, tombstones, boundary markers or public monuments commemorating important marriage alliances between clans. It seems

likely that there may have been more than one reason for which the stones were put up—just as modern society erects monuments for a variety of reasons—and that there may be some truth in all these explanations. Symbols were also used on small objects, such as the beautiful silver plaques in the Pictish treasure found buried at Norrie's Law in Fife; the designs are infilled with red enamel to make them show up clearly against the silver, and it may well be that the stones were similarly coloured. Amongst the carvings on the walls of the Wemyss caves are several recognisable Pictish symbols (no. 80), although no evidence survives to show whether caves were inhabited or used as workshops or sacred places.

Only rarely is it possible to be certain that a symbol stone is still in its original position, for most have been moved for one reason or another. An extreme example is the stone found built into the castle at Woodwrae near Aberlemno, which was then given to Sir Walter Scott, who displayed it at his home at Abbotsford in the Borders and subsequently presented it to the Society of Antiquaries of Scotland, with the result that it is now in the National Museums of Scotland in Edinburgh. More commonly stones have been moved out of the way of the plough to the edge of the field or into a nearby churchyard. The tall cross-slab beside the road at Aberlemno (no. 72) and the Cossans cross-slab (no. 73) are both known still to be in their original positions, and their topographical locations are therefore particularly interesting. At Aberlemno the stone was set up on a ridge running down the axis of Strathmore, while the Cossans stone was placed on a dry knoll amidst boggy marshland; both locations suggest that one of the functions of the stones was to mark territorial boundaries. Old records of a stone cairn beside the Aberlemno slab and graves beside Cossans indicate an additional funerary purpose.

Silver plaques from Norrie's Law

Symbol stone from Westfield Farm, Falkland
(now in Falkland Palace Museum)

The Lindores stone at Abdie (no. 71) is one of several along the southern shore of the Tay estuary, and it is likely that the maritime strategic value of the estuary was appreciated in Pictish, as in earlier Roman, times. Until recent quarrying destroyed all trace, there was a magnificent Pictish fortress on Clatchard Craig at Newburgh (NO 243178), situated to dominate access from the Tay via the Lindores Valley through the Ochil hills into the heart of Fife and beyond. This may have been flanked on the west by the small but highly defensible fort at Abernethy (see no. 70) and on the east by the great fort on Norman's Law (no. 94) both possible but as yet unproven candidates for the status of Dark Age forts. The only surviving known example of such a stronghold in this area is on Dundurn Hill (no. 91), but there must be others awaiting identification. There must also have been countless domestic settlements and farms in which the bulk of the Pictish population lived, but, although possible sites can be seen on air photographs as shadows in the soil, few have been recovered by excavation.

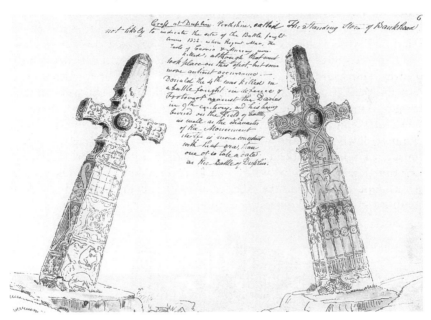

Cross at Dupplin, early 19th-century drawing

Several of the sculptures at Meigle (no. 78) and St Vigeans (no. 79) may have been architectural decoration, embellishing churches or other stone buildings in the way that the doorway into the round tower at Brechin (no. 69) is enhanced by carvings. Part of a stone arch carved with human figures and animals was found near Forteviot (now in NMS). It must originally have been part of a doorway into some important stone building in the late 9th or early 10th century, entirely appropriate to its location for it is known from historical records that Forteviot was a royal residence, first for Pictish and then for Scottish kings, from the 9th century onwards. The Dupplin cross (NO 050189), one of the few surviving free-standing crosses in eastern Scotland, is situated on the north side of the River Earn, opposite modern Forteviot, and a fragment of another such cross was found at Forteviot itself, both serving to underline the importance of the area. Indeed the magnificent Dupplin cross, set on a terrace high above the river, would almost certainly have been visible from the royal palace, and its rich carving has survived eleven centuries of weathering remarkably well.

Although the Picts were clearly aware of the tradition of free-standing crosses current amongst the Angles of Northumbria from around AD 700 and later amongst the Irish, they preferred the form of the cross-slab with its scope for decoration surrounding the cross, and it was only with increasing Irish influence in the 9th century that truly free-standing crosses began to appear, their decoration betraying both Irish and Northumbrian traditions. Although few such crosses survive, the number of fragments suggests that they were quite common in Tayside and Fife. The Camustone on the Panmure estate near Monikie (NO 519379) is a free-standing cross of 10th-century date with figural scenes including a crucifixion.

A special feature of Tayside Pictish monuments is a group of finely executed cross-slabs smaller in size than normal. They are late in date, belonging to the final years of the Pictish kingdom and to the early years after the Scottish takeover in the mid 9th century. A good example is the slab from Benvie, near Dundee (now in the McManus Galleries, Dundee), on which the well preserved motifs include two moustachioed horsemen similar to the figures on the Forteviot arch and the Dupplin cross. Other important examples of cross-slabs may be seen in the Meffan Institute, Forfar, including examples from Kirriemuir. Stones from St Madoes and Inchyra, beside the River Tay, may be seen in Perth Museum, from Inchbrayock in Montrose Museum, and a number of fine stones in the McManus Galleries in Dundee.

Sculptured fragment from Forteviot

Traditions of fine stone sculpture continued long after the Picts had become history. Fife and Tayside possess three superb examples of the hogback tombstone: at Inchcolm (no. 63), belonging to the mid 10th century, at Meigle (no. 78), late 10th century, and at Brechin (no. 69), dating to the early 11th century. This type of tombstone developed in 10th-century Yorkshire under Scandinavian influence, and it is a very distinctive, and often massively proportioned, monument. Meigle shows the classic house-shape with carved roof tiles while Brechin is the most elaborately decorated zoomorphic example in Scotland, one end sculpted into a great beast's head. Inchcolm is badly weathered and has lost much of the detail of its formerly intricate decoration, but it remains the earliest example of this type of tombstone in Scotland.

Aberlemno, back of cross-slab in churchyard

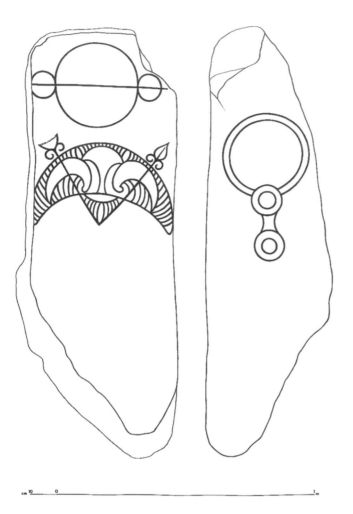

Abdie symbol stone

the sequence of carvings from Pictish times onwards is a graphic reminder of the many functions for which simple stone monuments have been used. The three original Pictish symbols are particularly well carved, especially the crescent and V-rod with its effective decoration. Above the crescent is a triple disc or cauldron symbol, here shown with a medial line to represent the chain by which the cauldron hung; the line was later adopted as the base line for the sundial. The back of the stone is undecorated, but one side bears a finely executed mirror symbol.

72 Aberlemno, Symbol Stone and Cross-Slabs, Angus

7th-8th/early 9th centuries AD.

NO 522558, three stones beside the B 9134 at Aberlemno between Brechin and Forfar. NO 522555, stone in churchyard, down minor road leading SE from B 9134 on the Forfar side of the roadside slabs (carpark behind church).

Historic Scotland; stones inaccessible beneath protective wooden jackets during winter months.

This group of stones makes an excellent introduction to the range and skill of Pictish carving, beginning with the most easterly of the three stones beside the road. This is an early Pictish monument, unshaped and incised on one face with a serpent, a double disc and Z-rod and a mirror and comb. A group of prehistoric cup-marks low down on the reverse of this slab suggests that the Pictish sculptor made use of an existing standing stone. Both this and and the next slab have been moved to their present positions in recent times, unlike the great cross-slab which remains in its original position. The small centre stone may also be a prehistoric standing stone, although there are indistinct traces of a crescent and a curving line. The tall, narrow cross-slab is likely to be the latest of the Aberlemno group; it stands almost 3 m high and is heavily ornamented on every face, although weathering and pollution have sadly blurred the details. The cross-head is sculpted in high relief with bosses and panels reminiscent of the jewelled metal crosses used inside churches, and the shaft is flanked by angels, panels of interlace and animals. The sides of the slab are carved with a running spiral pattern. The back is dominated by two huge

71 Abdie Churchyard, Symbol Stone, Fife

7th century AD.

NO 259163. From Lindores on the A 913, c 3 km SE of Newburgh, take the second or E minor road SW towards Grange of Lindores; the track to the church is immediately to the left after the railway bridge. The stone is in a small building on the right of the entrance to the churchyard.

The stone was found built into a garden wall in Lindores and had at some period been converted into a sundial with Roman numerals. It was also found convenient for a bench mark, the three-pronged symbol carved beneath the rectangular sundial. Traces of a large rectangle suggest that yet another use for the stone had been considered, and symbols, the crescent and V-rod and the double disc and Z-rod, both filled with decoration. The central panel contains a hunting scene, with a fine pair of trumpeters in the top right corner, and below are a centaur and the figure of David rending the jaws of a lion, alongside a sheep and a harp.

Better preserved and an outstanding example of Pictish art is the cross-slab in the churchyard, lovingly carved in the full range of a master craftsman's techniques, from light incision to high relief. The cross stands some 12 cm proud of its background, representing colossal effort in removing unwanted stone, and its surface is intricately carved with interlace patterns. The background is carved with amusingly intertwined animals showing strong Northumbrian influence. If you begin at the feet of the animal at the bottom of the left-hand panel, you will be able to trace its hind-legs and tail within the circle of its elongated body curving round to its forelegs, and then its neck curving backwards until its jaws grasp the hindquarters of the next animal. The back of the slab is framed within two serpentine animals whose heads confront one another at the top (the hole is not part of the original design but appears to have been bored in more recent times). There are two symbols: a rectangle and Z-rod and a triple disc, and beneath them a panel containing the only known battle-scene in Pictish art. The horsemen and foot-soldiers are carved in an ingenious combination of incision and low relief that creates a sense of perspective. Middle left is a group of three foot-soldiers, armed with shields (shown in profile) and spears; the central figure holds his spear on his right side and it is carved in relief, whereas the third soldier is carrying his spear in his left hand, lightly incised to show that it is further away.

Aberlemno is only some 10 km from the site of the battle of Nechtansmere, which took place in AD 685 near Dunnichen (a modern cairn at NO 509487 commemorates the battle, along with a cast of the symbol stone found nearby, which is now in the McManus Galleries, Dundee). It has been suggested that the Aberlemno battle-scene depicts the historic occasion of Nechtansmere, when the Picts defeated the Northumbrian army, and that the stone was erected some decades later to record the battle.

73 Cossans, Cross-slab, Angus

8th or 9th century AD.

NO 400500. 4 km S of Kirriemuir on the A 928, a track leads E to Cossans farm. The stone is in a field E of the farm.

Historic Scotland.

Traditionally known as St Orland's Stone, this impressive slab stands to a height of almost 3 m on a low rounded knoll; it was set up in the late 8th or early 9th century, and there are old records of stone cist-graves having been found close by. Its location suggests that it marked a boundary in the same way as the comparable cross-slab at Aberlemno (no. 72), as well as acting as a focus for burials. Eleven hundred years of weathering in this exposed position have damaged the sculptor's work, but this is nevertheless a particularly interesting stone, chiefly for its rare carving of a boat.

The entire length of the face of the slab is taken up by a ring-headed cross with a splayed base; ingeniously, the sculptor has carved the cross on two levels of relief so as to give a three-dimensional impression of a free-standing cross. The soft sandstone has allowed the creation of intricate spiral and interlace patterns over both levels of the cross, and an empty circular depression at the centre of its head may originally have held a decorative metal plaque. It seems likely that the knoll on which the monument stands was formerly surrounded by waterlogged marsh, and it is therefore very appropriate that the cross is itself surrounded by interlaced fish-monsters.

Two more fish-tailed beasts form a frame round the reverse side of the slab, enclosing, at the top, a crescent and V-rod and a double disc and Z-rod and figural panels below. An intriguing problem is posed by the central panel with its neatly cut recess: has some powerful symbol been deliberately removed? It must have been something important, for it had its own special decorative frame, open at the top as if to signify some connection with the symbols above. Below are two horsemen, each with a saddlecloth, and below them another pair of horsemen accompanied by two hunting dogs. Next comes the boat, a long vessel with upturned prow and stern, carrying at least four people and some large object in the prow. Unlike the boat carved in Jonathan's Cave (no. 80), no oars are depicted here, nor is there a sail. At the foot of the slab are carved two battling animals, one horned and the other cat-like, with pronounced claws and furiously arched back.

Dunfallandy, front of the cross-slab

74 Dunfallandy, Cross-slab, Perth and Kinross

8th century AD.

NN 946565. In Pitlochry, take the turning to Logierait and Dunfallandy; continue past Dunfallandy Hotel to cattle-grid on right and park. Walk on and take steep steps on left to stone.

Historic Scotland.

This splendid Pictish cross-slab has survived in good condition, its carving still crisp apart from the central panel of the cross-head, which must have been deliberately defaced. The rest of the cross bears intricate ornament and symmetrical arrangements of bosses on the arms, and the background is neatly filled with a series of animals and winged figures. Both sides of the slab have a raised decorative frame, that on the back taking the form of a pair of fish-tailed, animal-headed monsters, apparently licking a human head. There are several small symbols: a Pictish beast, double disc and crescent and V-rod above two clerics seated on either side of a miniature cross, another

Pictish beast and crescent and V-rod accompanying a horseman, and below a hammer, anvil and tongs.

A small Pictish cross-slab may be seen not far from Dunfallandy, in the churchyard at Logierait (NN 967520); although damaged, the lower part of a horseman survives on the back, along with a serpent twined round a straight rod, while the front bears a decorative cross.

75 Eassie Churchyard, Cross-slab, Angus

8th century AD.

NO 352474. The old church at Eassie is just N of the A 94, Glamis/Coupar Angus road, c 3.5 km W of Glamis; signposted.

Historic Scotland.

Although the back of the stone is worn and damaged, this remains an impressive cross-slab, and is particularly interesting for the lithe warrior striding purposefully alongside the shaft of the cross. His flowing cloak, small square shield and long spear are clearly visible. The cross itself is filled with interlace and key pattern, flanked at the top by angels and below, opposite the warrior, there are three animals including a fine stag. The stag and the two remaining cows (the tail and hind leg of a third is visible) on the back of the slab are all carved with spirals denoting their shoulder and hind-quarter muscles. There are also cloaked figures, a tree in a pot and symbols on the back, including the Pictish beast and a double disc and Z-rod. A rounded moulding separates the panels of designs.

76 Fowlis Wester, Cross-slabs, Perth and Kinross

8th-9th century AD.

NN 927240. Cast in the centre of the village and two stones in the church.

Historic Scotland, tall slab and cast.

There are two superb cross-slabs in the church. The first is a tall, elegantly tapering slab, which stood originally on the village green (where it has been replaced by a cast). In later times its role in village life included punishment, for an iron chain fixed to the cross-shaft probably attached the jougs or collar by which an offender might be held on public view. An unusual feature is the protruding arms of the cross: the two horizontal arms extend some 6 cm from the sides of the slab as an optical device to convey the impression of a free-standing cross. This is unique in Pictish art, but the device was used in Ireland and here perhaps betrays Irish influence. Unfortunately, the effects of weathering have all but obliterated the details of what was once a fine example of the sculptor's skill. Traces of interlace decoration survive on the shaft of the cross, key-patterning on the arms, and an arrangement of eight bosses round a central boss fills the centre of the cross-head. The back of the slab bore two insignificantly small symbols, a double disc and Z-rod at the top and a crescent and V-rod bottom left, together with horsemen, animals and a unique scene showing a man leading a cow with a bell round its neck, followed by a line of six bearded men walking abreast.

The other cross-slab lacks symbols and dates from the 9th century. It had been built into the fabric of the church and is therefore better preserved than the one that stood exposed to the weather on the village green. The carving is confined to one side and depicts a ring-headed cross on a splayed base, decorated with interlace, spirals and key-pattern. Motifs filling the background include Jonah being swallowed by the whale, two clerics seated on finely depicted chairs (note the animal-headed chairback on the left), and four standing figures in decorative robes. This stone is notable for the rich detail of its carving. The church itself was built originally in the 13th century and was attractively restored early this century.

77 Glamis, Cross-slabs, Angus

7th-8th centuries AD.

NO 385468. In the garden of the manse, opposite the church. NO 393465. On the N flank of Hunters Hill, SE of Glamis, on the S side of the A 94.

These two slabs share the distinction of illustrating the two main strands of Pictish decorative layout on opposing faces—one side of each bearing only symbols, the other side a cross with carved motifs in a wide range of iconography including symbols.

Fowlis Wester, cross-slab before removal to the church, front and back faces

The stone in the manse garden is far superior in artistic quality, at least to a modern eye, to the other, and it is interesting that they should both bear the serpent and the triple disc symbols.

One side of the slab in the garden bears three Pictish symbols on its rough and irregular surface: a serpent, a fish and a mirror. The sides and top have been shaped so that the slab tapers towards a pedimented head, 2.7 m high, but there is no decoration on the sides. The other face is carved with a cross in relief, entirely infilled with various interlaced designs. An odd feature of this cross is the presence of an incomplete incised ring linking the arms on all but the lower right quadrant, where the muzzle of the dog's head lies in the way, as if the addition of the ring had been a unsuccessful afterthought. Beneath the dog is a triple disc symbol, itself overlapping the dog. On the other side of the cross-shaft, two bearded men confront each other with axes, while above them is a cauldron with two pairs of legs sticking up. This may be part of a Pictish folktale, or it may be linked with the historically documented Pictish tradition of execution by drowning. Flanking the top of the cross are an animal and a centaur brandishing axes, and traces of animal heads may just be seen above the top of the cross.

Within the vestibule of the church is a fragment of another cross-slab, showing the interlace-filled base of the cross-shaft and the lower parts of a man and an animal, together with fragments of other stones.

The rough face of the slab on Hunters Hill bears an animal, a serpent and a mirror. The other side is sculpted in relief with an interlace-filled cross within a key-pattern frame. The background carvings include a winged figure, a beast-headed figure with an axe, several animals, a triple disc symbol and a flower symbol.

Meigle no. I

78* Meigle, Carved Stones, Perth and Kinross

8th-10th centuries AD.

NO 287445. On the B 954 just S of the village square; signposted

Historic Scotland.

More than thirty carved stones and fragments are known to have been found in Meigle, and there can be little doubt that an early ecclesiastical centre existed here, attracting important secular burials. Historical sources record the work of Thana, perhaps a monastic annalist, at Meigle in the mid 9th century, implying an appropriate setting for the

sculpture. Some fragments have been lost, but the remaining collection includes large and small cross-slabs, horizontal or recumbent graveslabs and a hogback tombstone, as well as an architectural fragment that may have decorated a 9th or 10th-century church (no. 22 in the collection). None of the stones need be dated earlier than about AD 800 and most are later, although several bear Pictish symbols including a finely executed 'Pictish beast' or 'swimming elephant' on the side of no. 5. The cross-slabs are mostly small in size, with the exception of nos 1 and 2. No. 1 is the earlier of the two and, although quite crudely composed, the scene on the reverse includes not only Pictish symbols (fish, 'elephant', serpent and Z-rod, mirror and comb) but also more exotic elements that must have been copied from an imported carving or manuscript: on the right is a kneeling camel, and on the left a winged figure identified as a Persian god. Cross-slab no. 2 is an imposing 2.4 m in height, carved in high relief but unfortunately much worn by weathering. A unique feature is the series of projections on the side and top, as if the slab were intended to be slotted into a wall or screen. The cross is massively proportioned, and the back of the slab is dominated by the central figure of Daniel, flanked on either side by two lions and possibly a lion cub. Above the lions on the left is a row of three horsemen, depicted by the overlapping outlines of their horses.

The small cross-slab no. 3 is of particular interest because of the details of the horseman on the reverse; his broad scabbard has a rounded chape or protective tip, silver examples of which were found in the treasure from St Ninian's Isle in Shetland. Instead of a stirrup (which were unknown at this period in Scotland), his foot appears to be braced in a slipper-like pocket at the point of the saddlecloth.

There are two fine tombstones designed to lie horizontally over their graves. The earlier of the two, the wedge-shaped no. 26, is a vigorously carved Pictish monument of the 9th century. The socket in the top at the higher end was probably intended to hold an upright cross at the head of the grave, and the end panel is carved with a beast pursuing a bearded man. Both sides and top are decorated with animal, abstract and human motifs, including a beautifully devised swastika of human bodies. Perhaps because of this taste for wedge-

shaped monuments, the hogback tombstone no. 25, carved in the late 10th century, was also made in this way instead of the normal house-shape, although it does bear the usual decoration in the form of roof-tiles. At the higher end of the ridge is a fine animal-head with long snout and flowing ears, very similar to the animal-heads decorating the base of the cross on no. 5. The hogback is clearly the work of local sculptor, adapting an exotic fashion in tombstones to local taste.

79 St Vigeans, Arbroath, Carved Stones, Angus

8th-10th centuries AD.

NO 638429. Take the A 933 NW from Arbroath towards Friockheim; St Vigeans is signposted on the right about 2 km from the town centre.

Historic Scotland.

The church at St Vigeans presents a striking sight, perched on a small steep knoll above the Brothock Burn. Although most of the present building belongs to a 19th-century restoration, the site has a long ecclesiastical history and bears the name of a 7th-century Irish saint, Vigianus. The collection of early stone-carving now housed in a converted cottage at the foot of the knoll was discovered during the re-building of the church, most of the

stones having been incorporated into its walls. Most were originally free-standing upright monuments, a few were recumbent or horizontal tombstones, and one or two may have been architectural pieces which once decorated an early church on the site. Overall, the collection is similar in range to that at Meigle (no. 76), and the absence of early symbol stones is a notable feature of both. Many of the St Vigeans stones have suffered badly from misuse as building material, and some survive only as fragments; only the most interesting of the 32 pieces will be treated here in detail.

Stone no. 1 is known as the Drosten Stone, after the first word of the unusual inscription set within a panel at the base of one of the narrow sides of the

slab. This is one of only nine inscriptions written in roman script that have been found in Pictland. It reads

DROSTEN:
IREUORET
[E]TTFOR
CUS

It is generally agreed amongst scholars that Drosten, Uoret and Forcus are personal names, the first two Pictish and the last Gaelic, and that the inscription is most probably commemorative. A Gaelic reading allows it to be translated as 'Drosten, in the time of Uoret, and Forcus'. The Pictish king, Uoret, reigned from 839 to 842. The stone was thus carved in the 9th century, a handsome tall cross-slab with prominent Pictish symbols created in relief on the back, above various animals, a bird and a fish, and hooded archer; this is one of the rare representations of a crossbow.

Although sadly mutilated (the carving on the back obliterated and the slab re-shaped), no. 7 retains enough of its sculptured face to give an impression of its former grandeur, with robed and seated clerics and fine interlacing on the cross. No. 11 is another damaged but still impressive cross-slab, with two robed clerics sitting on a bench and a quaint figure in baggy pleated trousers on the reverse. No. 8 is probably part of an architectural frieze, perhaps unfinished as one panel is empty. No. 14 is an elaborate recumbent tombstone, heavily decorated, with a slot at one end to take an upright cross.

80 Wemyss Caves, Fife

Mid 1st millennium AD.

Seek advice about access from the Environmental Education Centre at East Wemyss Primary School. Park on the front at East Wemyss. Walk NE along the shore first to the Court Cave (NT 342969) and then to the Doo Cave (NT 343970); the large mouth of Jonathan's Cave follows next (NT 345972) with the hidden mouth of the largely inaccessible Sliding or Sloping Cave (NT 346972) a little further E. A torch is helpful.

The caves formed in the sandstone cliffs to the north-east of East Wemyss have been the focus of antiquarian and archaeological interest since 1865 when Professor James Young Simpson visited them and found their walls 'to be covered at different points with representations of various animals, figures and emblems'. What particularly excited the discoverers was that several of the the incised markings could be compared to those on Pictish symbol stones, the significance of which was at that time becoming apparent as a result of John Stuart's work on cataloguing them. Careful drawings of the markings were made for the second volume of Stuart's *The Sculptured Stones of Scotland* (published in 1867) and these, amplified by photographic surveys in the early years of this century and again in the 1920s, have provided the basic record. Between 1984 and 1985 further drawing was undertaken, and it is clear that several areas of carvings have been lost, and perhaps even more sadly other markings in 'Pictish style' have been added; here we list only the most interesting and apparently authentic markings.

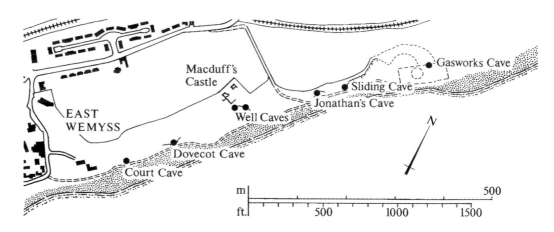

Wemyss Caves, location map of the caves

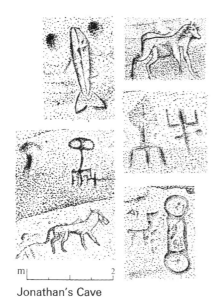

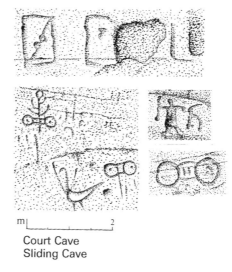

Wemyss Caves, drawings of selected portions of the carvings

m |_____| 2

Court Cave
Sliding Cave

m |_____| 2

Jonathan's Cave

The Court Cave has a main cavern and a smaller narrow cave at its entrance. In the narrow cave there is a figure brandishing a spear (possibly knobbed) and an animal; other symbols have flaked away. In the main cave, a marking sometimes described as a 'sceptre', a floriated rod flanking a symbol akin to a double-disc, is the clearest. There is a double-disc symbol on a higher ledge. Not all the other symbols on this wall, however, appear to be ancient for they were not included in the drawings of the last century, though several of the triangular motifs are visible in early photographs. It is in the Court Cave that James V is said to have met up with a gypsy band while travelling incognito; finding himself in some danger, tradition has it that he calmed the proceedings by throwing off his disguise.

The Doo Cave contained several interesting groups of symbols, but a collapse of the roof has meant that now only the hewn-out nesting hollows for the birds that give the cave its name survive. Simpson described the cave as 'one of the most magnificent of the series, being high in the roof, nearly a hundred feet in length, and about sixty or seventy in breadth. In some lights the cryptograms on its high walls and dome like ceiling show masses of beautiful and changing colour'. One of the most interesting symbols was a double-disc and Z-rod with a beast's head touching it; this may be closely compared in layout to the symbols on one of the silver plaques from the Norrie's Law hoard.

Wemyss Caves, carvings in Court Cave

Jonathan's Cave (or the Factor's Cave) contains many distinctive symbols of Pictish date, as well as several much later examples, including a 19th-century canon; particularly well-preserved are the double-disc symbols, an upright 'fish', several animals, and on the opposite wall an oared ship.

The Sliding Cave should only be visited with great care, but there are rectangular markings on one wall and double-disc on the other. A torch is essential.

No carvings have been reported in the Well Caves (NO 346971), which may be seen below Macduff's Castle, nor in the now collapsed Gasworks Cave at the north-east end of this stretch of cliff (NO 347973).

ROMAN TAYSIDE

Inchtuthil Roman fortress showing post-holes of internal buildings

East-central Scotland was the arena for Roman military operations on several occasions, notably during the advance of Agricola, and at Ardoch (no. 81) the area possesses perhaps the best preserved remains of a turf-and-timber fort anywhere in the Roman Empire. The names of several of the local iron-age tribes were recorded in the second century AD, including the *Venicones* in Fife and probably in Strathmore, and the *Caledonii* in the Grampians. Evidence of Roman activity in Fife is slight (there are temporary camps at Auchtermuchty, Bonnytown and Edenwood), but in Tayside aerial reconnaissance and a series of excavations have provided detailed information about a wide range of military installations; thus, although only a small group of sites are so well preserved as to be worth visiting, the unique range of sites—legionary fortress, forts, fortlets, watch-towers and temporary camps—visible on the ground underlines the importance of Strathearn and Strathmore to Roman studies.

The outline of the legionary fortress of Inchtuthil together with traces of the internal timber buildings can be seen clearly on the air photograph. Excavations undertaken between 1952 and 1965 have allowed the plans of these structures to be ascertained in considerable detail; architecturally, the most imposing were the *principia* (headquarters building), the hospital, workshop, and the granaries, but the examination of the officers' quarters and barracks revealed structural evidence of interest to the military historian. Outside the fort, in a separate defended compound, remains were uncovered of the temporary accommodation and baths used by senior officers before the completion of the fortress. The fortress was still under construction when it was abandoned as a result of the reorganisation of frontier forces some time after AD 86; the buildings were demolished and the revetting wall of the enclosing rampart was dismantled. Perhaps the most telling evidence of the organised withdrawal was the discovery of a pit containing and concealing iron objects that would otherwise have been of use to the native tribes; there were nine iron tyres and nearly ten tons of iron nails—875,428 were recovered in all. It is clear that abandoned Roman forts were pillaged for whatever might be useful; this may also be indicated by the discovery of pieces of rubble with mortar still adhering to them in the native fort at Clatchard Craig (NO 243178), which almost certainly derive from a Roman military installation, perhaps the fortress at Carpow, some 3.5 km distant.

Inchtuthil Roman tyres and nails

Roman nails

The tented camp of a Roman army in the field would have been laid out according to definite rules, with regular blocks or lines of tents for the troops' accommodation in the interior and a simple bank and external ditch forming the defensive perimeter; the entrances in each side might have been further protected by traverses or distinctive curving outworks. Many such camps have been discovered by aerial photography, and it has been suggested that it is possible to associate camps with specific seasons of campaigning by reason of differences in size, plan, or type of gateway defence. Camps of roughly 25 ha and 50 ha, for example, are thought to belong to the Severan advances of AD 208-11. Tayside contains one of the largest concentrations of temporary camps in Britain, an indication of its frontier status, and, although it is extremely rare to find any earthworks surviving even partially above ground, substantial portions of the larger camps at Ardoch (no. 81) and isolated fragments of the example at Innerpeffray (NN 916184) can still be seen; for the most part, however, their outlines appear only as cropmarks on air photographs, as at Dalginross (NN 774207) and Inchtuthil (NO 119394).

The importance of Tayside to Roman studies lies in the presence of well-preserved forts of the later first century AD, built and used for only a short time before being dismantled, and never subsequently built over either by later Roman occupation or in recent times; thus the completeness of our knowledge of the internal arrangements of Inchtuthil and Fendoch (NN 919283), as revealed by excavation, has made them two of the most studied sites in the Empire. Ardoch (no. 81) was indeed rebuilt on several occasions, but the remarkable state of preservation of the earthwork defences makes this an exciting site to visit. The watch-towers of the Gask Ridge (no. 83) form an unusually well-preserved group of sites and are associated with a Roman road, the line of which may still be traced. One of the most evocative sites to visit is the small watch-tower at the mouth of the Sma' Glen (no. 82), which affords extensive vistas not only over Fendoch and the farmland of Glen Almond, but also into the mountain fastness beyond the Highland Line.

**Roman
watch-tower
at Westerton**

Ardoch Roman fort

81 Ardoch, Fort, Perth and Kinross

Late 1st and mid 2nd centuries AD.

NN 839099. To the N of the village of Braco. Park in the village and follow the A 822 a little to the N; cross the bridge; the fort is signposted immediately to the E. The path from the gate leads to the centre of the W side of the fort.

The spectacular earthworks at Ardoch make this one of the most impressive forts in the Roman Empire. The fort has been partly excavated, but the sequence of building is not altogether certain; not surprisingly the best preserved features appear to belong to the latest phase of occupation. The rampart encloses an area of about 1.95 ha, the external ditches being particularly clear on the north and east sides; it is likely that this phase of the fort belongs to the late 150s. The rampart which lies a little way beyond the two innermost ditches on the north has been assumed to represent the northern limit of an earlier, and appreciably larger, fort, enclosing an area of some 2.5 ha. The excavations of 1896-7 indicated that the site had undergone several phases of occupation, the earlier of which dated to the Flavian period in the first century AD. The garrison in one of the earlier phases was the *cohors I Hispanorum*, whose

presence is recorded on a tombstone found during the 17th century (now in the Hunterian Museum, University of Glasgow).

The small rectangular earthwork situated near the centre of the interior of the fort is all that survives of a medieval chapel and its enclosing bank.

The importance of the site as a halting-place on a major axis of communication may be gauged by the number of temporary camps which have been detected in the fields to the north. For the most part these can only be seen as cropmarks on air photographs, but sections of the two largest camps, dating to the campaigns of Septimius Severus, survive as upstanding banks. These earthworks may still be seen in an area of heather-covered moorland on the west side of the A 822 just north of its junction with the B 827 to Comrie. Across the corner of the field the line of part of a 25 ha camp may still be seen to the east of a post and wire fence (NN 840107). At a point about 200 m west of the road junction (just before an electricity substation) strike to the north on the east side of the fence where a long stretch of the rampart and ditch of a 52 ha camp may still be traced; one of the two side entrances to the camp can be seen at the north end of the surviving defences (NN 839109).

**Fendoch Roman
watch-tower**

82 Fendoch, Watch-tower, Perth and Kinross

Late 1st century AD.

NN 909285. At the mouth of the Sma' Glen on the W side of the A 822; park in layby at the junction of the B 8063; there is a gate on the W side of the road, and the earthwork is on the top of the ridge 300 m to the NW.

Although there is now no trace of the rectangular timber watch-tower, the impressive earthen rampart and external ditch which enclosed it can still be seen. The splendid view from here into the Sma' Glen and down Glen Almond would have been even more remarkable from the top of a tower 5 m to 10 m high. The fort of Fendoch, of which barely any surface traces survive, lies at the southern edge of the grassy plateau 1 km to the south-east (NN 919283). The tower has been described as the 'eye' of the fort, for from Fendoch itself there is no view into the Sma' Glen, and we may envisage a signalling system, perhaps with beacon-fires or smoke, between the tower and the fort.

83 Gask Ridge, Watch-towers, Perth and Kinross

c AD 82-90.

The watch-towers in this sector were intended to control movement on the road between Strageath and Bertha, and the system may have been continued south to Ardoch and perhaps further. They should be seen as a sort of linear frontier, an early precursor of more complex barriers such as the Antonine Wall, but they were also distinct elements in a surveillance system of roadside installations which controlled movement of the native population into and out of Fife. The watch-towers between Ardoch and Kaims Castle (no. 84) have two ditches and thus appear to belong to a group distinct from the Gask Ridge series. The towers, separated by intervals which range from about 0.8 km to 1.5 km were some 3.5 m square with stout corner-posts, and excavations have revealed that some of these posts were connected by sleeper-trenches to provide additional support for the superstructure—a two-storey signalling tower of the type clearly illustrated on Trajan's Column; the pits in which these posts stood may be seen on the air photograph of Westerton (NN 873145); in some examples the tower was surrounded by an earthen rampart, probably surmounted by a timber breast-work, and by a ditch (over 3m wide and at least 1m deep), occasionally with an outer bank. The ditch was interrupted opposite the entrance (also visible on the air photograph) to allow access from the road; an indication of the road-line is given on the photograph by the roadside quarry-pits seen as dark patches. The general appearance of the watch-towers is shown in the reconstruction drawing, reminding us perhaps that, although the surviving traces are slight, the towers once formed part of an effective military communications-system, which successfully imposed Roman control over east-central Scotland.

Among the best preserved and most accessible sites are those listed below.

Parkneuk (NN 916184). Park at the entrance to the forestry track, walk along the track for about 50 m before turning east; the rampart, ditch, outer bank and three of the four post-holes were revealed by excavation in 1968.

Reconstruction of Roman watch-tower on the Gask Ridge by M Moore

Ardunie (NN 946187) Historic Scotland. Park at the bend in the road (NN 960188), walk west along the track, which is on the line of the Roman road, for some 1.3 km; the watch-tower is in a fenced enclosure to the south of the track. The ditch and causeway may still be seen.

On a rise to the north of the track at a point about 200 m west of the parking area there is the site of the tower of Roundlaw (NN 958188); excavations in 1972 showed the outline of the ditch and four rock-cut post-holes for the main uprights of the tower.

Muir o' Fauld (NN 982189) Historic Scotland. Park at the entrance to the forestry road at NN 985191 and walk to the west along the track (on the line of the Roman road) for 350 m; the watch-tower is signposted to the south of the track in a fenced enclosure. The rampart, ditch, causeway and outer bank can be seen.

Witch Knowe (NN 997195). Park at the entrance to the forestry track opposite the lodge to Gask House at NN 996194; a little to the east on the north side of the road there is an overgrown track; the watch-tower is in trees 90 m north of the broken gate. The ditch, causeway and outer bank can still be seen. Four post-holes of the watch-tower were discovered during excavations in 1900, each about 0.45 m in diameter and 0.6 m deep.

84 Kaims Castle, Fortlet, Perth and Kinross

Late 1st century AD.

NN 860129. On the A 822 4 km NE of Ardoch on the NW side of the road at Orchil. After seeking permission, enter by the gate to the SW of the pink house.

The rampart of the fortlet (some 21 m by 22.5 m internally) still stands 1 m in height within two outer ditches and an outer counterscarp bank. Although the fortlet was excavated in 1900, at the same time as several of the Gask Ridge stations (no. 83), no traces of internal structures were revealed and only areas of paving were discovered.

PREHISTORIC MONUMENTS

**Croft Moraig
stone circle**

Sir Walter Scott describes the pursuits and pleasures of *The Antiquary*, Mr Johnathan Oldbuck of Monkbarns, who 'measured decayed encampments, made plans of ruined castles, read illegible inscriptions and wrote essays on medals . . .' and would 'enter into a sea of discussion concerning urns, vases, votive altars, Roman camps, and the rules of castramentation.' The cabinets of curiosities of the early antiquaries have now given way to well organised museums, though this important phase of historical research is evoked both at Hospitalfield (no. 35) and in the Laing Memorial Museum at Newburgh; the interpretation and dating of field monuments, however, may still occasion very similar differences of opinion to those of Scott's antiquaries. In Fife and Tayside the range of upstanding early prehistoric monuments is in some respects more restricted than in other areas of Scotland; there are few chambered cairns for example, but many of the surviving forts, standing stones and round cairns are very impressive. The air photograph of hut circles and field systems at Drumturn Burn show how well an archaeological landscape can survive in upland areas.

The archaeological evidence comes not only from the surviving monuments, but also in the form of cropmarks and soilmarks of destroyed sites that may be traced on aerial photographs. In the last two decades intensive aerial prospection has revealed settlement sites of a wide chronological range, as well as ritual and burial monuments of considerable complexity. In order to highlight this important body of information we illustrate markings at Newton (NO 608465), where there are the pits of an agricultural boundary, the circular cropmarks of enclosures and two darker bottle-shaped or banana-like marks, which almost certainly indicate the positions of souterrains.

Hut circles and field systems at Drumturn Burn, Perth and Kinross

SETTLEMENTS AND FORTS

Excavations at Newmill (NO 084324) have clarified the interpretation of the souterrains of Angus and Perthshire; the stone-built underground gallery was associated with an unusually large timber-built house, the post-holes of which could still be traced and which are visible on the photograph. The souterrain appeared to be structurally integrated with the house, in the sense of being entered from within it, and the two were certainly contemporary structures. Although some souterrains are roofed with large flat slabs, at Newmill it is likely that the roof was of timber and that it was visible above ground-level. Neither the souterrain nor the associated house was rich in finds, but the excavator concluded that the souterrain had been a food-store and granary. From radiocarbon analyses we know that the souterrain was built about the first century AD and was abandoned in the late second or early third century. We should no longer think of them as 'Picts' houses', for they belonged to an earlier age than the Picts, and they were certainly not dwellings—they were the storehouses of the iron-age ancestors of the historical Picts.

Souterrains, ring-ditches and pit-alignment, Newton, Angus

Souterrain at Newmill, Bankfoot, Perth and Kinross

The timber house at Newmill was probably about 17.6 m in diameter, and it would have been an impressive structure. Houses of this period are evoked in a reconstruction illustrating building materials and roofing techniques in the McManus Galleries, Dundee. Timber was an important component of another class of prehistoric monument, the crannog, though today, if visible at all, these are small offshore islands. The island was the foundation for a house sometimes linked to the shore by a wooden or stone causeway. There is a concentration of such sites in Loch Tay, and excavations at Oakbank (NN 723442) have revealed a wealth of evidence about the environment and a variety of finds, including wooden platters, pegs, and even a whistle. Radiocarbon dates show that the site was flourishing in the second quarter of the first millennium BC.

Excavation may not only reveal a long sequence of building of hillforts but, with the advent of radiocarbon analysis, also provide material for more detailed chronological information. The timber-laced fort at Finavon (no. 93) has been shown to have been occupied as early as the 8th to 6th centuries BC. Objects discovered during excavation of the fort at Abernethy (NO 182153) showed that it was used in the 3rd or 2nd century BC, although its occupation may well have continued later. Excavations in advance of destruction by quarrying indicated that there were at least two phases of Dark Age fortification on Clatchard Craig (NO 243178) including a timber-laced rampart of 6th or 7th century AD and a later rampart, possibly of 8th-century date, which incorporated re-used stones with Roman mortar adhering to them. Forts such as Clatchard Craig and Dundurn (no. 91) have distinctive features of layout that distinguish them from iron-age sites, particularly in the use of craggy hilltop locations. Thus, unless there is clear evidence from excavation or from over-lying ramparts of the sequence of building, the hilltop forts of Tayside and Fife bear enigmatic testimony to the complex society of the iron age; among the most impressive are Barry Hill (NO 262503), Green Craig (NO 322215) and the Brown and White Caterthuns (no. 90).

In Glen Lyon and Strathtummel there are numerous round stone-walled forts which have long puzzled archaeologists; many are set on low-lying non-defensive positions and may represent the fortified houses of wealthy farmers. Excavations of one such ring-fort at Litigan provided material for a radiocarbon date of the 9th to 10th centuries AD, rather more recent than had formerly been suspected. At Aldclune a pair of ring-forts overlooking the River Garry was excavated in advance of roadworks (NN 894642); their use was found to range from the later centuries BC into the Pictish period, the later represented by a superb silver-gilt penannular brooch.

Green Craig fort, Fife

85 Ardestie, Souterrain, Angus

1st-2nd centuries AD.

NO 502344. Signposted on the N side of the A 92 Dundee-Arbroath road, to the NW of the Mains of Ardestie.

Historic Scotland.

This souterrain was discovered as a result of stone-clearance in 1949 and excavated by Dr F T Wainwright in 1949 and 1950. The shape of the souterrain was compared by Wainwright to that of a banana, with the entrance forming the stalk and the main curved chamber the banana itself. The short narrow passage leads down to the twin jambs of the entrance doorway. The souterrain was constructed with massive boulders at the base of the corbelled side-walls and with rougher stone-work, now partly reconstructed, forming the upper courses. Large flat slabs formed an irregular paving with a central drain for about two-thirds of its length. The drain was not an original feature of the souterrain construction, but was essential because the surrounding boulder clay did not allow water to run off naturally. But even the drain was not sufficient, and the souterrain was eventually abandoned; the roof and the upper courses of the wall appear to have been removed and the passage filled with earth.

Four surface structures, which were in use at the same time as the final phase of use of the souterrain, are visible on its south-west side. Only part of the north-west structure survives, but part of a broken rotary quern was found in the floor and a large cup-and-ring marked slab was found set into the wall. In the north-east corner of the adjacent structure there was a stone bench comprising a large flat slab supported by uprights; apart from another quern fragment, sherds and animal bones were found. The major feature of the third structure was a 'fire-bowl' with a well-preserved 'draught-vent' underneath the paving; among the debris was part of a Roman amphora and a pitted stone, which was probably used to produce fire. A narrow structure led from this series of surface buildings directly to the souterrain itself, but it is likely that this and the adjacent structure were not in use after the souterrain was filled in. A stone-lined tank originally lined with clay in order to make it water-tight may still be seen a little to the south.

Just how the souterrain and the surface structures should be interpreted in the light of the evidence from Newmill discussed in the Introduction is uncertain; on the one hand it seems not improbable that the roof of the souterrain itself was of timber rather than flat slabs, on the other hand the sophistication of the timber house at Newmill makes it unlikely that the surface features at Ardestie were roofed with individual timber and thatch wigwams as is sometimes suggested as a reconstruction. Another interpretation might be that the surface structures indicate paved industrial areas just outside the main roofed area involving activities that were perhaps hazardous (the 'fire-bowl') or noxious (a stone bench associated perhaps with butchery).

86 Barns of Airlie, Souterrain, Angus

1st-2nd centuries AD.

NO 305515. Situated below a stone wall at the end of the second field W of Barns of Airlie; check at the farm for permission and accessibility. A torch is essential.

This is one of the best preserved souterrains in Angus, for the roof remains intact except where a lintel has been removed to make access possible today. The gallery is some 19 m long and 2 m broad and is lintelled at a height of 1.8 m; the entrance passage, as yet unexcavated, is at the east end of the gallery. At Barns of Airlie several features of the construction of the souterrain may be appreciated in their relationship to one another: the massive basal course of boulders, with the upper corbelled courses of smaller slabs and boulders with the roof slabs above. The excavated finds were largely unremarkable, including quernstones as well as animal bones; one of the roof lintels bears eight cup-markings as well as serpent-like grooves, but whether the latter are of prehistoric or natural origin remains a matter for discussion.

87 Carlungie, Souterrain, Angus

1st-2nd centuries AD.

NO 511359. Signposted on the N side of the A92 Dundee-Arbroath road; this souterrain is within a field, but a narrow path through the crops is maintained.

Historic Scotland.

The souterrain was discovered in the course of ploughing in October 1949 and was excavated by F T Wainwright between 1950 and 1951; with Ardestie, which was excavated at the same time, Carlungie became a 'type-site' in souterrain studies until the work at Newmill, Perthshire, in 1977.

The souterrain is an L-shaped underground paved gallery set into a trench dug into the ground, with the side walls built of boulders and flagstones; the roof did not survive, and had it been of massive slabs or of timber there seems little doubt that it would have been visible above ground level. The souterrain is about 39 m in length and had been roofed at a height of not less than 2 m. There are entrance passages on the north and on the south-east, as well as a long narrow passage, which joins the main gallery about one-third of the way along its length. At the southern angle of the souterrain there is a small chamber, which has been interpreted as a workshop perhaps both for stone- and metal-working. There were eight paved areas on the surface to the north and east of the underground passage, but whether they were individual 'huts' or paved areas within a large timber structure is not certain.

88 Tealing, Souterrain, Angus

1st-2nd centuries AD.

NO 412381. Signposted from the A 929 Dundee-Forfar road; situated in a field W of farm; follow the path from the dovecote (no. 2).

Historic Scotland.

Accidentally discovered in the course of agricultural operations in 1871, this site, cleared out with some care and subsequently enclosed for protection, displays many of the classic features of

an Angus souterrain: a long curved passage, an expanded end and a constricted doorway. The excavations were recorded by Andrew Jervise, the eminent Angus antiquary, though not undertaken by him; he mentions several interesting features including the discovery of fallen roofing slabs within the passage. The souterrain measures about 24.3 m in length, 2.3 m in average breadth, and the corbelled walls still stand to a height of 2 m, with large boulders forming the basal course and rather smaller horizontally-laid blocks above. The finds, although now lost, formed an interesting assemblage, including domestic debris such as animal bones, broken pottery and quern stones as well as fragments of Roman pottery and glass (the latter less certainly associated); the Roman finds are of 1st or 2nd century AD date.

Near the entrance there is a large boulder decorated with cup-and-ring markings, which forms the lowest course of the wall on the north side.

89 Queen's View, Ring-fort, Perth and Kinross

Early 1st millennium AD.

NN 863601. The ring-fort is incorporated within a Forestry Commission trail at the E end of Loch Tummel. From the Queen's View Information Centre turn E along the B 8019, take the forestry track on the left past Allean Cottages; just beyond the barrier there is a forestry trail on the left side of the track (blue waymarkers); the ring-fort is 250 m to the W below the electricity transmission lines.

The fort is set on a terrace above Loch Tummel, a more defensible position than many examples, and, although there are now trees to north and south, there is an extensive view westwards along the loch. The major element is the stout stone wall, 3 m to 3.8 m thick, which encloses an area about 17 m in diameter. The entrance, which is on the west side, has upright jamb-stones to support a wooden door.

Brown Caterthun and White Caterthun, aerial view

90 Brown Caterthun and White Caterthun, Forts, Angus

Late 1st millennium BC-early 1st millennium AD.

NO 555668 and NO 547660.

Approached from a car park at NO 552660, the Brown Caterthun to the NE and the White Caterthun to the W. Extensive views from both.

Historic Scotland.

These two hillforts are impressive examples of prehistoric man's skills in engineering, using earth and stone to construct defensive ramparts and walls; like the great henge monument at Balfarg (no. 93) they illustrate a social order capable of marshalling a large work-force and considerable resources in terms of quarrying and timber.

The Brown Caterthun occupies the broad summit of the hill, with the outer defences set a little below the actual hilltop. The most impressive of the

several lines of defence is a rampart about 7 m in thickness, which encloses an area some 140 m by 190 m, and is now broken by nine entrances; several outer facing-stones can be seen, as well as stones of the entrance passages, particularly in the south-east flank. Within this fort there is a less well-preserved line of enclosure measuring about 90 m by 60 m internally. The main wall was additionally defended by double ramparts with a broad quarry ditch between them; breaks in the ramparts and causeways across the ditch line up with the entrances to the fort, and thus belong to the same period of defensive design. The outermost defences comprise two ramparts with an outer ditch; the entrances through these ramparts do not in all cases line up with the inner suite, and it is likely that they belong to a later phase of occupation.

The White Caterthun is crowned by a massive stone- walled fort measuring about 140 m by 60 m internally within a pair of walls, the inner measuring about 12 m in thickness and up to 3 m in

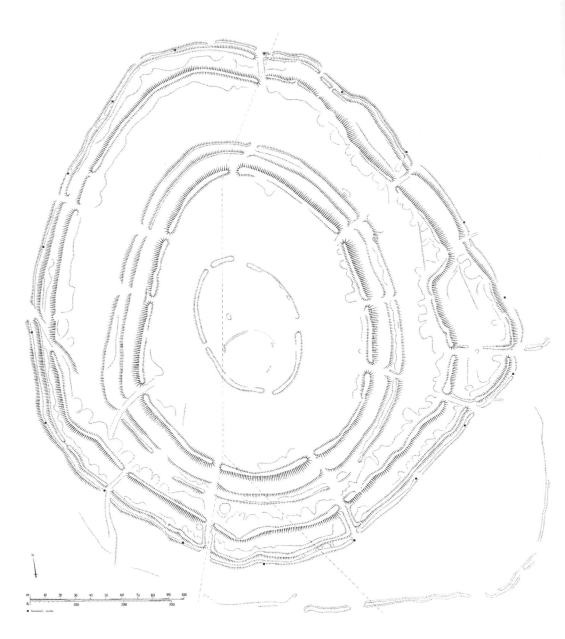

**Brown Caterthun,
plan**

height with the outer wall some 6 m in thickness. Within the fort there is a rock-cut cistern at least 3m deep at the west end as well as traces of a rectilinear enclosure of no great age. Outside the fort further lines of defence can be seen, including a rampart with internal quarry ditch and further enclosing banks lower down the slopes. As at the Brown Caterthun, there have clearly been several phases of defence, and it has been suggested that

the focus of defence shifted from hill to hill over a millennium or more, with the White Catherthun being a Pictish centre of power.

On the west side of the fort between the stone walls and the outer rampart there is a large boulder measuring about 2 m by 1 m, which bears about seventy cup-markings.

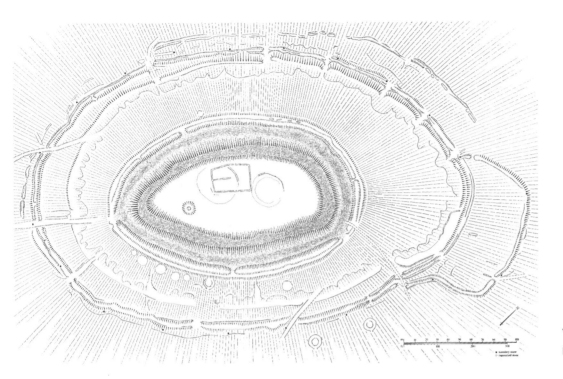

White Caterthun, plan

91 Dundurn, Fort, Perth and Kinross

7th-10th centuries AD.

NN 708232. At the E end of St Fillan's, take the South Loch Earn road and, immediately over the bridge over the River Earn, take the track signposted to Wester Dundurn. Follow the track past the farm entry towards St Fillan's Chapel and climb the NW flank of the hill.

The isolated and craggy hill of Dundurn commands extensive views to east and west along Strathearn and was an ideal choice of location for a Dark Age stronghold. Strathearn was the major route between Scottish Dalriada and southern Pictland, and it is likely that Dundurn was a Pictish fort deliberately situated in the borderland between the two. It is mentioned in the monastic annal compiled on Iona as having been under siege, *'obsessio Duin Duirn'*, in AD 683, although the annalist unfortunately saw no need to identify either the besiegers or the besieged. Excavations in the 1970s confirmed that the site had been occupied in the 7th century, probably in the form of a small timber fortification on the summit of the

hill; this was subsequently rebuilt in stone and a series of outer walls were built to enclose the terraces below. After the union of the Picts and Scots, Dundurn seems to have lost its strategic importance and the fort was finally abandoned sometime in the 10th or 11th century.

The visible walls take maximum advantage of the natural shape of the hill, with an oval citadel on the summit and four lower enclosures following the rocky terraces. At the west end of the hill, a series of less obvious earthen banks and scarps represent stock enclosures and cultivation terraces, which may be contemporary with the fort, but their date is uncertain and they could equally well belong to more recent times. The overall design of the fort is very similar to that of the contemporary Scottic stronghold at Dunadd in Argyll, and, like Dunadd, the objects found at Dundurn are of a high quality that confirms the importance of the site. They include an elaborately decorated leather shoe (luckily preserved by waterlogged conditions), a silver-plated bronze strap-end and a superb glass boss made of dark green and white glass swirled together and further decorated by blue and white spirals.

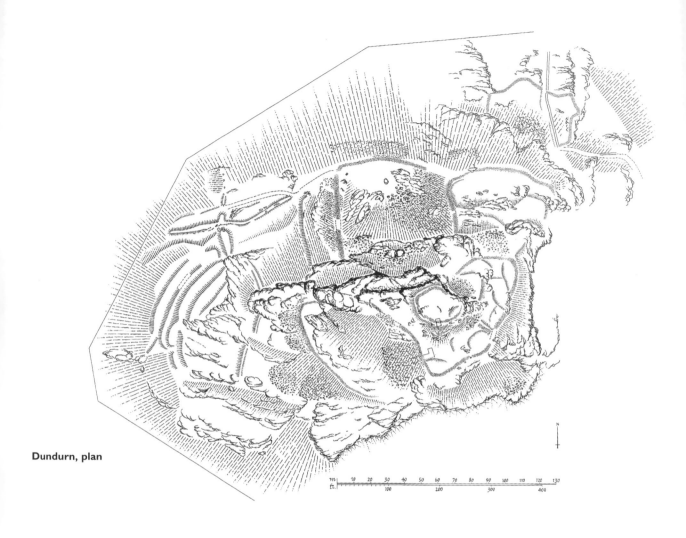

Dundurn, plan

92 East Lomond Hill and Maiden Castle, Forts, Fife

Late 1st millennium BC-early 1st millennium AD.

NO 244062 and NO 222068.

In the Lomond Hills section of the Fife Regional Park there are two interesting forts, one situated in a commanding position offering some of the most extensive views over the whole Region, the other set unusually on an isolated knoll in a small valley. Signposted on the S side of the A 912 between New Inn and Falkland, a narrow road leads up the East Lomond to a parking and picnic place. For Maiden Castle use Craigmead carpark on the Falkland to Leslie road at the col (NO 227061), follow the path to the

W, fork to the NW immediately after joining the main track; the fort is partly hidden from view by the plantation. Alternatively keep to the main track to the W of the carpark for 1 km, a collection of natural boulders signals four circular enclosures or hut-circles now heather-covered; Maiden Castle is visible below to the ENE; the ground is broken and tussocky.

Fife Regional Council: Fife Ranger Service.

The fort on East Lomond Hill occupies the summit as well as a lower terrace on the north. The hilltop is crowned by a large bronze-age cairn about 13 m in diameter, now surmounted by a geographical indicator. There are two encircling ramparts, the inner one surviving best on the north-west, but elsewhere the lines are shown by scarps. The lower terrace has also been defended by a rampart, best

**Maiden Castle
fort**

seen on the north-east. An enigmatic line of defence may be seen at the base of the knoll on the south flank where there is a further bank and ditch.

An indication that activity continued into the first millennium AD is provided by the discovery around 1920 of a slab bearing the incised figure of a bull in a rather effete Pictish style on the south side of the fort; the stone is in NMS, Edinburgh.

Maiden Castle is an isolated knoll which would in prehistoric times have been largely surrounded by marsh; the best-preserved part of the site is a rampart and ditch around the base of the hillock, but there are indications that there would originally have been other lines of defence higher up the flanks, though these are now indicated merely by scarps. The main entrance is at the east end, where there would have been an impressive gateway.

Two cup-and-ring marked stones, found to the east of Craigmead carpark at a point adjacent to the field-dyke (NO 231061), are now in Falkland Palace, as is a cup-and-ring marked stone found in 1890 at Glasslie, which is a little to the south-east.

93 Finavon, Fort, Angus

Mid 1st millennium BC.

NO 506556. The fort is to the N of the narrow road that runs between the A 90 and B 9134 between Finavon and Aberlemno at a point 1.5 km W of Aberlemno.

This fort occupies the summit of an isolated rocky hillock and comprises a massive wall enclosing an area about 150 m by 36 m with a further hornwork at the east end of the ridge; the wall has been of stone with a timber framework, which has burnt with such intensity that massive stretches of vitrified rubble have been formed. Excavations carried out between 1933 and 1934 by Professor V G Childe indicated that the wall was some 6 m thick and up to 4.9 m in surviving height externally; the vitrification was found only at the top of the wall, extending some 2 m into the wall core, perhaps because of the greater use of cross timbers in the upper part of the wall. The excavation revealed hearths and a possible oven, as well as pottery, spindle-whorls and the debris of metalworking. A deep rock-cut cistern was

Finavon fort, inner face of rampart during excavation

excavated at the east end to a depth of some 6.3 m. Further work in 1966, designed to provide dating evidence for the fort, revealed carbonised planks of wood, perhaps from hut floors, analysis of which yielded radiocarbon dates showing that the fort was in use between the 8th and 6th centuries BC.

94 Norman's Law, Fort, Fife

Late 1st millennium BC-early 1st millennium AD.

NO 305201. The summit of the hill is most readily approached from the S; ask for permission at Denmuir farm (NO 302188). Park at the farm and take the track leading NE from the farm.

The rocky summit of Norman's Law, commanding extensive views in all directions, has formed the natural focus for a series of defensive enclosures of several phases. The earlier phases may be indicated by the walls that take in the summit area (some 220 m by 75 m) and the lower terraces to the south, while the later phase of defence is probably the small fort on the summit, which measures about 50 m by 30 m within a wall up to 5 m in thickness with inner and outer facing-stones visible.

There are the traces of many round stone-walled houses on the summit and on the lower terraces,

some of them associated with small enclosures, several of which appear to be later than the periods of fortification.

BURIAL AND RITUAL MONUMENTS

The monuments of the third and second millennia BC are often impressive and puzzling at the same time; we can appreciate the engineering skills involved in setting up tall standing stones, but we are at a loss to know the reasons behind their erection. We know a little about the agricultural basis of the economy from such settlement sites as Grandtully, in Perthshire, and from recent important excavations at Balbridie in Kincardine, but the bulk of the archaeological evidence visible on the ground today is from burial sites (chambered cairns, cairns, and cists) or from monuments the interpretation of which is uncertain (henges, stone circles, standing stones, cup-marked stones).

The small number of stone neolithic monuments used to be taken to indicate a general sparseness of settlement in eastern central Scotland at this time, but intensive study of the aerial photographic evidence, coupled with excavation at Balfarg and Inchtuthil, has shown a range of interrelated monuments which had a part in the complex rituals associated with death and the disposal of the dead. One such site has been partly reconstructed at Balfarg (no. 95). The Inchtuthil example can be seen as the discordant cropmark on the centre left of the photograph in Chapter 9. An unusual earthwork that was formerly thought to belong to the Roman period because it was so straight, the Cleaven Dyke (no. 96), is probably of neolithic date, though this is not yet certain, and to be akin to the sort of linear earthwork known as a cursus.

Several complexes of ritual or ceremonial monuments dating to the third and second millennia BC have been explored in some detail; prolonged activity is shown by a variety of types of site in a localised group as at Balfarg and Balbirnie (no. 95). At Strathallan (NN 928163), rescue excavation in advance of a runway extension uncovered a series of sites including a henge monument (a circular earthwork comprising an inner ditch and outer bank) with two entrance causeways and an internal circle of large timber uprights. The henge was subsequently the focus for several periods of burials, some in cists and others, dating to the mid first millennium AD, in long graves. A large barrow, which was built to a complex design in about six phases, held ten burials, some inserted during its construction, and others rather later. Excavations at several sites, most notably at Balfarg, Strathallan, and Croft Moraig (no. 97) have shown that timber uprights played an important part in the initial layout. Tayside, particularly Perthshire, is unusually rich in stone circles and in related kerb-cairns such as Monzie (NN 882242), which is associated with a cup-marked stone, and Fowlis Wester (no. 100). The small stone circle at Sandy Road, Scone (NO 132265) has now been incorporated as an attractive feature in a housing development; in the course of its excavation a cinerary urn containing a cremation was found at the centre. More complex use of such sites may be illustrated at Croft Moraig (no. 97), Balbirnie (no. 95), and Meikle Findowie (NN 959386). The distinctive group known as 'four-posters', also often associated with burial deposits, is represented by Lundin (no. 101).

The standing stones of Fife and Tayside form one of the most interesting groups in Scotland, and the Ordnance Survey maps indicate many more stones than can be mentioned here. Single stones may have had a variety of functions: burial memorials, route markers and boundary markers for example. In recent years the suggestion has been put forward that some stones may have had a part to play in astronomical observation in prehistoric times, but the multiplicity of alignments of a single stone, the horizon and the sun or the moon makes this an unprovable possibility. Settings of pairs of uprights or alignments of three stones are also found in the area.

Paired stones are most commonly found in Perthshire, particularly in Strathearn and Strathtay, where there are some twenty-six examples; often there is one broad stone and one narrow stone. A well-proportioned pair may be seen from the road at Orwell (no. 104). A linear setting of three stones may be seen at St Madoes (NO 197210), but only two are still upright; a setting of particularly impressive stones dominates one corner of the golf course at Lundin Links (no. 102). Standing stones were clearly focal points in the community, for their transport and erection must have involved considerable organisation. One of the few standing stones to have been dated is that on the top of the barrow at Pitnacree (NN 928533), where the socket held a cremation deposit with charcoal; radiocarbon analysis suggested that the burial belonged to the early third millennium BC, and such stones were clearly important in the landscape of the third and second millennia BC.

Enigmatic carvings known as cup-markings and cup-and-ring markings are found on natural rock outcrops and on standing stones, as well as on large boulders and on cist slabs; no clue can be offered for the meaning of the cups or rings for they do not appear to form consistent patterns, and their importance to prehistoric peoples may have been more in the act of pecking them than in any 'message'. An origin in the neolithic period is demonstrated by the discovery of a cup-marked slab under the long barrow at Dalladies, in Kincardine, which may be dated to before 3000 BC. Cup-markings on standing stones cannot be dated precisely but are likely to belong to the third and second millennium BC: such stones include those at Easter Pitcorthie (NO 497039), Kynballoch, near Rattray (NO 185483), St Madoes, and Tuilyies, Torryburn (no. 105). Several decorated slabs have been found at the stone circle at Balbirnie, two associated with cist burials: a fine slab with crisply pecked markings was found behind one of the end slabs of a cist, while the side-slab of another was decorated with cup-and-ring markings.

One of the puzzling aspects of such markings is their presence in structures that we assume to be later than the second millennium BC, and it is sometimes difficult to decide whether the cup-marked boulders found in souterrains for example are merely included by chance or are in fact contemporary carvings illustrating a long tradition, but the former solution is normally preferred. Cup-and-ring marked boulders have been found in the souterrains at Ardestie (no. 85), Carlungie (no. 87) and Tealing (no. 88).

The greatest number of such carvings on natural rock surfaces in this area is in Strathtay. A surface that includes both cup-marks and cup-and-ring markings may be seen at Tullochroisk, to the south of the River Tummel (NN 984615). On Turin Hill, in Angus, there are several outcrops and boulders decorated with cup-marks and cup-and-ring markings. It has been noted that in Strathtay cup-and-ring markings more frequently occur on high ground, while simple cup-marks are often found on lower ground. Perhaps less surprisingly cup-and-ring markings are found on expanses of natural rock and simple cups are on boulders. At Croft Moraig (no. 97), a large cup-marked boulder was associated with the second period of the monument. Another impressive boulder is adjacent to the kerb-cairn at Monzie (NN 882242); either it was contemporary with the construction of the site or it may have acted as the magnet that attracted the builders to the spot.

In most parts of Scotland the earliest agricultural communities are represented not by their settlements but by their burial places; stone-and timber-built chambers covered by massive cairns were used to house the burials of a family or small interdependent community. The chambers were in use over many centuries and may thus also be seen as a statement of ownership or eventually of ancestral right to farm in the area. In Tayside and Fife only a small number of such sites have been identified and none is particularly well preserved; all are in the west of the region and it is not

surprising that they may most closely be compared with tombs in Argyll known as Clyde Cairns. The chambers are rectangular on plan and are subdivided into a number of burial compartments by transverse slabs. One of the simplest, and perhaps earliest, tombs is set into a natural mound at Cultoquhey House (NN 892234); more complex tombs survive at Kindrochat (NN 723229) and Rottenreoch (NN 842206). At Cultoquhey neolithic pottery and a leaf-shaped flint arrowhead accompanied an inhumation burial.

Several of the large round barrows of Strathtay may also belong to this period, but this can only be proved by excavation; at Pitnacree, for example, such examination revealed a complex mortuary structure associated with cremated burials dating to the mid fourth millennium BC. Pottery indicative perhaps of burials or more probably of settlement sites has been found at Grandtully (NN 927527), Clatchard Craig (NO 243178), Brackmont Hill (NO 437223), and Balfarg (no. 95). A large rectangular enclosure at Douglasmuir (NO 617481), excavated in advance of the laying of a gas pipe-line, was found to belong to the earlier fourth millennium BC; it measured about 65 m by 19 m and had been constructed of large posts set into post-holes.

At Creag na Caillich, above Killin, there is one of the few axe factory sites in Scotland; stone axeheads played a vital part in the economy of the early agriculturalists, allowing clearance of forests for fields, preparing timber for house-building as well as dressing posts for ritual monuments. Surviving axes from the area show that material from further afield, the Lake District and the Alps, for example, was also available.

In this chapter we have tried to show that the archaeological richness of Tayside and Fife comprises not only a wide array of monuments that may still be visited but also the more fugitive traces of man's past revealed by aerial prospection or by excavations in advance of destruction.

95 Balfarg and Balbirnie, Ritual Enclosure, Henge Monument and Stone Circle, Fife

3rd and 2nd millennia BC.

NO 281031 and NO 285029. To the NW of Markinch on either side of the A 92 Kirkcaldy-Cupar road. Balfarg is approached from the B 969 turning SE at the roundabout (now containing a modern stone circle!), signposted; the reconstructed posts of the ritual enclosure are part of a signposted trail to the E of the henge; Balbirnie is by a road at the N end of Balbirnie Park 240 m S of North Lodge.

Glenrothes Development Corporation.

These three sites, along with structures that were found between them, form one of the most important groups of monuments of neolithic and bronze age date in eastern Scotland. The visible monuments are a henge and a small stone circle, now re-sited to the south-east of its original position; excavations between them have, however, revealed a ditched enclosure, two timber structures, cairns and burials as well as a large quantity of pottery, the most important elements of which have been reconstructed. Although this site is earlier in date, most visitors will see the henge first.

The henge monument of Balfarg was excavated in advance of house-building, but the development was re-designed to allow the earthwork to form an open area, and now, with the partial digging out of the ditch, it offers a remarkable impression of the civil engineering skills of prehistoric man. The ditch encloses an area about 60 m in diameter; originally there would have been a large bank outside the ditch and together they would have formed a barrier around the central area. The entrance into the interior was across a narrow causeway on the west side. Several distinct phases of activity or construction were identified in the interior, the earliest involving the breaking of large numbers of pottery vessels and the burning of wood and bone. Later a circle of sixteen massive timbers was set up in pits with two unusually large timbers forming a detached 'porch' or entrance on the west side. These upright timbers are now marked by short posts, but the original posts may have been as tall as 4 m on the west side of the circle to judge by the depth of the post-holes. The henge remained the focus for the construction of further rings of uprights, this time of stone. The surviving evidence is not as clear as in the earlier phase because the stones appear to have been set in hollows rather than in deep pits; nevertheless it

Balbirnie stone circle as reconstructed

Balbirnie stone circle, decorated slab and Food Vessel

roofed. Pairs of post-holes within the enclosures have convincingly been interpreted as the foundation posts for raised platforms on which the dead were laid out until the flesh had rotted or until the appropriate ceremonial moment for burial came round. Whatever the precise nature of the rituals, the structures were in use in the middle of the fourth millennium BC and are among the earliest monuments in the area. Only one has been reconstructed and there is a detailed explanatory panel.

At Balbirnie three burial phases of activity could be identified, although the disturbed nature of parts of the site meant that aspects of the sequence were tentative. There is no doubt, however, that the setting up of the ellipse of ten stones was the first phase with a rectangular kerbed area at its centre perhaps only a little later. Sherds of Grooved Ware pottery, in a style akin to that from Balfarg, were found within the filling of one of the sockets for one of the uprights. The purpose of the central setting is, however, obscure (it should be remembered that the crazy-paving within the reconstructed site is entirely modern). Perhaps a long time after the original building of the circle, the site was used as a burial-place. Two cists were constructed in pits which cut across the corners of the central setting, and this implies that its purpose had been forgotten by this time; the more central cist had been robbed in antiquity, and the burial which it contained had been scattered. The pit cutting through the north-west corner of the setting

may be suggested that there had been two concentric rings. The two impressive standing stones near the entrance causeway are, however, the only remaining features of this phase. The final period of prehistoric activity on the site is represented by the burial of a young person in a pit at the centre of the henge; the burial, accompanied by an unusual handled Beaker and a flint knife, was covered by a large slab weighing about two tons, which has been replaced in its original position.

The road leading out of the Henge circle of houses joins one of the main roads of the development and at this point a tarmac path leads to the reconstruction of the timber enclosure. Excavation revealed two timber-built structures, perhaps the main uprights of palisaded enclosures, for on structural grounds they could not have been

Balbirnie stone circle, cist and central setting in the course of excavation

contained an undisturbed cist; when the capstone was removed the cist was found to be almost filled with earth and cremated bone (an adult female and a child), with a complete Food Vessel and a flint knife on the floor. One of the supporting stones behind the south end slab was decorated with seventeen cup-marks. Another small cist to the north-north-east of the centre contained a burnt bone toggle, while a disturbed cist to the south-east had a side slab decorated with cup-markings and cup-and-ring markings; a cast of this slab has been used in the reconstruction.

Finally the interior of the circle had been covered by cairn material, perhaps covering smaller independent cairns that had protected the cists, and the cairn was used to receive deposits of cremated bones—as many as sixteen individuals—underlining the continued respect for the site as a focus for burials. After excavation in 1970 and 1971 the main elements of the site were re-erected by Glenrothes Development Corporation at a point some 125 m SE of the original position.

96 Cleaven Dyke, Cursus Monument/Bank Barrow, Perth and Kinross

4th or 3rd millennium BC.

Between NO 175397 and NO 154409 in North and South Woods to the NE of Meikleour. Park on the A 93 at about NO 168402. The earthwork runs NW and SE through this point, but the most rewarding walk is to the NW.

The earthwork extends for a length of some 2.3 km and consists of a bank up to 10 m wide and almost 2 m high in places, flanked by two distinct ditches. The apparent straightness of the earthwork and its proximity to Inchtuthil encouraged archaeologists to attribute it to the Roman period. Careful planning has shown that it is not altogether straight and that it is likely to have been built in stages. Excavation has shown it to be a ritual monument of 4th or 3rd millennium date, related to types of site more common in southern Britain and known as cursus monuments or bank barrows.

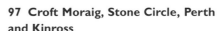

97 Croft Moraig, Stone Circle, Perth and Kinross

3rd and 2nd millennia BC.

NN 797472. On the S side of the A 827 Aberfeldy-Kenmore road about 6 km WSW of Aberfeldy. Park carefully at the entrance to the farm; the gate is at the roadside.

This setting of large boulders was excavated in 1965 and was shown to have a complex sequence of building and use at three main periods: a post setting of upright timber posts; a central oval arrangement of stones; and finally the main stone circle, which surrounded the oval setting. At the centre of the setting there was a flat stone with a charcoal-filled hollow, perhaps a hearth.

In the second period the timbers were forgotten and eight large boulders set up in an oval arrangement (6 m by 7.6 m) with three outlying stones on the southern arc; the ground surface on which the boulders were set had been carefully flattened with earth, which contained quantities of neolithic pottery. The stones were erected in shallow sockets and were supported by packing- stones around their bases. One stone in the north-east arc is decorated with several small cup-markings. The stones are all of similar size (between 1.4m and 1.6m) and are set on approximately the same axis as the earlier timber horse-shoe. Probably associated with this period is the outermost line of stones on the site forming a band of massive boulders and smaller stones, broken on the north-east and south-west. On the same axis as the oval setting there is a large slab, the upper surface of which bears about twenty-three cup-markings, two of which have partial rings.

The last phase of activity on the site is represented by a circle of nine stones and two outlying stones; the circle also incorporates the three outlying stones of the earlier phase. The two impressive stones beyond the circle on the east-south-east imply a change of axis from that of the first two phases. Beyond the two stones, excavation revealed deep grave-pits, but the acid soil conditions meant that no burial remains survived.

This interesting sequence may be compared to the various phases represented at Balfarg and Balbirnie (no. 95) and illustrates the range of ritual structures in timber and stone in the neolithic and early bronze age.

---

98 Easter Pitcorthie, Standing Stone, Fife

2nd millennium BC.

NO 497039. On the N side of the B 942, 350 m W of Easter Pitcorthie farmhouse.

This large standing stone (some 2.4 m high) is unusual in that its south face has been decorated with thirty-three cup-markings and two dumb-bell shaped motifs. In the mid 19th century the farmer dug round the stone and found that the socket in which it had been set contained cremated bones, a phenomenon paralleled at Orwell (no. 104).

99 Fortingall, Stone Circles, Perth and Kinross

2nd millennium BC. NN 745469. Just to the E of Fortingall village on the S side of the road. Park near the hotel.

There are three settings of stones in the field, two of which were excavated in 1970. The first now comprises three uprights, but excavation revealed that there were originally eight set out in a rectangular arrangement with the largest stones at the corners. There are four stones of the second setting, but it too had originally comprised eight uprights. Charcoal and cremated bones survived from the prehistoric period, but it is likely that the sites had been deliberately slighted in Victorian times, for a beer bottle was discovered under one of the toppled stones. The third setting consists of a massive boulder at the centre with two taller flanking stones, a layout that has been compared to that of the recumbent stone circles of Grampian.

On the flat river-terrace to the south-east of the village there is an unusual medieval earthwork of a class known as homestead moats (NN 734466); described on early editions of Ordnance Survey maps as *Praetorium* and thought of as part of a Roman camp, it is in fact a rectangular moat with an inner and formerly an outer bank, within which there would originally have been timber buildings and perhaps a wooden stockade associated with the inner bank. The ditch is about 15 m broad and the central area is about 1.5 m above the level of the surrounding ground. There is an entrance causeway on the eastern flank of the moat. Such sites are sometimes interpreted as medieval hunting lodges.

Further to the west there is a ditched enclosure with a cup-marked stone (NN 731465), and to the west near Bridge of Lyon (and visible from the road) there is a neolithic long cairn (NN 729465), measuring some 32 m in length and 12.5 m in breadth at its wider end; to the south-west of the moat there is a fine standing stone some 2 m high (NN 731464).

100 Fowlis Wester, Cairn, Standing Stone, and Stone Circle, Perth and Kinross

2nd millennium BC.

NN 924249. At the crest of the road N of Fowlis Wester, there is a gated track to the W; park near the gate and walk 600 m to the W.

Situated on the Moor of Ardoch above Fowlis Wester, a position that offers commanding views over Strathearn towards the Ochil Hills, there is an interesting group of monuments excavated in 1939; it comprises two standing stones (although one is now fallen), a cairn with a circle of boulders around it, and a ruined circle of standing stones. The upright stone is some 2 m high and bears a single cup-mark. Excavation revealed a deposit of cremated bone, charcoal and quartz chippings on the east side of the stone; on the same side there was a pit carefully packed with white water-rolled stones. The cairn to the south-west belongs to a distinct group of sites known as kerb cairns, for the perimeter boulders, or kerb, form the most remarkable element; the cairn is some 4.8 m in diameter and is best preserved on its southern half. At its centre excavation revealed traces of burning and patches of cremated bone as well as deliberately positioned quantities of white quartz. The inner face of one of the south-western kerb stones was decorated with three cup-marks. Four stones of the surrounding circle survive, but the stone-holes of the other seven could be clearly traced. The second circle and a fallen standing stone may be seen a little to the west, but the circle has been more severely damaged and none of its stones now remains upright.

track is a setting of four standing stones to the south-east; this is a 'four-poster' setting of stones on the top of a mound. The stones were erected around a deposit of cremated bone, pottery and burnt wood; finally cairn material was heaped over the interior, spilling out beyond the standing stones. The pottery includes sherds of a cord-ornamented Beaker and a Collared Cinerary Urn; these may well represent prolonged activity on the site rather than a short period of burial ritual.

 Lundin Links standing stones

101 Lundin, Standing Stones, Perth and Kinross

Mid 2nd millennium BC.

NN 880505. To the NE of Aberfeldy, on the S side of the Grandtully to Aberfeldy road A 827, a farmtrack leads across the former railway at NN 877505.

The first monument to be encountered is a small standing stone set up in an unusually inconspicuous position (NN 878506), perhaps indicating the site of a burial. Farther along the

102 Lundin Links, Standing Stones, Fife

2nd millennium BC.

NO 404027. The stones are within the golf course of the Lundin Ladies Golf Club and intending visitors must check at the club-house; the stones may readily be viewed from the road to the W without impeding play.

This impressive group of stones has been the subject of conjecture for centuries; the *New Statistical Account* offers the theories current in the 1840s, including a Roman origin, or perhaps the gravestones of Danish chiefs who were defeated by Banquo and Macbeth, or most probably Druidical remains. For the modern prehistorian, the mention of the discovery of 'ancient sepulchres' nearby is an interesting link to other stones, including Orwell (no. 104). An astronomical significance for the stones has also been suggested. There is a pair of stones with a third at a point 30 m to the north; in the late 18th century there was a fourth stone which lay broken nearby. The single stone is about 5.5 m tall, and the pair measures about 4.1 m and 4.6 m in height respectively.

103 Newbigging, Cup-and-ring-marked Stone, Perth and Kinross

2nd millennium BC.

NO 155352. The stone has been moved from its original position (NO 152352) to a point at the edge of a field near Newbigging farmhouse, just beside a gate.

This boulder, moved to its present position in 1981, is profusely decorated with cup-marks and cup-and-ring markings on what is now its uppermost surface. The major figure is a cup-mark surrounded by up to five broken arcs; the way in which much of the decoration is enclosed within a linear 'frame' on three sides is also unusual.

104 Orwell, Standing Stones, Perth and Kinross

2nd millennium BC.

NO 149043. At the N end of Loch Leven, to the N of the A 911 and N of Orwell farm; clearly visible from the road.

This pair of shapely stones stands on a slight rise. In the 19th century, several cists and burials were discovered in the course of ploughing nearby, and the stones were clearly a focal point for burial and ritual in the bronze age. The stones are unusual in having been explored in recent times too, for in 1972 following the toppling of the western stone the area round each was excavated and the western stone subsequently re-erected. This stone (2.8 m in height and 2.95 m in girth at the base) had been set in a small hollow, and a small deposit of cremated bone was found a little to its south-west. The eastern stone is an impressive whinstone monolith (3.8 m in overall height), set in a socket measuring about 1.5 m in diameter and 0.75 m deep. A remarkable find was the discovery of two cremation deposits within the stone-hole on the south-west side, presumably inserted during the erection of the stone; they had been carefully interred one above the other with a flat slab separating them. The remains of several people were present, as well as bones of pig and dog.

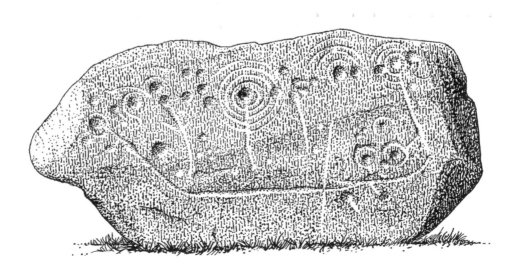

Newbigging cup-and-ring marked boulder

105 Tuilyies, Torryburn, Standing Stone, Fife

2nd millennium BC.

NT 029865. On the S side of the A 985 at a point 700 m NE of Torryburn.

This spectacular stone is 2.4 m in height and is decorated with many cup-markings on its east side; the deeply weathered grooves, which are its most noticeable feature, are, however, natural. In the absence of excavation, the boulder setting a little to the south cannot be satisfactorily explained.

106 West Mains, Auchterhouse, Cairn, Angus

Early 2nd millennium BC.

NO 315376. On the summit of West Mains Hill, 700 m NNE of the farm of West Mains.

This spectacular cairn, situated at a height of 289m OD and thus a conspicuous landmark from several directions, measures some 70 m in diameter and 2.5m in height. It was excavated in 1897 when the various stages in the building of the mound were revealed: at its centre there was a double cist, the corners of which were sealed with clay to make it watertight; the cist was surrounded by boulders and this central setting was covered by a mound of turves and edged with a kerb of large boulders; finally the mound was covered with stones. The central cist contained two heaps of cremated bones and a bronze dagger in one compartment, and a cremation deposit in the other. Perhaps because the cist was so carefully sealed, not only do the bronze dagger blade and the bronze rivets by which the hilt was attached survive in good condition, but also fragments of the ox-horn hilt and mountings for a sheath, which was probably made of skin.

107 Clach na Tiompan, Chambered Cairn, and Standing Stones, Perth and Kinross

3rd and 2nd millennia BC.

NN 829328. From the A 822 between Fendoch and Amulree, there is a private road W of Newton to Auchnafree; the cairn is on the N side of this road 6km WNW of Newton.

None of the small number of chambered cairns in Tayside is well preserved or readily accessible, but the location and unusual length of the cairn at Clach na Tiompan make it an interesting site to visit. Situated on a terrace some 15 m above the north bank of the River Almond, the cairn must have formed the centre of the religious life of a small farming community. Some sense of the duration of this activity is given by the fact that the long cairn is almost certainly a structure of several periods, because four burial chambers have been incorporated into its final length, although their sequence of building is a matter of conjecture.

Tuilyies standing stone (Left)

Clach na Tiompan chambered cairn, blocked entrance to the south-east chamber in the course of excavation

The cairn, aligned north-west and south-east, is some 57 m long and up to 11.5 m broad at its south-east end. The best-preserved chamber was found near this end; the main compartment was composed of four large slabs and a capstone with two small compartments leading from an impressive façade of upright slabs on the south-west. The final blocking of the entrance was still in position, as shown on the photograph, with six slabs carefully wedged into position to prevent access to the tomb. No burial remains were discovered, as the tomb had been rifled, perhaps when the road was built in the last century.

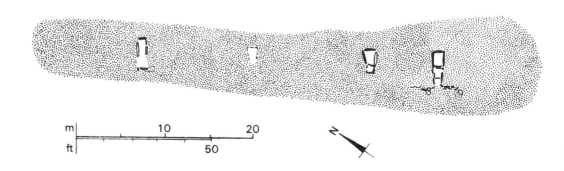

Clach na Tiompan, plan

m | 10   20

ft | 50

MUSEUMS

Alyth Folk Museum, Commercial Street. Domestic and rural artefacts from Alyth and district.

Anstruther, Scottish Fisheries Museum: see no. 7.

Arbroath, Abbot's House, Arbroath Abbey: see no. 43.

Arbroath, Arbroath Museum, Signal Tower, Ladyloan: see no. 22.

Arbroath, St Vigeans Museum: see no. 79.

Auchterarder, Glenruthven Weaving Mill. The only working steam textile-engine in Scotland; displays of local textile production.

Blair Atholl, Atholl Country Collection, Old School. Displays of local life and trades; a blacksmith's smiddy, crofter's stable and byre.

Blair Atholl, Mill. A well preserved and now reconstructed water-mill originally built in the 17th century.

Brechin, Brechin Museum, St Ninian's Square. A display of local prehistory, the burgh and cathedral.

Buckhaven, Buckhaven Museum, College Street. Displays on the history of the burgh, particularly its role in the East Coast Fisheries.

Burntisland, Burntisland Museum, High Street. Displays on the history of the burgh, and the Firth of Forth ferry service.

Ceres, Fife Folk Museum, The Weigh House: see no. 30.

Crail Museum, Marketgate, illustrates the development of this royal burgh.

Culross, The Study and The Town House (NTS) form an important introduction to the architecture and development of the royal burgh (no. 26).

Dundee, Barrack Street Museum. Local geology and wild life.

Dundee, Broughty Castle Museum, Broughty Ferry: see no. 55.

Dundee, Frigate *Unicorn*, Victoria Dock. The oldest British-built ship afloat.

Dundee, North Carr Light Vessel, Victoria Dock. This light vessel, an important beacon in the North Sea between 1938 and 1975, forms an interesting complement to shore- or rock-stations, such as the Bell Rock (no. 22).

Dundee, Polar Exploration Ship *Discovery*, Discovery Point.

Dundee, McManus Galleries. A fine building by Gilbert Scott contains displays on social and local history, art and archaeology, including the material from the Roman fort at Carpow and a good selection of Pictish stones.

Dundee, Verdant Works: see no. 10.

Dunfermline, Andrew Carnegie Birthplace Museum, Moodie Street. The weaver's cottage and loomshop of the period of Andrew Carnegie's birth in 1835 have been carefully recreated.

Dunfermline Museum, Viewfield Terrace. Displays on local archaeology and history, including the production of linen.

Dunfermline, Pittencrieff House. A 17th-century mansion house with exhibitions on costume as well as bee-keeping.

East Wemyss Environmental Education Centre, Primary School. Displays on mining, local history, and the nearby caves (no. 80).

Forfar, Meffan Institute. Displays on local archaeology, history, folk life, and industry; fine displays of carved stones from Kirriemuir and Forfar area.

Glamis, Angus Folk Museum: see no. 1.

Glenesk, Folk Museum. Displays on life in the glens in the 19th century.

Inverkeithing Museum, The Friary. Exhibitions on local history, particularly Rosyth Dockyard, housed in 14th-century friary.

Kinross, Michael Bruce Cottage Museum, Kinnesswood. The cottage of the mid 18th-century poet; the village life of the period is recreated.

Kinross, Kinross Museum, High Street. Exhibitions on local archaeology and industry.

Kirkcaldy, Kirkcaldy Museum and Art Gallery. Displays on local archaeology, natural and social history; a fine collection of Scottish painting. The nearby Industrial Museum houses a forge and an exhibition on the linoleum industry.

Leven Museum, Greig Institute, Forth Street. Local history.

Meigle Museum: see no. 78.

Montrose Museum and Art Gallery, Panmure Place. Fine displays of local history and archaeology, including Pictish stone from Inchbrayock, maritime gallery and wildlife.

Muthill Museum. Local history and folk life.

Newburgh, Laing Memorial Museum. The museum, first opened in 1896, houses the collection of an eminent Victorian historian and antiquary, Alexander Laing (1808-92).

Perth Museum and Art Gallery, George Street. Social and natural history; extensive art collection; material from medieval Perth; Pictish stones from St Madoes and Inchyra.

St Andrews, St Andrews Preservation Trust Museum, North Street. Housed in a 17th-century building, the museum illustrates local life in the last century, including grocer and chemist shops.

St Andrews Cathedral Museum: see no. 67.

St Vigeans Museum, Arbroath: see no. 79.

BIBLIOGRAPHY

Apted, MR *The painted ceilings of Scotland 1550-1650*, Edinburgh, 1966.

Barclay, G *Balfarg: the Prehistoric Ceremonial Complex*, Glenrothes, nd.

Breeze, DJ *Roman Scotland: a guide to the visible remains*, Newcastle-upon-Tyne, 1979.

Breeze, DJ *The Northern Frontiers of Roman Britain*, London, 1982.

Cant, RG *Old St Andrews*, St Andrews, 1945.

Cant, RG *Central and North Fife: its Landscape and Architecture*, Cupar, 1965.

Cant, RG *The East Neuk of Fife: its Burghs and Countryside*, Anstruther, 1968.

Cant, RG *Historic Buildings in Angus*, Forfar, 1968.

Cruden, S *The Scottish Castle*, Edinburgh, 1960, third edition, 1981.

Dunbar, JG *The Historic Architecture of Scotland*, London, 1966; revised edition, 1978.

Fawcett, R *Scottish Medieval Churches*, Edinburgh, 1985.

Fawcett, R *Castles of Fife: a Heritage Guide*, Glenrothes, 1993.

Fawcett, R *Medieval Abbeys and Churches of Fife*, Glenrothes, 1995.

Fenton, A and Walker, B *The Rural Architecture of Scotland*, Edinburgh, 1981.

Fife Regional Council *The Capital in the Kingdom: the Archaeology of Medieval Dunfermline*, Glenrothes, 1994.

Frere, SS and St Joseph, JKS *Roman Britain from the Air*, Cambridge, 1983.

Gifford, J *Fife*, Buildings of Scotland, London, 1988.

Hanson, W and Maxwell, GS *Rome's North West Frontier*, Edinburgh, 1983.

Hay, GD and Stell, GP *Monuments of Industry*, Edinburgh, 1986.

Hay, G *The Architecture of Scottish Post-Reformation Churches 1560-1843*, Oxford, 1957.

Henderson, I *The Picts*, London, 1967.

Hume, JR *The Industrial Archaeology of Scotland: I The Lowlands and Borders*, London, 1976.

Jackson, A *The Pictish Trail*, Kirkwall, 1989.

Lamb, AC *Dundee: its Quaint and Historic Buildings*, Dundee, 1895.

MacGibbon, D and Ross, T *The Castellated and Domestic Architecture of Scotland*, Edinburgh, 5 vols, 1887-92.

MacGibbon, D and Ross, T *The Ecclesiastical Architecture of Scotland*, Edinburgh, 3 vols, 1896-7.

McKean, C and Walker, D *Dundee, an illustrated architectural guide*, Edinburgh, 1993.

Pride, G *The Kingdom of Fife, an illustrated architectural guide*, Edinburgh, 1990.

Ritchie, A *Scotland BC*, Edinburgh, 1988.

Ritchie, A *Picts*, Edinburgh, 1989.

Ritchie, G and A *Scotland: Archaeology and Early History*, London, 1981.

Royal Commission on the Ancient and Historical Monuments of Scotland *Inventory of Monuments and Constructions of Fife, Kinross* *and Clackmannan*, Edinburgh, 1933; *North-East Perth: an Archaeological Landscape*, Edinburgh, 1990; *Dundee on Record: Images of the Past*, Edinburgh, 1992; *South-East Perth: an Archaeological Landscape*, Edinburgh, 1994.

Simpson, AT and Stevenson, S *Town Houses and Structures in Medieval Scotland*, 1980.

Small, A and Thoms, LH *The Picts in Tayside*, Dundee, nd.

Tabraham, C *Scottish Castles and Fortifications*, Edinburgh, 1986.

Wainwright, FT (ed) *The Problem of the Picts*, Edinburgh, 1955, and Perth, 1980.

Wainwright, FT *The Souterrains of Southern Pictland*, London, 1963.

Walker, B and Gauldie, WS *Architects and Architecture on Tayside*, Dundee, 1984.

Walker, DM *Dundee Architecture and Architects 1770-1914*, Dundee, 1955.

There are also guide booklets or leaflets to individual monuments in the care of Historic Scotland and the National Trust for Scotland.

INDEX OF PLACES

Printed in Scotland for HMSO by (3808)
Dd 0293082 C50 02/96